INTERNATIONAL POLITICAL ECONOMY SERIES

General Editor: Timothy M. Shaw, Professor of Political Science and International Development Studies, and Director of the Centre for Foreign Policy Studies, Dalhousie University, Halifax, Nova Scotia

Recent titles include:

Pradeep Agrawal, Subir V. Gokarn, Veena Mishra, Kirit S. Parikh and Kunal Sen
ECONOMIC RESTRUCTURING IN EAST ASIA AND INDIA: Perspectives on Policy Reform

Deborah Bräutigam
CHINESE AID AND AFRICAN DEVELOPMENT: Exporting Green Revolution

Steve Chan, Cal Clark and Danny Lam (*editors*)
BEYOND THE DEVELOPMENTAL STATE: East Asia's Political Economies Reconsidered

Jennifer Clapp
ADJUSTMENT AND AGRICULTURE IN AFRICA: Farmers, the State and the World Bank in Guinea

Robert W. Cox (*editor*)
THE NEW REALISM: Perspectives on Multilateralism and World Order

Ann Denholm Crosby
DILEMMAS IN DEFENCE DECISION-MAKING: Constructing Canada's Role in NORAD, 1958–96

Diane Ethier
ECONOMIC ADJUSTMENT IN NEW DEMOCRACIES: Lessons from Southern Europe

Stephen Gill (*editor*)
GLOBALIZATION, DEMOCRATIZATION AND MULTILATERALISM

Jeffrey Henderson (*editor*), assisted by Karoly Balaton and Gyorgy Lengyel
INDUSTRIAL TRANSFORMATION IN EASTERN EUROPE IN THE LIGHT OF THE EAST ASIAN EXPERIENCE

Jacques Hersh and Johannes Dragsbaek Schmidt (*editors*)
THE AFTERMATH OF 'REAL EXISTING SOCIALISM' IN EASTERN EUROPE, Volume 1: Between Western Europe and East Asia

David Hulme and Michael Edwards (*editors*)
NGOs, STATES AND DONORS: Too Close for Comfort?

Staffan Lindberg and Árni Sverrisson (*editors*)
SOCIAL MOVEMENTS IN DEVELOPMENT: The Challenge of Globalization and Democratization

Anne Lorentzen and Marianne Rostgaard (*editors*)
THE AFTERMATH OF 'REAL EXISTING SOCIALISM' IN EASTERN EUROPE, Volume 2: People and Technology in the Process of Transition

Stephen D. McDowell
GLOBALIZATION, LIBERALIZATION AND POLICY CHANGE: A Political Economy of India's Communications Sector

Juan Antonio Morales and Gary McMahon (*editors*)
ECONOMIC POLICY AND THE TRANSITION TO DEMOCRACY: The Latin American Experience

Ted Schrecker (*editor*)
SURVIVING GLOBALISM: The Social and Environmental Challenges

Ann Seidman, Robert B. Seidman and Janice Payne (*editors*)
LEGISLATIVE DRAFTING FOR MARKET REFORM: Some Lessons from China

Caroline Thomas and Peter Wilkin (*editors*)
GLOBALIZATION AND THE SOUTH

Kenneth P. Thomas
CAPITAL BEYOND BORDERS: States and Firms in the Auto Industry, 1960–94

Geoffrey R. D. Underhill (*editor*)
THE NEW WORLD ORDER IN INTERNATIONAL FINANCE

Henry Veltmeyer, James Petras and Steve Vieux
NEOLIBERALISM AND CLASS CONFLICT IN LATIN AMERICA
A Comparative Perspective on the Political Economy of Structural Adjustment

Robert Wolfe
FARM WARS: The Political Economy of Agriculture and the International Trade Regime

International Political Economy Series
Series Standing Order ISBN 0–333–71708–2 hardcover
Series Standing Order ISBN 0–333–71110–6 paperback
(*outside North America only*)

You can receive future titles in this series as they are published by placing a standing order. Please contact your bookseller or, in case of difficulty, write to us at the address below with your name and address, the title of the series and the ISBN quoted above.

Customer Services Department, Macmillan Distribution Ltd
Houndmills, Basingstoke, Hampshire RG21 6XS, England

Globalization and the Dilemmas of the State in the South

Edited by

Francis Adams
Department of Political Science and Geography
Old Dominion University
USA

Satya Dev Gupta
Department of Economics
St Thomas University
Canada

and

Kidane Mengisteab
Department of Political Science and Geography
Old Dominion University
USA

First published in Great Britain 1999 by
MACMILLAN PRESS LTD
Houndmills, Basingstoke, Hampshire RG21 6XS and London
Companies and representatives throughout the world

A catalogue record for this book is available from the British Library.

ISBN 0–333–72949–8

First published in the United States of America 1999 by
ST. MARTIN'S PRESS, INC.,
Scholarly and Reference Division,
175 Fifth Avenue, New York, N.Y. 10010

ISBN 0–312–22263–7

Library of Congress Cataloging-in-Publication Data
Globalization and the dilemmas of the state in the south / edited by
Francis Adams, Satya Dev Gupta, and Kidane Mengisteab.
p. cm. — (International political economy series)
Includes bibliographical references and index.
ISBN 0–312–22263–7 (cloth)
1. International economic integration. 2. Developing countries—Economic policy. 3. Free Trade—Developing countries. 4. Structural adjustment (Economic policy)—Developing countries. I. Adams, Francis. II. Gupta, Satya Dev. III. Kidane Mengisteab. IV. Series.
HF1418.5.G58177 1999
337—dc21 98–53721
CIP

10 9 8 7 6 5 4 3 2 1
08 07 06 05 04 03 02 01 00 99

Printed and bound in Great Britain by
Antony Rowe Ltd, Chippenham, Wiltshire

Contents

List of Tables and Figures

Tables

Figures

Acknowledgements

This project benefitted from the advice and assistance of numerous individuals to whom we would like to express our gratitude. We are especially indebted to Tim Shaw, the general editor of this international political economy series. Tim provided invaluable support and insight throughout each stage of this project. His mastery of the theory and practice of development, and careful attention to detail, greatly contributed to the overall success of the volume. Aruna Vasudevan, commissioning editor at Macmillan, was also instrumental in guiding this project to a successful conclusion. Her generous assistance and unwavering patience were greatly appreciated.

We would also like to thank Karen Gould, Dean of Arts and Letters at Old Dominion University, who provided administrative support for this project. A research grant from her office helped finance the final preparation of this volume. Elaine Dawson, also with the College of Arts and Letters, provided copyediting and wordprocessing assistance. Her hard work was critical to the timely and successful completion of this volume. Keith Povey also contributed to the final preparation of this anthology. His close reading of the text and superb copyediting were immensely helpful. Additional assistance was provided by Lynn Allen, Supad Ghosh, Susan Kent and Susan Morris.

The chapter by Christine Chin and James Mittelman was originally published in *New Political Economy* (vol. 2, no. 1 (1997), pp. 25–37). Because the authors treat many of the central themes of this volume, we felt inclusion of this article would enhance the overall coherence and unity of the project. We appreciate receiving permission to reprint this article from Carfax Publishing Ltd (P.O. Box 25, Abingdon, Oxfordshire OX14 3UE, United Kingdom), which publishes *New Political Economy*.

Of course, this book would not have been possible without our superb group of contributors. Edited volumes can be a difficult undertaking without the full support and commitment of all those involved. Fortunately, our contributors were conscientious in the preparation of their chapters, flexible in adjusting their work to meet our needs, and exceptionally prompt in meeting our multiple requests. The fact that the project went from the idea stage to final production in little over a year is a testament to their remarkable responsiveness and cooperation.

Although this project could not have been completed without the assistance of the above individuals, we are, of course, solely responsible for its shortcomings.

FRANCIS ADAMS
SATYA DEV GUPTA
KIDANE MENGISTEAB

List of Abbreviations

ACFTU	All China Federation of Trade Unions
AFRC	Armed Forces Revolutionary Council
AIS	FIS armed attachment
ANC	African National Congress
ASEAN	Association of Southeast Asian Nations
BNI	Bureau of National Investigations
BTA	Business Travelling Allowance
CAP	Permanent Agrarian Congress
CBI	Confederation of British Industry
CBN	Central Bank of Nigeria
CCP	Chinese Communist Party
CD	Campaign for Democracy
CDHR	Committee for the Defence of Human Rights
CDR	Committees for the Defence of the Revolution
CDSI	Council for the Discernment of the State's Interest
CEPAL	United Nations Economic Commission for Latin America and the Caribbean
CLO	Civil Liberties Organization
CNC	National Peasants Confederation
CNOP	National Confederation of Popular Organizations
COE	Collective-owned enterprise
CONPAZ	Coordinating Group of Nongovernmental Organizations for Peace
COSATU	Congress of South African Trade Unions
CRP	Constitutional Rights Project
CTM	Confederation of Mexican Workers
CVC	Citizens' Vetting Committee
ECLAC	United Nations Economic Commission for Latin America and the Caribbean (or, as it is known in Latin America, CEPAL)
ECOSOC	UN Economic and Social Council
EPR	Popular Revolutionary Army
ERP	Economic Recovery Programme
ESA	Employment Standards Act
ESAF	Enhanced Structural Adjustment Facility
EU	European Union

EZLN	Ejercito Zapatista de Liberación Nacional (Zapatista National Liberation Army)
FA	*Frente Amplio* (Broad Front)
FDN	Democratic Front for National Reconstruction
FDI	Foreign direct investment
FFS	Secular socialist forces
FIE	Foreign-invested enterprise
FIS	Islamic Salvation Front
FLN	National Liberation Front
FMC	Cuban Women's Federation
FOS	Federal Office of Statistics
FSE	*Fondo Social de Emergencia* (Emergency Social Fund)
GATT	General Agreement on Tariffs and Trade
GDP	Gross domestic product
GEAR	Growth, Employment and Redistribution strategy
GIA	Armed Islamic group
GTUC	Ghana Trade Union Congress
IFI	International financial institution
IFP	Inkatha Freedom Party
IMF	International Monetary Fund
INCC	Interim National Coordinating Committee
JFM	June Fourth Movement
MNC	Multinational corporation
MOSOP	Movement for the Survival of Ogoni People
MST	*Movimento dos Sem Terra* (the Landless Movement)
MTI	Movement of Islamic Tendency
NAFTA	North American Free Trade Agreement
NAPM	National Alliance for People's Movement
NCD	National Commission for Democracy
NDC	National Defence Committee
NDM	New Democratic Movement
NDP	National Democratic Party
NEDLAC	National Economic Development and Labour Council
NEP	New Economic Policy
NFA	National Framework Agreement
NGO	Non-governmental organization
NIC	National Investigations Committee
NIC	Newly industrializing country
NRI	Non-resident Indian

OECD	Organization for Economic Cooperation and Development
OLS	Ordinary least-squares (regression)
OPEC	Organization of Petroleum Exporting Countries
PAMSCAD	Programme of Action to Mitigate the Social Costs of Adjustment
PDC	People's Defence Committees
PNDC	Provisional National Defence Council
PRC	People's Republic of China
PRD	Party of the Democratic Revolution
PRI	Institutional Revolutionary Party
PRLG	People's Revolutionary League of Ghana
PROCAMPO	Programme of Direct Support of the Countryside
PRONASOL	National Solidarity Programme
PSWU	Public Service Workers Union
PTA	Personal Travelling Allowance
RCD	Constitutional Democratic Rally
RDP	Reconstruction and Development Programme
RMALC	Mexican Action Network on Free Trade
SAP	Structural adjustment policy
SAP	Structural adjustment programme
SIF	Social investment fund
SOE	State-owned enterprises
TNC	Transnational corporation
UBA	United Bank for Africa
UNCTAD	United Nations Conference on Trade and Development
UN	United Nations
WDC	Worker's Defence Committees
WTO	World Trade Organization
YSTF	Youth and Students Task Force

Notes on the Contributors

Francis Adams is Assistant Professor of Political Science at Old Dominion University. His research interests include international political economy, multilateral development banks and foreign economic assistance. His regional focus is Latin America. He is the author of *From Economic Nationalism to Neo-Liberalism* and various articles on political development, Third World debt, and North–South relations. His forthcoming book examines US economic assistance programmes in Latin America.

Samir Amin is Professor and Director of the Third World Forum in Senegal. He is past director of the African Institute for Economic Development and Planning, and has taught development economics at the Universities of Poitiers, Paris and Dakar. His books include *Accumulation on a World Scale*, *Unequal Development*, *Imperialism and Unequal Development*, *The Arab Nation*, *The Law of Value and Historical Materialism*, *The Future of Maoism*, *Eurocentrism*, *Delinking: Towards a Polycentric World*, *Maldevelopment: Anatomy of Global Failure*, *The Empire of Chaos*, *Rereading the Postwar Period: An Intellectual Itinerary*, and *Capitalism in the Age of Globalization*.

Christine B. N. Chin is Assistant Professor of International Relations in the School of International Service at American University. Her research and teaching interests are in the areas of Southeast Asia, international political economy and culture studies. Her current research project is on Southeast Asian responses to globalizing structures and processes. She is the author of *In Service and Servitude: Foreign Female Domestic Workers and the Malaysian 'Modernity' Project*.

Manochehr Dorraj is Associate Professor of Political Science at Texas Christian University. He is a specialist in the fields of comparative politics, international relations and political economy, with a regional focus on the Middle East. He is the author of *From Zarathustra to Khomeini: Populism and Dissent in Iran*, the editor of *The Changing Political Economy of the Third World*, and the co-editor of *Middle East at the Crossroads: The Changing Political Dynamics and the Foreign Policy Challenges*.

Susan Eckstein is Professor of Sociology at Boston University and past President of the Latin American Studies Association. She has authored over four dozen articles on economic, social and political developments in Latin America, and a number of books including *Back from the Future: Cuba under Castro*, *The Poverty of Revolution: The State and Urban Poor in Mexico*, and *The Impact of Revolution: A Comparative Analysis of Bolivia and Mexico*. She has also edited *Power and Popular Protest: Latin American Social Movements*.

Satya Dev Gupta is Professor and Chair of the Department of Economics at St Thomas University, Canada. Formerly, he held teaching positions at McGill University, the University of Toronto, the University of the West Indies and the University of Delhi. He has published several papers in the fields of international economics, regional economics and econometrics. He is the author of *The World Zinc Industry* and editor of *Globalization, Growth, and Sustainability*, *Dynamics of Globalization and Development*, and *The Political Economy of Globalization*.

Richard Harris is Professor of Global Studies at California State University, Monterey Bay. His current interests centre on globalization, the political economy of the post-Cold War period, and the effects of neo-liberal policies in Latin America. He is the author of *Cuba in Transition* and *Marxism, Socialism, and Democracy in Latin America* and co-editor of *Capital, Power, and Inequality in Latin America*.

Julius O. Ihonvbere is Professor of Government at the University of Texas at Austin, and currently serving as programme officer in the Governance and Civil Society Unit of the Ford Foundation. His research interests are in state–civil society relations, demilitarization, democratization, structural adjustment, globalization and human rights in the developing world with a special interest in Africa. He has published several articles in leading journals and a number of books including *Nigeria: The Politics of Adjustment and Democracy* and *Economic Crisis, Civil Society and Democratization: The Case of Zambia*.

Xiaobo Lu is Assistant Professor of Political Science at Barnard College, Columbia University and a member of the East Asian Institute at Columbia. His research interests include political corruption, political economy of post-communist transition and the role of bureaucracy in economic development. He has published articles on these subjects and is co-editor (with E. Perry) of *Danwei: Changing Chinese Workplace in Historical and Comparative Perspective*. He is currently finishing a book-length manuscript on political corruption in China.

Kidane Mengisteab is Professor and Chair of the Department of Political Science and Geography at Old Dominion University. His current research interests include the relations between globalization and democracy. He is the author of *Ethiopia: Failure of Land Reform and Agricultural Crisis* and *Globalization and Autocentricity in Africa's Development in the Twenty-first Century*. He is the co-editor of *Beyond Economic Liberalization in Africa*.

James H. Mittelman is Professor of International Relations at American University, Washington, DC. He has also held the Pok Rafeah Chair in International Studies at the Institute of Malaysian and International Studies, Universiti Kebangsaan, Malaysia. His most recent books include, as co-author, *Out from Underdevelopment Revisited: Changing Global Structures and the Remaking of the Third World;* as editor and contributing author, *Globalization: Critical Reflections*; and as co-editor and contributing author, *Innovation and Transformation in International Studies*.

W. Ofuatey-Kodjoe is Professor of Political Science at Queens College and the Graduate Center of the City University of New York. He is also Executive Officer of the PhD programme in political science at the City University of New York, and the Director of the Fellowship Programme at the Ralph Bunche Institute of the United Nations. He has published several articles and books, including *The Principle of Self-Determination in International Law* and *Pan-Africanism: New Directions in Strategy*.

Mustapha Kamal Pasha is Associate Professor of International Relations at the School of International Service, American University. He specializes in comparative and global political economy, South Asian politics, and social theory. His current research focuses on civil society, the cultural impact of globalization, and comparative political economy of South Asia. His publications include *Colonial Political Economy: Recruitment and Underdevelopment in the Punjab* and *Out*

From Underdevelopment Revisited: Changing Global Structures and the Remaking of the Third World (with James H. Mittelman).

John Weeks is Professor of Development Economics and Director of the Centre for Development Policy and Research at the School of Oriental and African Studies. He has also worked with numerous United Nations agencies. His current research interests are macroeconomic policy in developing countries and the impact of globalization on wage labour in underdeveloped countries. He is author or editor of over ten books, including *Capital and Exploitation* and *A Critique of Neoclassical Macroeconomics.*

Behzad Yaghmaian is Associate Professor of Economics at Ramapo College of New Jersey. He has written in the areas of international political economy, Third World studies and the political economy of Iran. His recent research has focused on the political economy of neoliberalism, the World Bank/IMF policies of export-led growth, and the political economy of everyday life in developing countries.

1 Globalization and the Developing World: An Introduction

Francis Adams, Satya Dev Gupta and Kidane Mengisteab

Globalization is the defining characteristic of our time. The modern system of independent nation states and distinct national economies is being replaced by a single transnational political economy. Power and authority are steadily shifting to global institutions and corporations. National governments have seen their sovereignty and control over domestic political and economic affairs rapidly diminish.

While globalization clearly effects all countries, the degree of change has not been uniform throughout the world. A distinction should be drawn between the industrialized nations of the north and the developing nations of the south. Whatever *sovereignty* governments in the developing world managed to obtain with decolonization is now rapidly eroding. This is largely due to the rising supremacy of transnational corporations which are typically based in the North and supported by their home governments. The traditional model, where the nation state was perceived as the premier authority for maintaining security and promoting development, is now being replaced by a *neoliberal* model premised on the dictates of the market and the preferences of supranational organizations.

Throughout Latin America, Africa, the Middle East and Asia the state traditionally played a central role in the economic affairs of these nations. The largest industries were owned by the government, the state assumed primary responsibility for the provision of basic goods and services, and wages, prices and interest rates were tightly controlled. Governments also maintained highly restrictive foreign trade and investment regimes to protect domestic economies from global market forces. This *state-centric* model was deemed necessary to overcome a legacy of dependency and underdevelopment.

In recent years the state in developing countries has disengaged from the economy. Governments have sold off public corporations, delegated the provision of basic services to the private sector, and deregulated their domestic economies. Governments have also jettisoned protectionist trade and investment policies by slashing import restrictions and creating incentives to attract foreign capital. Neoliberalism, reflected in the decline of the welfare state and the unfettered mobility of capital, has become the new orthodoxy.

The transition from states to markets in the developing world has not been a smooth process. Neoliberal reforms have clearly *intensified* inequality and division. Some social groups have profited from the movement towards free markets and have consistently supported the reform programme. Other groups have been adversely affected and attempted to block reform. Economic restructuring has heightened social polarization. Many scholars of the developing world have examined the causes and consequences of globalization. At the same time, less attention has been paid to the formidable *dilemma* which globalization poses for the Third World state. There are compelling pressures, largely emanating from the international environment, to carry out free market reforms. At the same time, these reforms often produce social resistance and political turmoil at home. Devising effective strategies for maintaining reform in the face of societal opposition is the single greatest challenge confronting these governments.

Governments in the developing world have two broad policy alternatives. The first is to rely on coercion. Military and police force could be deployed to deactivate popular sectors and eliminate all forms of independent political activity. The second alternative is to compromise with opposition groups. Governments could make concessions which slow the implementation of reform or soften the social costs. In most cases, some combination of these two strategies is deployed. The *primary objective* of this project is to understand and explain variation in strategic choice cross-nationally.

GLOBAL IMPERATIVES

The transition from state to market in the developing world is frequently traced back to the mid-1970s, when accumulating foreign debts and reduced export earnings led to chronic liquidity and foreign exchange shortages. New commercial lending also dried up as banks began to lose confidence in the ability of these nations to repay their past loans. In order to continue purchasing vital imports many developing nations turned to the International Monetary Fund (IMF) for assistance.

IMF support was contingent on selling off government-owned businesses, making deep cuts in social programmes, lifting price controls on basic necessities, and reducing wage rates. The Fund also advocated greater integration in global markets. Developing nations were encouraged to remove trade and exchange controls and to institute incentives to attract foreign direct investment. Together these reforms reflected the IMF's preference for a market-based allocation of resources within and between nations.

The World Bank also introduced policy-based loans in the early 1980s. These loans were specifically designed to help nations reduce their current accounts deficits, improve their balance of payments position, and help service their foreign debts. To receive World Bank assistance developing nations were required to adopt the same type of neoliberal reforms. This philosophy is evident in the World Bank's 1996 report, *Global Economic Prospects and the Developing Countries.* In particular, the report states that:

> [i]ntegration matters because there is an association between growth performance and integration. Fast growth tends to promote a more open economy, reflecting policies common to both, and hence lagging integration is a sign of underlying policy deficiencies. Additionally, integration tends to promote higher growth through the channels of better resource allocation, greater competition, transfer of technology, and access to foreign savings.

The increasingly influential role of the World Trade Organization (WTO) should also be acknowledged. In the past, developing nations were allowed to maintain higher tariff barriers than the industrialized nations of the north. However, this 'Generalized System of Preferences' (GSP) has been eroded in recent years. Under the most recent 'Uruguay Round' agreement, developing countries which seek expanded access to northern markets are required to reduce their own trade barriers at home. This agreement also removes many restrictions on foreign investment and brings intellectual property rights and service industries into the multilateral trade regime.

Since the advanced industrialized countries have comparative and competitive advantages in these areas, it should be emphasized, the multilateral trading regimes created at the WTO coincide closely with the interests of developed nations. It is thus not surprising that the neoliberal reforms advocated by the international institutions have been equated with a new era of economic colonialism. The political influence of these international institutions is important. Globalization is sometimes considered the *inevitable* and *irreversible* product of technological change and the power of capital. But as a number of the contributors to this volume demonstrate, these institutions have a powerful bias in favour of free markets and corporate enterprise. They have clearly played a major role in promoting economic liberalization.

Transnational corporations (TNCs) have obviously contributed to global economic change, and there has been a spectacular growth in the number and size of TNCs during the past two decades. New transportation and communications technologies have made it profitable for private firms to assemble a product from components produced in many different countries. Production is now organized on a global basis as corporations routinely shift operations from one venue to the next in search of the most profitable investments. Mergers and acquisitions are the preferred route to overseas production. Transnational corporations have become extraordinarily powerful actors on the global stage. There are about 40 000 TNCs, with nearly 300 000 foreign affiliates, and their sales exceed the value of total world exports. Furthermore, as the United Nations' 1996 *World Investment Report* notes,

> [a]bout 90 per cent of the parent firms in the world are based in the developed countries, while two-fifths of foreign affiliates are located in the developing countries . . . the world's 100 largest TNCs – just 0.3 per cent of the TNC universe – control most international production. The largest corporations have annual budgets and total products which far surpass those of many developing nations.

Transnational corporations exercise considerable influence in the developing world. Because these corporations control most international trade, developing countries are dependent on them for access to export markets. These firms are also the single greatest source of capital and new technologies for developing countries. Since they can shift production from one country to the next, governments which act contrary to their interests could lose access to foreign markets, capital and technology. As TNCs have extended their operations internationally they have sought the progressive removal of all obstacles to the free deployment of their resources. Developing nations are limited in their ability to tax these corporations or require strict labour and environmental standards. In many respects, these nations are pressed into a 'race toward the bottom' as they seek to outbid one another to attract and maintain foreign investment.

Advances in information technology and the push for financial liberalization programmes, a major component of the structural adjustment programmes, and the recent developments at the WTO, have *internationalized* the financial markets at a pace much faster than the internationalization of production. Portfolio investment has now become the largest source of external finance. A *trillion* dollars is spent every day in cross-border purchase of corporate stocks or government bonds. However, in general, portfolio flows move more because of risk diversification and the pursuit of short-term capital gains than for the purposes of acquiring productive assets. As a result, portfolio flows have fluctuated widely, destabilizing financial markets in countries throughout the developing world.

Once again, governments are only successful in attracting portfolio investment if they demonstrate a commitment to privatization, deregulation and liberalization. These measures are considered essential for ensuring a profitable investment climate. Measures which deviate from free markets, on the other hand, are dismissed as inimical to growth and induce the export of capital abroad. Since capital flight erodes the value of a nation's stocks, bonds and currency, this constitutes an additional source of pressure to maintain an open economy.

The transition from state to market in the developing world largely reflects the imperatives of the international economy. While foreign exchange, debt and liquidity crises have weakened the position of developing countries, international institutions and corporations have seen their power expand. The internationalization of production and capital markets severely limits policy choice in the South. Because these nations are increasingly dependent on access to foreign markets, capital and technology, there seems to be no alternative to neoliberal reform.

THE DOMESTIC ARENA

While market-oriented reform in the developing world is largely a function of pressures emanating from the international economy, there are *internal* forces which also favour reform. A careful analysis of these internal forces requires recognition of different levels of economic diversification in the developing world.

Some countries, such as Brazil, Mexico, China, and the newly industrializing countries of East and Southeast Asia have attained a significant level of global competitiveness. There are also a number of other countries which have developed highly competitive labour-intensive industries. Many of the major businesses within these countries are linked to the global economy and their process of accumulation largely depends on these links. These businesses benefit from the globalization process and support free market reform. Workers that are employed by competitive export industries also gain from globalization. Finally, large-scale commercial farmers and the cash-crop-producing segment of the peasantry benefit from greater access to external markets.

At the same time, there are a number of groups which are adversely affected by globalization and have resisted free market reforms. Infant industries typically require some form of protection from external competition and are generally resistant to unqualified globalization. Import substituting industries would also be disadvantaged, since the process of accumulation in these industries is based on the domestic market. While they might support internal liberalization, they would generally oppose global openness. Similarly, capital- and technology-intensive industries which are not in a position to compete with the established transnational corporations are more nationalist than globalist. Most of the domestic working class opposes neoliberal reform. This group tends to lose from the retrenchment of subsidies and social programmes, and from higher prices associated with deregulation and devaluation. The working class is also hurt by the loss of public-sector employment and face stagnant and declining real wages as foreign trade and investment depresses local labour markets. The subsistence peasantry, the largest social group in the less-diversified developing countries, such as those of sub-Saharan Africa, has little to gain from globalization.

SOCIAL MOBILIZATION AND RESISTANCE

Globalization has clearly worked against the interests of diverse social groups in the developing world. Global openness undermines the already precarious position of *subaltern groups* and intensifies domestic inequalities. Small-scale entrepreneurs, the working poor and subsistence peasants have all seen their relative position decline.

The emergence of widespread resistance to globalization thus comes as no surprise. Neoliberal reform has spurred the development of a wide spectrum of non-governmental organizations which have been at the forefront of efforts to block reform. Some labour unions and opposition political parties have also mobilized against neoliberalism. In some countries, revolutionary groups have emerged with the explicit objective of scaling back market reforms. Governments have thus had to grapple with protests and demonstrations, strikes and work stoppages, land seizures, riots and civil disobedience, and even armed rebellion. At times, this opposition has successfully toppled governments. Those governments which have managed to retain power have seen their authority diminish.

COERCION AND COMPROMISE

As noted above, the globalization process places contradictory pressures on the Third World state. While there are compelling pressures to adopt market-oriented reforms, these reforms threaten the economic well-being of diverse social groups. This has led to organized resistance from a wide spectrum of groups in civil society. Devising strategies to maintain reforms in the face of such opposition, without *jeopardizing* political stability, is the central challenge for the Third World state today.

Developing countries have sometimes deployed military and police force to *deactivate* popular sectors and eliminate all forms of autonomous political activity. This generally includes suspending the constitution and replacing the rule of law with arbitrary political authority. Authoritarian leaders also move to eliminate other bases of political power: the legislature is shut down, civilian courts disbanded, and elections cancelled. Political opponents are typically imprisoned, tortured, executed or forced into exile. To maintain high levels of economic growth and inflows of foreign capital, the state actively intervenes to break up demonstrations, strikes and land seizures. Repression is generally linked to the emergence of a coalition of governmental, industrial and military elites whose preeminent objectives are political stability and rapid economic growth. Popular movements are considered a serious threat to these twin objectives.

Although coercion is frequently deployed as a short-term solution to generalized crisis, it is rarely a stable form of political rule in the long run since it is inherently difficult to legitimize or institutionalize political authority under authoritarian regimes. Legitimation is difficult for two reasons. First, the exclusionary nature of the regime, and obvious class bias, undermine its ability to mediate social relations or gain the consent of large segments of civil society. Second, deliberate and repressive demobilization only increases social polarization and intensifies opposition movements. The increasing size and strength of the opposition weakens the regime's initial base of support and jeopardizes the regime's survivability. Political turmoil is even more of a problem in a globalized economy since foreign investors and the domestic elite will send their money out of the country at the first sign of trouble. As capital flight increases, the nation's currency depreciates. A precipitous decline in the currency can send the economy into a recession, further undermining a government's legitimacy and stability.

Because sole reliance on coercion only *intensifies* the opposition, precipitates capital flight and undermines state legitimacy, it is generally not considered an effective long-term solution. As a result, governments in the developing world have often made concessions with oppositional groups. The most common approach is to weaken the reform programme. Privatizations are slowed, deregulation is limited to only certain sectors of the economy, and new forms of protection are put in place for domestic industries. Governments have also offered various forms of compensation to those groups most adversely affected by reform. New social programmes are created to lessen the social costs experienced by the poor and working class.

At the same time, governments are limited in the extent to which they can compromise with the opposition. The very nature of the reforms makes it increasingly difficult to offset the social costs involved. A streamlined state is not able to maintain the same level of patronage and social programmes as it was accustomed to in the past. Moreover, weakening reform programmes reduce financial support from international financial institutions and encourage capital flight. Attempts to raise wages or control interest rates only leads transnational corporations to shift production to some other part of the world. Third World governments are thus caught in a difficult position: *both* coercion and compromise carry considerable risks. Sole reliance on either strategy would almost certainly jeopardize the reform programme. Governments have thus attempted to balance the use of repression with the granting of concessions. Repression is deployed to deactivate direct challenges to authority, while concessions are used to divide and coopt the more moderate elements of the opposition.

This book examines the political economy of reform in the developing world. Our central focus is the challenges posed by globalization for the Third World state. The book begins with thematic chapters which consider the broad parameters of globalization and its effects on developing countries. This is followed by a series of case studies from Latin America, Africa, the Middle East and Asia. These chapters provide detailed empirical analysis of economic and political transformation throughout the developing world. Our overriding objective is to better understand and explain the political economy of change in the South.

THEMATIC ISSUES

The thematic section begins with Samir Amin's overview of the most salient characteristics of globalization. Amin demonstrates how this new era of capitalist development is not a random process but rather the consequence of a very deliberate strategy. The anti-state ideology of neoliberal reformers serves the private interests of transnational capital. For Amin, globalization is producing both new forms of polarization and inequality and new transnational social movements. The scope and character of globalization is not predetermined but will depend on the balance in the relationships between nations at any given moment and the specific internal social relations of these nations.

The chapter by Christine Chin and James Mittelman also considers alternative forms of resistance in the context of globalization. Their chapter delves into the constitutive role of power in shaping cultural critiques of economic globalization as well as patterns of struggle. The authors revisit the works of three theorists of resistance, Antonio Gramsci, Karl Polanyi and James Scott, in an attempt to reconceptualize anti-globalization resistance movements today. Chin and Mittelman demonstrate how globalization has led to changing notions and practices of work, family and politics as people seek to negotiate a semblance of control over the expansion of market forces and diverse spheres of their everyday lives. As political and economic power becomes more diffused and less institutionalized, so too will forms of resistance.

For his part, John Weeks contends that the ideology of globalization of markets has been used to justify the loss of control by governments over economic policy in the developing world. The argument that it is an inexorable and irreversible process is an ideological assertion that seeks to forestall policy changes that would limit the destructive tendencies of capital. For Weeks, neither theory nor practice suggests that the development of global markets leads inevitably to a policy regime corresponding to the unmitigated interests of capital. The chapter also points to the growing hegemony of finance capital over productive capital and considers the range of policy measures which could be implemented to constrain the movement of finance capital.

CASE STUDIES

The second part of this book includes a number of case studies of the political economy of reform in Latin America, Africa, the Middle East and Asia. These case studies, which have either a regional or country-specific focus, provide detailed comparative analysis of political choice in the developing world.

This section begins with three chapters on Latin America. Richard Harris provides a regional overview of both legal and extralegal resistance to neoliberal reforms. The chapter categorizes the various types of popular resistance in Latin America and the alternative responses taken by governments in the region. Harris points to two alternative approaches to contain popular resistance to economic liberalization: a tactical approach which relies on repression, and a more strategic approach which attempts to maintain resistance within manageable limits. International financial institutions have played a major role in development of the second type of measures. Harris goes on to outline an alternative project to the neoliberal agenda which responds to the needs and interests of the diverse multiclass spectrum of social movements and grassroots organizations.

Mexico is a prominent example of neoliberal reform in Latin America. Francis Adams outlines the reforms which have been implemented during the past decade and considers their effects on diverse societal groups. He also chronicles various manifestations of resistance to these reforms, including insurrection, strikes and work stoppages, popular mobilizations, independent political activity, and civil disobedience. The last section examines the political strategies which state elites have deployed in response to these grassroots challenges. While coercion has sometimes been used to deactivate popular sectors, Adams demonstrates how state elites have frequently negotiated with their most vocal opponents, adopting compromise measures and compensatory programmes which lessen the social costs of adjustment. It has been this delicate balance between coercion and compromise which has allowed the Mexican government to generally maintain the reform programme intact despite widespread social dislocation.

Cuba also represents an important case study of the political and economic challenges posed by globalization. For Susan Eckstein the adoption of market-oriented reforms in this country is the product of both a changing external environment and strong domestic pressures. This chapter examines the rising chorus of discontent in Cuba and the response of the state. For Eckstein, institutional arrangements have patterned both civil disobedience and state actions. Although the Cuban government has sometimes repressed opposition groups, it has also enacted compensatory measures to ameliorate the most adverse social consequences of these market reforms.

We then present three case studies from Africa. Post-apartheid South Africa is one of the few African states which has adopted a *consociational* power-sharing arrangement as a strategy of state building. In his chapter, Kidane Mengisteab demonstrates how this arrangement attempts to unify different races, ethnic groups and social classes under a shared political and economic system and to integrate disjointed economic sectors into a complementary system on the basis of negotiated terms that are acceptable to all groups. This carefully crafted arrangement is generally credited for making a peaceful transition possible in South Africa by securing the interests of minorities from domination by majorities and by assuring the economically deprived majorities that the state would quickly address their plight. At the same time, the South African state faces internal and external pressures to comply with the conditions of globalization. For Mengisteab, globalization imposes constraints on autonomous policy-making by individual countries and thus undermines consociational arrangements. The government in South Africa has attempted to maintain its consociational strategy of transformation despite the pressures of globalization.

In the following chapter, Julius Ihonvbere examines how the patterns of production and politics in contemporary Nigeria limit the nation's ability to effectively exploit the opportunities created by globalization or resist the negative consequences of integration. The non-hegemonic nature of the state and the weakness of the dominant elites makes it difficult for the Nigerian state to articulate a viable and holistic approach to capitalist growth. As a result, state elites have sought to contain domestic opposition by closing democratic spaces, repressing opponents, and reconstructing political discourses. The chapter concludes with an assessment of the potential for democratic transition and economic development in Nigeria.

The chapter by W. Ofuatey-Kodjoe investigates the political strategies employed by the regime of John Rawlings in Ghana to overcome internal opposition to IMF-mandated neoliberal reforms. In 1982 there was a serious debate within the Ghanaian government regarding economic policy. The rhetoric of the government at the time was anti-IMF and in favour of 'self-reliant' policies. It thus came as a surprise to many observers when the government adopted the structural adjustment policies of the IMF. Although neoliberal economic policies have been generally detrimental to the poor and working class, the Rawlings regime has been successful at weathering internal opposition to the economic reforms. As Ofuatey-Kodjoe demonstrates, the government has managed to survive through a combination of political repression, including imprisonment without trial of labour leaders and other activists, cooptation of community leaders and civic groups, and the extensive use of patronage and appeasement.

The Muslim world is the focus of chapters by Manochehr Dorraj and Behzad Yaghmaian. For Dorraj, North African and Middle Eastern states have frequently used populist politics to bestow nationalist legitimacy on authoritarian regimes. While populist symbolism and rhetoric may be effective culturally, traditional economic schemes of self-sufficiency and autonomous economic development have been eroded in the face of global interdependence. As the economic crisis mounts throughout the Muslim world, and the state has proved incapable of providing for the basic needs of people, many Islamic groups have emerged as agents of social welfare and providers of goods and services. Drawing primarily on case studies of Algeria, Egypt and Jordan, Dorraj argues that these groups constitute an alternative source of power. This has induced many authoritarian regimes to grant political and economic concessions to their strongest domestic opponents.

The chapter by Yaghmaian outlines the various stages in which structural adjustment reforms have been implemented in Iran and considers the distributional effects of these reforms, placing special emphasis on the social and psychological impacts that are not typically considered in economic analyses. In the absence of organized civil society and the institutions of collective action, Yaghmaian argues, a process of retreat to personal struggles for survival occurs leading to diverse manifestations of individually crafted coping mechanisms. The internalization of discontent thus shields the state from collective opposition to its policies. However, because state elites fear eventual breakdown of civil society, they have retreated from the full implementation of neoliberal reform.

The last two chapters examine the political economy of globalization in Asia. Mustapha Pasha's chapter critically examines the effects of liberalization on social equality in South Asia. The author demonstrates how liberalization and privatization has been detrimental to precisely those sectors least capable of competing in a marketplace. Drawing upon the comparative experience of India, Pakistan and Sri Lanka, Pasha explores various forms of resistance. Under pressures from domestic opposition to globalization, a new compromise between the state and societal actors often follows concessions to specific political elements generally contributing towards the rise of new centres of patronage. Neoliberalism, in seeking to depoliticize the political economies of the south, ends up activating new political passions and spawns new structures of patronage.

In the final chapter, Xiaobo Lu examines the changing nature of industrial relations in China. Before the neoliberal reforms, the state provided full and permanent employment and all essential social services. During the past two decades both the ownership of production and the nature of industrial relations have shifted. Workers in the state sector have been adversely affected by globalization and have actively resisted the reforms. This chapter examines how the political leadership of China has responded to this shift in industrial relations. Focus is placed on changing relations between the state and workers as reflected in work mobility, social welfare, income and labour rights protection. The author posits that the state will continue to play a significant role in managing industrial relations. The pace, scope and sequence of changes in industrial relations are determined by both leadership choice and the structural constraints from the pre-reform past as reflected in the entrenched *danwei* (work unit) system in China.

Globalization has had a profound impact on the political and economic character of Latin American, African, Middle Eastern and Asian nations. This book explores the challenges posed by globalization in the developing world. The transition from state to markets has clearly polarized these societies. Governing elites have been scrambling to devise effective strategies which maintain neoliberal reforms without jeopardizing their political stability. This book considers alternative responses of the state in the South in an attempt to better understand and explain the political challenges posed by globalization.

Part I
Thematic Issues

2 For a Progressive and Democratic New World Order

Samir Amin

The page of the post-World War II era has been turned, but this is not simply 'due to the end of the Cold War'. The transformation is defined by the collapse of the three societal models that shaped the life and struggles of the postwar period (1945–80): the welfare state of the developed capitalist West, Sovietism, and the projects of national liberation in the Third World countries. A 'return' to these models is impossible, and the desire for such a return is little more than the expression of a helpless nostalgia on the part of groups that have, in any case, largely lost their capacity to act. At the same time, the developments we have experienced over the past 15 years are not acceptable, because in our view the economy must be made to serve the people, and not the other way round.

These developments can be summarized in quite simple terms: we are speaking of growing social distortions as they take a dramatic turn in the majority of countries in the west, the former eastern bloc, and the south. Massive and permanent unemployment has reappeared within the Triad (the United States, Europe and Japan), the welfare state has been eroded, and a new phenomenon of exclusion/marginalization has become a permanent feature of the landscape. In the countries of the former eastern bloc and the south, the situation is even more dramatic. Rare exceptions involving some southern countries with dynamic economies deserve further discussion.

We do not accept the dominant argument that these developments are 'the price we have to pay for a period of transition' that will eventually lead to a new, allegedly healthier and more dynamic economy from which all will benefit. However, can we say that these social distortions are really a new phenomenon in the history of capitalist expansion? Or was the postwar era the exception in this history – an exception that can be explained as a result of the fact that power relationships, after the defeat of fascism, were more favourable to the labouring classes and peoples of the world than at any previous time? In that case, the current situation would be a return to normal (that is, a return to the law of accumulation and pauperization, according to Marx's theses).

The 'Third World' has broken apart into a group of emerging countries, which have now entered the industrial age and even developed the capacity to compete in world markets, and a group of marginalized and excluded countries.

Emerging Countries

The capitalist countries of Eastern Asia (Korea, Taiwan and Singapore), along with China, have registered high growth rates, while these rates were collapsing almost everywhere else in the world. These countries are not actively competing to provide industrial products in world markets. In addition to being economically dynamic, they are less affected by aggravated social distortions (though there is considerable cross-national variation), less vulnerable (because of an intensification of intraregional relationships that is specific to East Asia, and similar in degree to what has happened within the European Community), and characterized by effective intervention by the state, which plays a key part in carrying out national development strategies, even when these national strategies are turned outwards.

Marginalized Countries

The industrial capacity of Latin American countries and India is equally significant. However, regional integration is less advanced in their case (20 per cent for Latin America versus 60 per cent for eastern Asia or the European Community), and state intervention is less coherent. Because growth rates remain modest in these regions, the aggravation of already huge inequalities is even more dramatic.

Excluded Countries

Overall, the countries of Africa and the Arab and Islamic world are still trapped in an obsolete international division of labour. They remain exporters of primary products, either because they have not entered the industrial age or because their industries are fragile, vulnerable or uncompetitive. Here, social distortions mainly appear in the form of swelling masses of pauperized and excluded people. There is absolutely no sign of progress towards regional integration (intra-African or intra-Arab). Growth is almost non-existent. Although this group includes both 'rich' countries (oil-exporting countries with small populations) and countries that are poor or extremely poor, it does not include any country that behaves as an active agent in the world system. In this sense it is truly marginalized.

Active and marginalized peripheries are not distinguished solely by the competitiveness of their industrial production. There is also a political difference. Dominant powers in the active peripheries, and behind them society as a whole (whatever the social contradictions within that society), have a project and a strategy to carry it out. This is obviously true of China, Korea and, to a lesser extent, certain countries in Southeast Asia, India and some Latin American countries. These national projects are confronting the projects of imperialism, which currently dominate the world, and the result of this confrontation will shape the world of tomorrow. Marginalized peripheries, on the other hand, have little independent strategy of their own. As a consequence, their thinking is done for them by imperialist circles which retain the exclusive power to initiate 'projects' for these regions (such as the African, Caribbean, Pacific project of the European Community, or the 'Middle East' project of the United States and Israel), projects which are not opposed, in fact, by any local project. These countries are therefore passive subjects of globalization. The growing differentiation between these groups of countries has shattered the concept of the 'Third World' and ended the common front strategies of the Bandung era (1955–75).

However, as we shall see, there is no general agreement on how to assess the nature and prospects of capitalist expansion in the countries of the former Third World. For some people, the most dynamic emerging countries are in the process of 'catching up' and are no longer 'peripheries,' even if they are still at an intermediate level within the world hierarchy. For others, including myself, these countries represent the true periphery of tomorrow. The centres/peripheries contrast, which from 1800 to 1950/1980 coincided with the opposition between industrialized and non-industrialized economies, is based today on new and different criteria that can be defined through analysis of the five monopolies exercised by the Triad:

- globalized finance,
- technological innovation,
- access to global resources,
- means of communication and information, and
- weapons of mass destruction.

What of marginalized regions? Is this a phenomenon without historical precedent? Or does it embody on the contrary a permanent tendency of capitalist expansion, one that was momentarily checked, in the aftermath of World War II, by power relationships that were more favourable to peripheries as a whole? The argument states that this exceptional situation was the basis of the Third World's 'solidarity' – despite the variety of countries of which it was composed – in its anticolonial struggles, its demands with regard to primary products, and its political will to impose its own modernization and industrialization, which Western powers attempted to prevent. It is precisely because the successes achieved on these fronts have been uneven that the coherence and solidarity of the Third World have been eroded. As noted elsewhere in this volume, the dominant ideology proclaims that 'there is no alternative' and that the peoples of the world must 'adjust' to the so-called rationality and efficiency requirements of the market economy.

WHAT IS NEW IN THE WORLD CAPITALIST SYSTEM?

A number of major features of today's general economic situation have been defined and seriously studied. At this point, it will be sufficient if we outline the most important of these features:

- First, the same fundamental options, known as neoliberalism, inspire the economic policies of almost every government in the world. In the countries of the Triad and within the European Community, these options are associated with recognized goals: deregulation, more flexible labour markets, unlimited privatization (including the privatization of traditionally public services), cuts to social spending, emphasis on combatting inflation (supported by tight monetary policies and high positive real interest rates), uncontrolled openness to international capital transfers, and so on. In many southern and eastern countries these options are reinforced by the implementation of draconian 'structural adjustment' programmes (SAPs) and, in some cases, by what is known as 'shock therapy.'

  However, this general description must be qualified by important distinctions concerning the countries of East Asia (Korea, China, Taiwan and to a lesser extent, Southeast Asia), which are not really playing the neoliberal game. These countries implement the kind of coherent industrialization policies that other countries have given up, and that are practically 'planned' in that government interventions are designed to provide energetic support for their requirements.

- Second, a crisis is being experienced by almost every country in the world. Symptoms include weak economic growth (zero or negative growth for many Eastern European countries and for marginalized areas of the Third World), weak investments in productive activity, and the rise of unemployment. We have already mentioned the aggravation of distribution inequalities that accompanies these changes. Stagnation persists, even though official rhetoric still focuses on 'recessions' and 'upturns.'
- Financialization is a third defining characteristic of this era. This is reflected in the domination of short-term, speculative concerns, imposing themselves at the expense of long-term choices favouring productive investments.
- Fourth, as globalization advances, so does the subordination of national policies to the hazards of this unbridled capitalism, made uncontrollable through fundamental neoliberal choices such as flexible exchange rates and freedom of financial transfers.

Together, these factors lead almost everywhere to economies running at several different speeds: certain sectors, regions and companies (especially among the large multinationals) record strong growth rates and large profits, while others stagnate, regress or disintegrate. Labour markets are segmented to adjust to this situation.

Once again, is this a genuinely new phenomenon? Or is a multi-speed system in fact the norm throughout the history of capitalism? The phenomenon would merely have been attenuated for exceptional reasons during the postwar period (1945–80), when social relations had imposed systematic government interventions (on the part of the welfare state, the Soviet state and the national state in Third World countries of the Bandung era) that made it easier to generalize the growth and modernization of productive forces by organizing the regional and sectional transfers that shaped this growth. On at least two levels, these transformations bring decisive long-term effects.

Giant corporations are certainly not a new development in the history of capitalism. However, it has been rightly pointed out that some aspects of their evolution are new. Until now, large corporations – even the ones known as multinationals – have been in the first place (and particularly in terms of who owned their capital) national firms whose activity had extended beyond the frontiers of their country of origin. In order to deploy themselves, they needed the active and positive support of their government. Today they have become powerful enough to develop their own strategies of expansion outside (and sometimes against) the assumptions of government policies. Therefore, they want to subordinate these policies to their own strategies. Anti-government neoliberal discourse conceals this objective to legitimize the exclusive purpose of defending the private interests represented by these corporations. The 'freedom' being demanded is not freedom for all; it is freedom for corporations to pursue their interests at others' expense. From this point of view the neoliberal discourse is perfectly ideological and dishonest.

On another level more directly related to current technological revolutions, work processes are now being radically modified. Assembly-line production (the Taylorist model) is being replaced by new forms that are profoundly affecting the structure of social classes and their perception of the problems and challenges faced by workers. Here too we find important elements of the problems related to the segmentation of labour markets.

Financialization can be analyzed as a product of this crisis. Surplus capital, which under existing structures cannot find an outlet in the expansion of productive systems, embodies a serious danger for the dominant class – the danger of a massive devaluation of capital. Management of the crisis therefore demands that financial outlets be provided in order to avoid this worst possible outcome. High interest rates, flexible exchange rates, the foreign debt of the Third World and Eastern European countries, the American deficit, privatization and the financialization of pension funds are means to this end. However, the flight forward into financialization does not offer a way out of the crisis; on the contrary, it leads to imprisonment in a stagnationist spiral because it worsens distributional inequality and forces companies to play the financial game. In this sense financialization is not merely synonymous with the domination of financial institutions (banks, insurance companies, pension funds); it also means that financial assumptions dominate the management of all corporations.

The 'Asian miracle' has received considerable attention. The Asia/Pacific region is frequently viewed as the centre of the emerging future, and taking over the role of Europe/North America in dominating the planet. In a more sober vein, the Asian phenomenon has given rise to assertions which deserve serious attention. These assertions question both the theory of the polarization inherent in worldwide capitalist expansion (a theory that is unfortunately often confused with vulgar versions of 'dependency'), and the strategies of disconnection suggested as ways of meeting the challenge of polarization. There is supposed to be evidence that catching up is possible, and that it is more likely to be achieved by active integration into world markets (in the vulgar version of this argument, this can ultimately mean an export-oriented strategy) than by an illusory disconnection (which is deemed to have caused the Soviet catastrophe). Internal factors, including the 'cultural' factor, would therefore explain why some have succeeded in imposing themselves as agents actively shaping the world, while others have failed and become marginalized and disconnected against their will.

If we are to make genuine progress in discussing these complex issues, we need to distinguish the various levels of analysis dealing with internal social structures and forces acting at the level of the world system. In my view the Soviet evolution, for example, is chiefly explained by the nature of the system's social options (the 'capitalism without capitalists' project). An active and controlled integration into globalization is very different from an economic strategy based on giving priority to exports; each is founded on a different internal hegemonic social bloc. East Asian countries have been successful precisely to the extent that they have subjected their external relationships to the requirements of their internal development – have refused, at least until recently, to 'adjust' to dominant tendencies at the world level. This is in fact the definition of delinking, which some too hasty readers have confused with autarky.

Polarization, like any other aspect of capitalist society, has not been defined once and for all in some immutable form. What has certainly changed is the way in which it expressed itself for a century and a half through the contrast between industrialized and non-industrialized countries – a contrast that has in fact been challenged by the peripheries' national liberation movements, which have forced the centre itself to adjust to transformations brought about by the industrialization (however uneven) of the peripheries. Can this fact justify the assertion that East Asia is in the process of 'catching up' with Triad centres? This conclusion seems premature. The thesis I am presenting here leads to a very different conclusion: through the action of the Triad's five monopolies, the globalized law of value produces polarization in new forms, subordinating the industry of dynamic peripheries. China, if it chooses further integration into the international division of labour, will not escape this evolution. [This basic reality is stressed by Xiaobo Lu later in this volume. – *Ed.*]

The evolution of China's development will weigh heavily in the global balance, simply because of the weight of this country. The various possibilities in this regard should therefore be thoroughly discussed. I will attempt to make explicit the conditions, internal and external, that govern various scenarios, all of which are equally possible and which can be classified in several ways.

In one scenario, China disintegrates; the northern and western regions are 'marginalized', and the southeast becomes a compradorized region within the Southeast Asian constellation, which is industrialized but nonetheless dominated by the United States and Japan.

Another scenario is that the Chinese national project is pursued on the basis of the success of the 'three positives': (1) social redistribution of income maintains solidarity throughout the region, (2) regional redistribution reinforces the interdependence of China's regional internal markets, and (3) control over external relations continues to be subordinated to the requirements of the national project.

This last scenario deteriorates under the influence of what I have called the 'fourth and major negative', that is, the attempt to pursue the national project without modifying the framework of the existing power system (the Party State described as Leninist). This deterioration could lead either to the breakup of the country (first scenario) or to the crystallization of a more overt, and probably not very democratic, form of national capitalism.

In the third scenario, the current projects shift towards the left as popular social forces reinforce their power, and the country moves forward in the long transition to socialism.

THE GLOBAL MANAGEMENT OF THE CRISIS

The requirements of the economic management of the crisis are expressed in the economic policies described above. However, this dimension of the management of the system cannot work on its own without the support of appropriate political forms, for neoliberalism engenders nothing but chaos and leads to the multiplication of seemingly insoluble conflicts. This is why I have argued that it is not a viable alternative, but merely a method for managing the crisis (this point has given rise to disagreements which meaning should be clarified).

We would probably all agree that the structure of political life was profoundly modified when the page of the postwar era was turned.

Political life and struggles traditionally took place within the framework of political states whose legitimacy was not questioned (a government might be challenged, but not the state itself). Behind the state, political parties, trade unions, a few major institutions (that is, business partners), and the sphere defined by the media as 'the political class' formed the basic structure of the system in which political movements, social struggles and ideological currents found expression.

It is apparent that almost everywhere in the world, all of these institutions have lost part or all of their legitimacy. The people 'don't believe in them anymore'. In their place a variety of 'movements' have taken centre stage, focusing on the demands of environmentalists or women or the struggle for democracy or social justice, or asserting community identities (ethnic or religious). The status of these movements, their patterns of organization or non-organization, their methods of expression (in some cases purely declamatory, in others acting through the channels of political life such as parties and elections, and sometimes resorting to violence) vary from one country to the next, and often from one moment to the next. Extreme instability is therefore a characteristic of this new political life. The way in which these demands and movements combine with a radical critique of society (that is, of actually existing capitalism), or fit into globalized neoliberal management, deserves to be discussed in concrete terms. Some of these movements are or can be part of a conscious and organized refusal of the societal project of dominant powers; others, on the contrary, are not interested in fighting this project.

Dominant powers know how to make this distinction and do in fact make it. Overt or concealed support for some, determined opposition to others; such is the rule in this new, chaotic and agitated political life. The left must also make its own analyses and remember them in defining its strategies for mobilization and action.

One of the major themes of the neoliberal offensive carried out by dominant powers is an all-encompassing anti-state ideology. We have already noted that this offensive serves the private interests of large corporations seeking to free themselves from possible government intervention, because the government might be responsive to the interests of others. However, this does not mean that the world could really function as a pure market, without governments. Large corporations themselves, and capital in general, need a government able at the very least to act as a police officer. The functions of this police officer, at the national and world levels, vary according to the situation.

In the countries of the periphery in the widest sense – integrated and dynamic peripheries of Asia and Latin America, potential new peripheries of Eastern Europe, marginalized peripheries of the African and Islamic worlds – the useful police officer function excludes any serious attempt at democracy. Here, the theme of democracy is cynically invoked to shoot down an adversary (socialist or populist), but is never invoked against an ally or an agent. In this area, the double standard prevails. At times, however, the violence of the political crisis is such that it imposes an appearance of democracy of the type I have referred to as 'little, low-intensity democracy', pseudopluralist and pseudo-electoral, as a way of managing the 'transition'. The era of dictatorships and authoritarian regimes, whether military, theocratic or other, is far from over.

In developed capitalist countries the conflict between the aspirations of popular majorities and the results produced by current policies, the helplessness of states to deal with the forces unleashed by globalization (a helplessness that is accepted and even willed by the classes that dominate the state), and frighteningly effective forms of media manipulation have produced a genuine crisis affecting the idea and practice of democracy.

Generally speaking, contemporary capitalism works within a system of 'low intensity democracy'. Postmodernist ideology seeks to justify this situation by denigrating major struggles over fundamental choices and choosing instead to laud the management of daily life at ground level. The proliferation of NGOs is to a large extent an answer to this strategy of depoliticization of the peoples of the world. Far from constituting the basic structure of a powerful civil society emerging to face the state, these reorganizations accompany the management of society by the dominant forces of capital. A strong civil society goes hand in hand with extensive politicization, living and active class organizations (parties, trade unions and others), and a state that is strong because it is genuinely democratic. A weak state is the best vehicle for the weakening of democracy and civil society.

This management system cannot do without police officers capable of acting at the global level. In this respect, all dominant forces accept that the United States (that is, American military forces equipped with remote-controlled weapons of mass destruction) shall fulfill this function. There is no conflict between globalization as it is proposed by these dominant forces of capital and American hegemony. Neither

Japan, the European Community, nor any of the countries that make up the Community have any real ambition to reduce this power, even if at times, in some European countries, there is a feeling that 'it would be nice if things were otherwise'. The antistate discourse is aimed at all states, except the United States, in its hegemonic political and military functions.

There is an overall political strategy of global management. This strategy is carried out by the United States and supported by the other major powers. This point is certainly the object of controversies and contradictory analyses that need to be discussed. The debate should not be avoided as some kind of stale 'conspiracy theory'. There is no conspiracy, but the adversary does have a general strategy. In my opinion, the goal of this strategy is to maximize the fragmentation of potential antisystemic forces by supporting the breakup of state forms of social organization. Let us have as many Slovenias and Chechenyas as possible! The use or indeed the manipulation of identity demands is highly appreciated in this context.

The issue of community identity and specificity – especially along ethnic or religious lines – is therefore one of the central issues that must be debated with the greatest possible seriousness and sense of responsibility. The basic democratic principle implying genuine respect for diversity, whether national, ethnic, religious, cultural or ideological, must be fully respected. Diversity cannot be managed in any other way than through the sincere practice of democracy, otherwise it is doomed to become a weapon adversaries use for their own purposes.

Historically, left-wing forces have often been deficient in this area – though not always, of course, and not to the extent that is often asserted today. One example among others is Tito's Yugoslavia, which was practically a model of coexistence of nationalities on a genuinely equal footing. In the Third World of the Bandung era, national liberation movements often succeeded in uniting different ethnic and religious communities against the imperialist enemy, and the first generation of ruling classes in African states was often genuinely transethnic. Rare, however, were the powers capable of managing this diversity democratically and maintaining achievements. The weakness of their democratic propensities produced results as regrettable as their management of other problems faced by their societies. Powerless to deal with the crisis when it came, the ruling classes resorted to desperate expedients and often played a key part in encouraging a retreat into community as a way of prolonging their 'control' over the masses.

However, even in many authentic bourgeois democracies in which the fundamental freedoms are respected, community diversity has certainly not always been handled appropriately. Great Britain in Ireland, racism in the United States, and the treatment of native people in Latin America, are a few examples, as are non-democratic regimes like those of the former Soviet Union. Many other examples might be invoked. The very real problems of oppressed peoples must be addressed. We cannot do otherwise than respect diversity, which actually existing systems fail to honour. A serious debate on the issue of specificity and the culturalist ideology is therefore necessary. In my opinion (which many do not share), the success of culturalism is proportional to the deficiencies of democratic management of diversity. By culturalism I mean the assertion that these differences are 'paramount' and should be given 'priority' (over class differences, for example); they are sometimes even considered 'transhistorical', that is, founded on historical invariants (this is often the case of religious culturalisms, which then easily slide towards obscurantism and fanaticism).

In order to see more clearly in the jungle of identity claims, I submit for discussion a criterion that strikes me as essential. Progressive movements are those whose demands combine with the struggle against social exploitation and for the extension of democracy in all dimensions. In our current phase, progressive movements are therefore those that help open people's eyes to the reality of globalized neoliberal management. That is, those that clearly refuse to support, tolerate or ignore the objectives of unbridled capitalist globalization, the subjection of workers and peoples, and 'low intensity' democratic management. On the other hand, movements that claim to be 'without a social programme' are reactionary movements that perfectly serve the interests of dominant capital. Dominant capital supports these movements, even while the media denounce the very people who become the victims. These movements are used and in some cases even manipulated.

In conclusion, I will revert here to the scenarios for the future that follow from the basic assumptions of the deployment of capital's project for globalized domination. On the basis of what has been said above, variations of the one big scenario are possible:

1. European variations: German Europe? with or without the euro? Latin-Americanization of Eastern Europe? Breakup (or downplaying) of the European Community?

2. East Asian variations: regional Asia–Pacific integration around Japan and the United States? Regional integration of eastern Asia, minus Japan, around China? Breakup of China?

The 'big' project, in any case, is already formulated in terms of neo-imperialist regionalizations (along the lines of 'sharing the burden'), defining geostrategic southern spaces behind each of the powers constituting the Triad:

1. USA/Canada/Latin America (definition of this space has begun with the integration of Mexico through the North American Free Trade Agreement (NAFTA)).
2. USA/Israel/oil-producing countries of the Persian Gulf/Arab Mashrek.
3. European Community/Maghreb/sub-Saharan Africa.
4. European Community (or Germany)/Eastern Europe, or, alternatively, Germany/USA/Eastern Europe/former Soviet Union.
5. Japan/Association of Southeast Asian Nations (ASEAN) or Japan/USA/Asia–Pacific.

Here also, two observations probably deserve further discussion. First, is the neo-imperialist project compatible with the emergence of about 15 regional and subregional poles enjoying 'privileges' in their region, but continuing to act as faithful relays under 'open' globalization? Germany and Japan immediately spring to mind. Others include Brazil in South America, Israel in the Middle East, South Africa in southern Africa, Turkey (and/or Iran) in west central Asia, and Korea in eastern Asia. Second, is it possible for some of the subregional poles to 'rebel' and extend their autonomy in conflict with globalization/American hegemony? On what conditions? Brazil and the Mercosur initiative, for instance, might provide an example if Mercosur were to increase its distance from liberal dogmas.

In this general context, it is easy to imagine a new stage of capitalist expansion based on the accelerated growth of active peripheries (China, East Asia, India, Latin America) and a renewal of growth in Eastern Europe, the former Soviet Union and the European Community, while the marginalized African and Islamic world is left to its convulsions. Intensified exchanges between the world's various dynamic regions would certainly support this project. However, in my view, the further we go in this direction the more exchanges between the regions in question will intensify and the more the new polarization founded on the Triad's five monopolies will increase. In this perspective the disparities between regional levels of development would not decrease; on the contrary, the distance between the centres and the new periphery would widen.

This scenario could be disrupted in various ways. For example, a renewal of class struggles is foreseeable and already visible (France, 1995; Korea, January 1997). The movement will spread and progressively erode the power of dominant capital's offensive. It may thus prepare the conditions for the emergence of the alternative that we will be considering in the fourth section of this chapter. Another possibility is that the ruling classes and hegemonic blocs of certain countries may also act to inflect the model in a direction more favourable to them, thus enlarging their margin of autonomy. I am thinking firstly of China – especially if the social solidarity which endows its project with a marked national character should be reinforced by the intervention of currently excluded popular forces – but also of Korea, India and Brazil.

OUTLINE OF AN ALTERNATIVE ECONOMY SERVING THE PEOPLE

Any alternative that is going to embody respect for all people must inevitably start with the reinforcement, through their struggles, of their power in their national societies. In the absence of such developments, discourses on alternatives remain pious hopes, academic exercises and the wishes of intellectuals. 'Pleas' based on 'reason' or general interest, addressed to existing powers, will never have any effect because the policies carried out by these powers are sufficiently rational and efficient from the point of view of the social interests they defend. The results they produce (unemployment, inequalities, exclusion) are their true objectives, while the rhetoric of politicians who deplore them are pure hypocrisy. Nor can we rely on the spontaneity of struggles in hopes that they will invent a coherent alternative of themselves.

A profoundly responsible discussion of the lineaments of an alternative is therefore, and will remain, indispensable for all analysts and actors of social change. Fortunately, debates of this type are numerous and often rich. However, they usually take place within a country or a region, and for this reason the global dimension of problems and solutions is often missing. Other debates, equally important, immediately focus on the planetary aspect of problems. But these debates often present the opposite flaw: world problems are not related to national problems, which are ignored or simplified.

We must reject the idea that globalization is a take-it-or-leave-it proposition – take it as it is, in its unbridled form designed to answer the needs of large corporations, or leave it and choose confinement in some autarkic absurdity. Globalization, like everything else, can be embodied in many possible alternatives defined by the balance in the relationships between nations at any given moment, and, behind them, the specific internal social relations of these nations. Just as the reinforcement of the popular classes is an absolutely necessary condition for the emergence of alternatives at the national level, the reinforcement of peoples at the peripheries (active and marginalized) is essential within the world system. How can this be achieved? Certainly not through 'humanitarian' rhetoric (or interventions), nor through 'cooperation' as it is developed even in the most well-intentioned circles.

In this case, as in internal matters, we are dealing with power relationships that can be modified only by the parties involved, that is, the countries of the peripheries, whether active or marginalized. I am suggesting that emphasis should be put on giving priority to the construction of large regional groups. However, these zones must not be defined as they are in the neo-imperialist project (as zones of specific responsibility for each member of the Triad, that is, as vehicles for unbridled globalization), but, on the contrary, as blocs of resistance to globalization capable of forcing the renegotiation of north/south relationships. Obviously, we are all thinking of the Latin American, African, Arab and Southeast Asian blocs, for no single country in these regions has enough weight to modify the heavy constraints imposed on it by unbridled globalization. The only possible exceptions are China, India, Brazil and Russia. The regionalization I am suggesting seems to me the only reasonable and effective way of opposing the polarizing effects of the Triad's monopolies. Specifically, it would be possible to define the essential orientations of the regionalization projects I am suggesting, that is, the priorities that the projects ought to serve.

Of course, the transformations of the international order I am advocating will become feasible only if, and to the extent that, the nature of power is itself transformed in the countries of the periphery as popular, national and democratic hegemonic blocs replace dominant comprador blocs. At that point, it will be possible to look again at the major issues related to the world order to propose orientations and objectives for major negotiations that could organize a controlled interdependence, designed to serve the peoples of the world, in the following issue areas:

1. Renegotiation of 'market shares' and the rules of access to them. This project, of course, challenges the rules of the World Trade Organization (WTO), which, behind the rhetoric of 'fair competition', is exclusively occupied with defending the privileges of oligopolies active at the world level.
2. Renegotiation of the systems of capital markets, in order to end the domination of financial speculation operations and channel investment towards productive activities in the north and south. This project challenges the functions, and perhaps even the existence, of the World Bank.
3. Renegotiation of monetary systems in order to set up regional arrangements and systems ensuring the relative stability of exchange rates and organizing their interdependence. This project challenges the International Monetary Fund (IMF), the dollar standard, and the principle of free and floating exchange rates.
4. The beginning of a worldwide taxation system, involving, for instance, the taxation of rents derived from the exploitation of natural resources and their redistribution throughout the world according to appropriate criteria and for appropriate purposes.
5. The demilitarization of the planet, beginning with the reduction of the most powerful forces of mass destruction.
6. The democratization of the United Nations (UN) through the creation of a second assembly more representative of popular social forces within member countries.

Considered as a whole, the proposals outlined in the previous paragraphs embody a kind of programme for building economies that serve the peoples of the world. Would this be a capitalist or a socialist economy? It is important to debate this point. My perception is that it would associate elements of both in an undeniably conflictual relationship, imposing a compromise at this stage between the assumptions of capitalism and those that are independent of capitalism. This is a stage in the long transition from world capitalism to world socialism.

3 Conceptualizing Resistance to Globalization

Christine B.N. Chin and James H. Mittelman

Assessments of resistance to globalization are necessarily influenced by the manner in which one conceptualizes these processes. Too often, both terms are used promiscuously, the former as a buzzword or catchall and the latter in many different ways, sometimes as a synonym for challenges, protests, intransigence or even evasions. Hence, we seek to juxtapose alternative explanations of resistance and highlight the complexities of conceptualizing it. The purpose of this chapter, then, is to explore the question: What is the meaning of resistance in the context of globalization?

Perhaps the most potent force restructuring world order at the turn of the millennium, globalization encompasses multiple changes in the economy, politics and culture. Among the main feature of economic globalization is a fundamental shift towards an integrated and coordinated division of labour in production and trade. The global division of labour comprises new technologies, especially in communications and transportation; a reorientation in emphasis from the old Fordist production systems toward post-Fordism, with pressures for greater flexibility in the workforce and heightened patterns of specialization; and distinctive regional divisions of labour tethered to the growth mechanisms of the world economy. Today, cross-border flows – undocumented workers, finance, knowledge and information – take on new proportions and transcend territorial states. What is new as well is the reduction of effective regulatory control over this activity.[1]

Concurrent to these accelerations and decelerations in different zones of the global economy are political responses to economic globalization. To delimit the politics of globalization one must first come to terms with the concept of globalization itself. Broadly speaking, there are two interpretations. The strong thesis advanced by some of the purveyors of globalization holds that it is a totalizing or homogenizing force washing across all shores and battering down the barriers that stand in its way.[2] In fact, much of the discomfort with the literature on globalization focuses on this strong argument about a 'borderless world'.[3] Whereas the enthusiasts of globalization overwork the category and engage in economic overdetermination, some critically-minded scholars embrace a less demanding and, in our view, a more compelling claim. Globalization is not only about a series of intensifications in the dynamics of capitalism (that is, competition and accumulation), but also fundamentally about interactions – changes in different spheres of social activity, the ways that they compress time and space, and their varied impact on strata in zones of the world economy. In this sense, globalization may be construed as a partial, incomplete and contradictory process – an uneasy correlation of economic forces, power relations and social structures.

A major asymmetry in the globalization trend is between its economic and political levels. Although it would be wrong to concede the neoclassical premise that economics and politics are separable realms, it is clear, at least in analytical terms, that globalization's hegemonic project is neoliberalism and that liberal democracy cannot keep pace with its spread. In the space opened by this disjuncture, resistance movements are on the rise. But they cannot solely be understood as a political reaction to globalization. Rather, in the teeth of globalizing tendencies, resistance movements shape and are constitutive of cultural processes. Such is the main thesis to be developed in this chapter.

For us, and in brief, culture may be regarded as interest- constituted social processes that create specific and different whole ways of life, of which material social life is an inextricable part.[4] There is no dearth of culturally laden manifestations of resistance to globalization. Culminating in the election of a Government of National Unity, led by the African National Congress, in South Africa in 1994, the worldwide anti-*apartheid* movement against a racial monopoly of the means of production, buttressed by substantial flows of foreign capital, may be the foremost example of a movement against globalization from above. There are numerous illustrations of more localized resistance, such as the Zapatista armed uprising among the Maya Indians against the Mexican government's neoliberal reforms, symbolically launched on 1 January 1994, the day of the inauguration of the North American Free Trade Agreement. But it would be facile to conceptualize resistance only as declared organized opposition to institutionalized economic and military power. One must dig deep to excavate the everyday individual and collective activities that fall short of open opposition. To grasp resistance to globalization, one must also examine the subtexts of political and cultural life, the possibilities and potential for structural transformation.

We begin to delve the constitutive role of power in shaping cultural critiques of economic globalization as well as patterns of struggle by revisiting the works of three master theorists of resistance, even if their writing was not explicitly directed at the contemporary phase of globalization: Antonio Gramsci's concept of counterhegemony, Karl Polanyi's notion of countermovements, and James C. Scott's idea of infrapolitics. For the sake of brevity, our compass is limited to these authors; other conceptualizations and systematic empirical referents cannot be provided within the space allotted to us. We hold that the trialectic of Gramsci–Polanyi–Scott, set forth through a critical evaluation of each author's work in the next three sections of this chapter, offers a sound basis for reconceptualizing resistance movements. The conclusion then probes the convergence and contrasting emphases within the triad, and also suggests directions for further study and exploratory research.

RESISTANCE AS COUNTERHEGEMONY

Ostensibly, Gramsci's analysis of social change as explicated in *Selections from the Prison Notebooks* neither could have anticipated nor accounted for globalization.[5] The notes were written between 1929 and 1935 while Gramsci, a member of Parliament and the general secretary of the Communist party, was imprisoned by the fascist regime in Italy. In his discussions of state–society relations, Gramsci was concerned particularly with orthodox Marxist and bourgeois liberal theoretical frameworks that privileged 'economism' by reducing transformations in all aspects of social life to economic determinants.

Gramsci's theoretical efforts to transcend economism are applicable to conceptualizing late twentieth-century resistance. In place of economism, he developed the concept of hegemony. Hegemony encompasses whole ways of life; it is a dynamic lived process in which social identities, relations, organizations and structures based on asymmetrical distributions of power and influence are constituted by the dominant classes. Hegemony, then, is as much economic as it is 'ethico-political' in shaping relations of domination and subordination.

The institutions of civil society such as the church, family, schools, media and trade associations give meaning and organize everyday life so that the need for the application of force is reduced. Hegemony is established when power and control over social life are perceived as emanating from 'self-government' (that is, self-government of individuals embedded in communities) as opposed to an external source(s) such as the state or the dominant strata.[6] Since hegemony is a lived process, different historical contexts will produce different forms of hegemony with different sets of actors, such as the nineteenth-century 'passive revolution' of the Risorgimento, in which the bourgeoisie in Italy attained power without fundamental restructuring from below, and the early twentieth-century proletarian revolutionary leadership in Russia.

The processes of establishing hegemony, however, can never be complete because the hegemonic project presumes and requires the participation of subordinate groups. While hegemony is being implemented, maintained and/or defended, it can be challenged and resisted in the interlocking realms of civil society, political society and the state. Different forms and dimensions of resistance to hegemony are subsumed under the rubric of counterhegemony. Implicit in the counterhegemonic project are 'wars of movement' and 'wars of position', in which people engage in openly-declared collective action against the state. Wars of movement are frontal assaults against the state (for example, labour strikes or even military action), whereas wars of position can be read as non-violent resistance (for example, boycotts that are designed to impede everyday functions of the state).[7] The objective of both types of war is to seize control of the state.

Wars of movement and position are expressions of counterhegemonic consciousness at the collective level. They represent moments in history when individuals come together in violent and non-violent confrontations with the state. The question remains, how and why does counterhegemonic consciousness emerge in everyday life, leading to openly-declared collective action?

Gramsci's discussion of common sense in the development of counterhegemonic consciousness is crucial to explaining historical and/or contemporary forms of resistance. Common sense that is held and practiced in everyday life is neither linear nor unitary; it is the product of an individual's relationship to and position in a variety of social groups:

> In acquiring one's conception of the world one always belongs to a particular grouping which is that of all the social elements which share the same mode of thinking and acting. We are all conformists

> of some conformism or other . . . *When one's conception of the world is not critical and coherent but disjointed and episodic, one belongs simultaneously to a multiplicity of mass human groups* . . . The starting point of critical elaboration is the consciousness of what one really is, and is 'knowing thyself' as a product of the historical process to date which has deposited in you an infinity of traces, without leaving an inventory.[8] (Emphasis added)

Importantly, the coexistence of conformity and resistance in common sense can give rise to inconsistencies between thought and action, which help explain contradictory behaviour on the part of a subaltern group which may embrace its 'own conception of the world' while still adopting conceptions borrowed from dominant classes:

> [T]he co-existence of two conceptions of the world, one affirmed in words and the other displayed in effective action, is not simply a product of self- deception . . . It signifies that the social group in question may indeed have its own conception of the world, even if only embryonic; a conception which manifests itself in action, but occasionally and in flashes . . . *But this same group has, for reasons of submission and intellectual subordination, adopted a conception which is not its own but is borrowed from another group; and it affirms this conception verbally and believes itself to be following it, because this is the conception which it follows in 'normal times' that is when its conduct is not independent and autonomous, but submissive and subordinate.*[9] (Emphasis added)

By arguing that individuals and groups possess critical consciousness – albeit 'in flashes' – of their subordinate positions in society, Gramsci acknowledged the ambiguity of resistance and dismissed the overly deterministic and unidimensional explanation of false consciousness.

Nevertheless, in the discussion of thought and action, Gramsci was careful not to suggest that submission in the face of domination is the simple product of the subaltern's rational calculation of costs and benefits (in the sense that resistance would be futile at best, or would elicit retaliatory action, at worst). The fragmentation of social identity which characterizes and is characterized by simultaneous membership in different groups means that it is possible, if not probable, that the subaltern can be progressive on certain issues and reactionary on others in the same instance.

A Gramscian reading of resistance would have to explicate the development of counterhegemonic consciousness that informs wars of movement and position, as well as national–popular actions led by organic intellectuals from all walks of life who can meld theory and *praxis* to construct and embed a new common sense that binds disparate voices and consciousness into a coherent programme of change. In his time, Gramsci called for organic intellectuals to infuse common sense with a philosophy of praxis that encourages subaltern groups' critical understanding of their subordination in society. The objective is a 'national–popular' movement constituted by alliances between the leaders (in league with their organic intellectuals) and the led (subaltern). Whereas wars of movement and position capture the state, the national–popular movement provides the new basis for whole ways of life.

Gramsci did not offer programmatic ways that a philosophy of praxis could transcend the fragmentation of identity and interests. With contemporary globalization, the interpenetration of forces at the local, national, regional and world levels implies that different peoples enter into alliances that can be and are ever more contradictory – for example, low-wage female factory workers in Free Trade Zones who also are members or supporters of Islamicist movements in Southeast Asia. A new common sense has to address effectively or make coherent women's critical understanding of the tensions, limitations and opportunities inherent in their identities as daughters or wives in the household, as low-wage workers on the factory floor, as citizens, and as Muslims in the local, national and transnational Islamic communities.

Moreover, globalization begets openly-declared forms of resistance that may or may not have the state as a target. In a context in which liberal, authoritarian and ex-communist states in transition alike are becoming conveyor belts for transnational capital, if and when it occurs the driving force(s) of openly-declared resistance against the state must be analyzed within the larger context of the contradictory ways in which state structures and policies assume 'educative' functions that nurture a new kind of citizenry and civilization commensurate with the requirements of transnational capital, while trying to maintain the legitimacy with which to govern.[10]

Although wars of movement and position may still be discerned, sometimes in nascent form, the compression of time and space has created new venues of and for resistance. Contemporary social movements simultaneously occupy local, national, transnational and/or global space as a result of innovations in, and applications of technologies that produce instantaneous communication across borders (for example, the Internet, facsimile machines, cellular mobile phones and globalized media). The Gramscian framework of resistance must be stretched to encompass new actors and spaces from which late twentieth-century counterhegemonic consciousness is expressed. In the following section, we discuss the possibility of further considering social movements as a form of resistance.

RESISTANCE AS COUNTERMOVEMENTS

In *The Great Transformation: The Political and Economic Origins of Our Time*, Karl Polanyi argued that the causes of global political, economic and social crises of the 1930s leading to World War II, may be traced to state-supported implementation of the 'self-regulating' market system during the eighteenth and nineteenth centuries.[11] The movement to install and expand the self-regulating market sparked protective measures or countermovements to reexert social control over the market – hence, the notion of a double movement.

Polanyi understood resistance in the form of countermovements as having arisen from, and affecting, different and whole ways of life. Protecting workers from the commodification process implies defending the social relations and institutions of which they are a part:

> *In disposing of a man's labour power the system would, incidently, dispose of the physical, psychological, and moral entity 'man' attached to that tag. Robbed of the protective covering of cultural institutions, human beings would perish from the effects of social exposure*; they would die as victims of acute social dislocation through vice, perversion ... [N]o society could stand the effects of such a system of crude fiction even for the shortest stretch of time unless its human and natural substance as well as its business organization was protected against the ravages of this satanic mill.[12] (Emphasis added)

The movement–countermovement framework allows one to conceptualize contemporary social movements as a form of resistance since the latter are, in the main, defined as 'a form of collective action (a) based on solidarity, (b) carrying on a conflict, (c) breaking the limits of the system in which action occurs'.[13] The level of analysis would have to be extended from the national to the transnational and/or global levels since some contemporary social movements – for example, those that concern environmental destruction, women's rights and indigenous peoples' rights – appear to bypass the state in search of transnational or global solutions.

There are two implicit problems in the counter/social movement framework. Collectivity is assumed in the notion 'movement' and this has the effect of constructing counter/social movements as united fronts in and of themselves. In the past decade or so, the fragmented nature of the feminist movement is evidenced in the internal conflict and domination generated from differences of race, religion, class and nationality, in spite of and because of attempts to address national and global patriarchy.[14]

That which also is imputed in counter/social movements is the presence of organizational structure. This may be the case with some social movements (for example, Greenpeace and Friends of the Earth in the environmental movement), but 'submerged networks' with no clearly defined organizational structure have also formed in an era of globalization. Participants in submerged networks live their everyday lives mostly without engaging in openly-declared contestations:

> They question definition of codes, nomination of reality. They don't ask, they offer. They offer by their own existence other ways of defining the meaning of individual and collective action. They act as new media: they enlighten what every system doesn't say of itself, the amount of silence, violence, irrationality which is always hidden in dominant codes.[15]

The presence of submerged networks gives new meaning to resistance. Even though participants can mobilize to protest state policies, open engagement or confrontation with the state or even transnational corporations is not the immediate or even ultimate objective. In the absence of openly-declared collective action, resistance has to be read as the ways in which peoples live their everyday lives. Submerged networks affirm that even though resistance can be manifestly political and/or economic, it is shaped by and shapes whole ways of life. In advanced industrialized societies, examples of submerged networks are those in which families and their friends make it a point – in their consumption habits – to refuse to buy tuna fish caught using methods that destroy entire dolphin populations, and/or those who purchase only consumer products from companies that actively practice environmental conservationism. Such acts have economic consequences in the corporate world, and political consequences for policy-makers. Significantly, submerged networks are sites of emerging alternative values and lifestyles.

In Egypt, for example, submerged networks exist in the informal sector of the *sha'b*. Networks radiate from the family – the basic unit of social organization in the *sha'b* – to include ties that transcend class, occupation and kin. The 'familial ethos' governs the allocation and distribution of material and symbolic resources in the *sha'b*.[16] In the present unspoken pact between the Egyptian state and the *sha'b,* state legitimacy is maintained by the distribution of basic goods and services to the *sha'b* in return for political acquiescence. Participants of the *sha'b* acquiesce to, as much as they engage in, resistance against the state. Members of the Islamic movement, who also are members of the *sha'b*, have been known to and can draw on submerged network ties to smuggle arms and, on occasion, to mobilize and organize mass protests against the state.

The notion of the Polanyian double movement thus has a distinct advantage of neatly encapsulating openly-declared demands on the national, transnational and/or global levels, for protective measures against various dimensions in the implementation and expansion of the self-regulating market. As discussed, however, the movement–countermovement framework neither forwards analysis of differences within countermovements nor anticipates undeclared forms of resistance, both of which have emerged and must be addressed in conceptualizing late-twentieth-century resistance to globalization.

RESISTANCE AS INFRAPOLITICS

In 1990, James C. Scott introduced the idea of 'infrapolitics' as everyday forms of resistance conducted singularly and/or collectively, and that fall short of openly-declared contestations. What began as his attempt to understand the conditions for peasant rebellions in Southeast Asia and the absence of openly-declared resistance in a village in rapidly industrializing Malaysia, gradually led to the conceptualization of 'infrapolitics' to explain the changing meaning of politics and resistance in most forms of day-to-day dominant–subordinate relations.[17]

Scott warned that in the context of increasingly complex societies, the absence of openly-declared contestations should not be conflated with acquiescence. It is in the realm of informal assemblages such as the parallel market, workplace, household and local community, when people negotiate resources and values on an everyday basis, that 'counterhegemonic consciousness is elaborated'.[18] These are the sites of infrapolitical activities that range from foot-dragging, squatting and gossip, to the development of dissident subcultures.

Taken at face value, such activities cannot tell us anything about counterhegemonic discourse until we account for the conditions from which they emerge. Infrapolitics are identified by juxtaposing what Scott calls the 'public' and 'hidden transcripts'. Public transcripts are verbal and non-verbal acts carried out by the dominant party or, 'to put it crudely, the *self* portrait of dominant elites as they would have themselves seen'.[19] They are the public record of superior-subordinate relations in which the latter appears to willingly acquiesce to the stated and unstated expectations of the former. Hidden transcripts, on the other hand, consist of what subordinate parties say and do beyond the realm of the public transcript or the observation of the dominant. In the context of surveillance structures set up by the dominant class(es) or the state, hidden transcripts record infrapolitical activities that surreptitiously challenge practices of economic, status and ideological domination.

The study of infrapolitics, we believe, is premised on what sociologists call ontological narratives.[20] Ontological narrativity does not refer to the mode of representation or the traditional 'story-telling' method of historians (that is, method of presenting historical knowledge) considered non-explanatory and atheoretical by mainstream social scientists. Rather, ontological narratives are the stories that social actors tell, and in the process come to define themselves or to construct their identities and perceive conditions that promote and/or mitigate the possibility for change.[21]

Even though hidden transcripts record contestations over material and symbolic resources and values in everyday life, they do not occur in a localized vacuum. Infrapolitical activities are the product of interactions between structure and agency – the ways that real and perceived constraints and opportunities affect the behaviour of subordinate groups. Scott's analysis of infrapolitical activities thus falls short of capturing the complexities inherent in undeclared forms of everyday resistance. In his study of landlord–peasant relations in a rural Malay village, Scott asserted that analysis of state structures and policies were important *only* to the extent that they impinged on local class relations.[22] Especially during the 1980s and in the context of national agricultural development policies and fluctuating global prices of commodities, landlord–peasant relations were shaped by impingements on, and interactions among, the rural community, state structures and policies, as well as the transformations marking a globalizing economic system.

Superior–subordinate relations such as those of the landlord–peasant, manager–worker, husband–wife, and state official–squatter are embedded in the whole ways of life of which state structures and policies play an important part. Take, for instance, policies designed to normalize the patriarchal nuclear family-form as most natural in and for the expansion and maintenance of capitalist free markets, and/or that privilege scientific/technical education at the expense of the humanities. Such policies frame worldviews as they directly and indirectly affect all aspects of social life from the rate of urbanization, housing development and employment opportunities, to the control and distribution of resources in the household.

In increasingly complex social contexts, subalterns do not have an unproblematic unitary identity. Nor can their behaviour be explained by implicit reference to the economic model of the self-interested utility maximizer. Put simply, infrapolitical activities are not the mere product of subaltern decisions to conduct undeclared resistance in the face of surveillance structures set up by the dominant strata. Class is but one (albeit important) modality of identity in landlord–peasant or other forms of dominant–subordinate relations. The different and possibly conflicting modalities of subaltern identity can be as real and, under certain conditions, as constraining on behaviour as the actual or perceived futility and fear of openly-declared resistance in the face of domination. By putting a unidimensional face on resistance, Scott inadvertently assigns a similar unidimensional face to domination, even though he analytically distinguishes economic, status, and ideological domination.

In this connection, Gramsci reminded us that subaltern identities are embedded in complex overlapping social networks in which individuals simultaneously assume positions of domination and subordination (perhaps as a husband or wife, an elder or junior, a manager or office clerk, and a donor or recipient of aid). Analysis of the manner in which particular combinations of identity are expressed in the context of structural constraints can help explain why, given systems of surveillance (in which rewards and punishments inhere), some conform while others engage in infrapolitical activities of different types. Conversely, this approach also deepens analysis of the changing nature of domination.

Hidden transcripts have the potential to facilitate understanding of the *internal politics* of subaltern groups. The phenomenon of 'domination within domination' occurs in cases in which contradictory alliances are formed between the dominant and the subordinate that, in turn, dominate others. Although Scott acknowledges this point, his emphasis on class without sufficient attention to the interactions between class and non-class forces undermines the efficacy of the infrapolitical framework. The immediate focus on class presumes that the development of class consciousness stands apart exclusively from other modalities of identity.

It is, indeed, possible to argue that class contestations in the context of surveillance can and do lead to infrapolitical activities that are grounded in material life. This argument is made possible *only* after having considered how and why the class dimension comes to be privileged and expressed over other modalities of identity. To do otherwise would reaffirm what Gramsci called 'economism', and subsequently relegate non-economic considerations to the ambit of superstructure.

Infrapolitics are embedded in whole ways of life, of which the material dimension is a necessary part. They embody contestations over the processes of grounded identity construction, maintenance, and transformation, of which the symbolic and material dimensions of class are intertwined with other modalities of identity such as age, gender, race-ethnicity, religion, nationality and/or sexuality. The identification, juxtaposition and analyses of public and hidden transcripts can foreground the conditions in which certain dimensions of counterhegemonic consciousness develop, and how different or even conflicting perspectives within hidden transcripts are negotiated and/or (not) resolved in everyday life.

Resistance conceptualized as infrapolitical activities offers a viable avenue for generating theoretically-grounded studies of everyday responses to globalizing structures and processes. If conducted with sensitivity to the complex interplay between or among multiple identities in the context of structural constraints, the study of public and hidden transcripts may reveal changing notions and practices of work, family and politics, for example, as peoples seek to negotiate a semblance of social control over the expansion of market forces in diverse spheres of their everyday lives.

AN EMERGING RESEARCH AGENDA

The conduct and meaning of resistance are culturally embedded. This foundational proposition is no less applicable or relevant in conceptualizing contemporary resistance to globalization, as it was to

Table 3.1 Comparison of targets and modes of resistance

	Main target	*Mode of resistance*
Gramsci	State apparatuses (understood as an instrument of education)	Wars of movement and position
Polanyi	Market forces (and their legitimation)	Countermovements aimed at self-protection
Scott	Ideologies (public transcripts)	Counterdiscourses

Gramsci, Polanyi and Scott's analyses of social change in different historical periods. The three master theorists acknowledged, implicitly and explicitly, that resistance arises from and is constitutive of specific and whole ways of life.

From this foundational argument, however, the theorists diverged in their respective discussions of the forms and dimensions of resistance. Gramsci and Polanyi, focused on the collective level, whereas Scott drew attention mainly to the level of the individual in everyday life. As delineated by the grid below (see Table 3.1), the main targets and modes of resistance differ from one theorist to another: Gramscian wars of movement and position against the state, Polanyian countermovements against market forces, and Scott's infrapolitical activities in the face of everyday domination.

Differences in levels of analysis, main targets and modes of resistance should not be reasoned by way of the intellectual proclivities of each theorist *per se*. Rather, these conceptual tensions among the theorists correspond to, and reflect, the changing conditions of social life; from Gramsci to Polanyi to Scott, as societies became more complex, so too did the targets and modes of resistance. Contemporary transformations in social life in general, and state–society relations in particular, imply that all three major targets and modes of resistance coexist and are modified in the globalizing process.

Taken as an important conversation and debate, the grid forms a trialectic that may be profitably fastened to neoliberal globalization. The trialectic points to possibilities of identifying and contesting forms of domination, expanding political space, and opening new venues – hence the redefinitions of politics. Seen from the observation points of this trialectic, a conceptualization of contemporary resistance to globalization sensitizes one to the following shift in ontology, suggested below.

Forms of Resistance

As political and economic power becomes more diffused and less institutionalized, so too will forms of resistance. Undeclared forms of resistance conducted individually and collectively in submerged networks parallel openly-declared forms of resistance embodied in wars of movement and position, and countermovements. Depending on the context, everyday activities such as what one wears (for example, the veil in Muslim societies or the 'dashiki' in the African-American community), or buys and consumes may qualify as resistance – as much as that of organized strikes, boycotts, and even armed insurgencies against states and transnational corporations throughout the world. One of the key challenges here is to problematize the absence of openly-declared forms of resistance. Doing so can explicate the changing meaning of politics as a result of interactions between forces of change on the local, national, regional, and global levels.

Agents of Resistance

In the past, agents of resistance were synonymous mostly with union workers, armed rebel/peasants, and political dissidents including students and certain intellectuals, as class contestations assumed overt political and/or military dimensions. In the present, agents of resistance are not restricted to such actors. They range from blue-collar and white-collar workers, and to clerics, homemakers, and middle managers. It is important to note that even state elites can resist the wholesale implementation of neoliberal development paths, for example those who insist on 'Asian-style democracy' in the midst of establishing open markets and free trade. It is the complex ways in which symbolic resources and values articulate with the material conditions of life in different societies that produce a variety of organic intellectuals, a more encompassing group in the current phase of globalization. Class contestations only partly form *the* basis of resistance. Instead, agents of resistance emerge from interactions between structure and agency that lead to the contextual privileging of particular intersections of different modalities of identity – class-nationality-gender-race/ethnicity-religion-sexuality. Implicit in the designation of different peoples as agents of resistance is an expansion of the boundaries associated with the traditional sites of political life.

Sites of Resistance

Resistance is localized, regionalized and globalized at the same time that economic globalization slices across geopolitical borders. What this means, in part, is that the 'public–private' dichotomy no longer holds, for most (albeit not all) dimensions of social life are affected, in varying and interconnected ways, by globalizing forces. Everyday life in the household and the informal market can facilitate as well as resist such forces in distinctly material and/or symbolic ways. Another closely related phenomenon is the development of cyberspace, a site in which resistance finds its instantaneous audience via the Internet or WorldWideWeb. Counterdiscourse is a mode of late-twentieth-century resistance in cyberspace. We have to bear in mind, however, that although states in general are incapable of effectively monitoring and/or censoring cyberspatial counterdiscourse, this particular mode of resistance is open mainly to those who have access to computers, modems and the Internet.

Strategies of Resistance

By strategies, we refer to the actual ways that people, whose modes of existence (for example, through job loss, encroachment on community lands, or undermining of cultural integrity) are threatened by globalization, respond in a sustained manner towards achieving certain objectives. While forms of struggle differ, groups may adopt varied means to contest, scale up or down, and link objectively and/or subjectively to their counterparts in other countries or regions. Local movements become transnational or global with sustained access to communication technologies that construct and maintain communities of like-minded individuals – for example, community activists and scholars meet at different fora for the exchange of information and plans. An emerging strategy of 'borderless solidarity' is to link single issues such as environmental degradation, women's rights and/or racism, and to highlight the interconnectedness of varied dimensions of social life. Analyses of this may bring to bear the conditions and methods by which commonality can be achieved in spite of and because of the fragmentation of identities and interests as political life is transnationalized and globalized. Nonetheless, evolving global strategies of resistance do not entirely make obsolete the state. Under certain circumstances, strategies of resistance can and do pit state agencies against one another. For example, in the case of shipping toxic waste to the developing world, state agencies in charge of environmental protection may join in protests while their counterparts responsible for industrial development continue to encourage the kinds and methods of industrialization that cause environmental destruction. Studies of global, transnational and local resistance, then, must take into account transformations in state structures, whether or not strategies of resistance manifestly engage the state.

Quite clearly, an ontology of resistance to globalization requires grounding. When contextualized, the elements of *forms*, *agents*, *sites* and *strategies* may be viewed in terms of their interactions so as to delimit durable patterns and the potential for structural transformation. The trialectic of Gramsci–Polanyi–Scott calls for conceptual frameworks that link different levels of analysis. Integration of the local with the global can foreground the conditions in which different forms, agents, sites, and strategies of resistance emerge from the conjunctures and disjunctures in the global political economy.

Notes and References

1. See especially Gary Gereffi, 'The Elusive Last Lap in the Quest for Developed-Country Status', in James H. Mittelman (ed.), *Globalization: Critical Reflections* (Boulder, Col.: Lynne Rienner, 1996); James H. Mittelman, 'Rethinking the International Division of Labour in the Context of Globalization', *Third World Quarterly*, vol. 16 (1995), pp. 273–94, and 'Global Restructuring of Production and Migration', in Y. Sakamoto (ed.), *Global Transformation: Challenges to the State System* (New York: United Nations University Press, 1994), pp. 276–98.
2. See especially Kenichi Ohmae, *The Borderless World: Power and Strategy in the Interlinked Economy* (New York: HarperCollins, 1990).
3. See especially Paul Q. Hirst and Grahame Thompson, *Globalization in Question: The International Economy and the Possibilities of Governance* (Cambridge, Mass.: Basil Blackwell, 1996).
4. Our definition of culture is borrowed from Raymond Williams. For a more detailed conceptualization of culture see Williams's book, *Marxism and Literature* (Oxford: Oxford University Press, 1977).
5. Antonio Gramsci, *Selections from the Prison Notebooks,* ed. and trans. Quinten Hoare and Geoffrey Nowell Smith (New York: Lawrence & Wishart and International Publishers, 1971).
6. *Ibid.*, p. 268.
7. *Ibid.*, pp. 229–30. Gramsci also linked wars of position to 'passive revolution' of the dominant classes – that is, revolution from above – that sidesteps the need for fundamental restructuring from below. See section, 'Function of Piedmont', pp. 105–20.
8. Gramsci, *Selections from Prison Notebooks*, *op. cit.* p. 324.

9. *Ibid.*, pp. 326–7.
10. See, for example, Christine B.N. Chin, *In Service and Servitude: Foreign Female Domestic Workers and the Malaysian 'Modernity Project'* (New York: Columbia University Press, 1998).
11. Karl Polanyi, *The Great Transformation: The Political and Economic Origins of Our Time* (Boston: Beacon Press, 1944). For a discussion of different forms of the state and of the ways they relate to the market as well as world order, see Robert W. Cox, *Production, Power, and World Order: Social Forces in the Making of History* (New York: Columbia University Press, 1987).
12. Polanyi, *The Great Transformation*, *ibid.*, p. 73.
13. Alberto Melucci, 'The Symbolic Challenge of Contemporary Social Movements', *Social Research*, vol. 52 (1985) p. 795.
14. See especially, bell hooks, *Feminist Theory: From Margin to Center* (Boston: South End Press, 1984), and *Ain't I a Woman: Black Women and Feminism* (Boston: South End Press, 1981); and Chandra Mohanty, Ann Russo and Lourdes Torres (eds), *Third World Women and the Politics of Feminism* (Bloomington: Indiana University Press, 1991).
15. Melucci, 'The Symbolic Challenge,' *op.cit.*, p. 812.
16. 'The *sha'b* literally refers to a collective mass, people, or Egyptian nation, but is used in its adjectival form to identify lifestyles, neighbourhoods, tastes, and cultural practices which are identified with more indigenous phenomena', Diane Singerman, *Avenues of Participation: Family, Politics and Networks in Urban Quarters of Cairo* (Princeton: Princeton University Press, 1995), pp. 10–11.
17. James C. Scott, *The Moral Economy of the Peasant: Rebellion and Subsistence in Southeast Asia* (New Haven: Yale University Press, 1976), *Weapons of the Weak: Everyday Forms of Peasant Resistance* (New Haven: Yale University Press, 1985), and *Domination and the Arts of Resistance: Hidden Transcripts* (New Haven: Yale University Press, 1990).
18. Scott, *Domination and the Arts of Resistance*, *ibid.*, p. 200.
19. *Ibid.*, p. 18.
20. Margaret R. Somers, 'The Narrative Constitution of Identity: A Relational and Network Approach', *Theory and Society*, vol. 23, no. 5 (1994), pp. 605–49.
21. See especially, Judith Butler and Joan W. Scott (eds), *Feminists Theorize the Political* (New York: Routledge, 1992); Clifford Geertz (ed.), *Local Knowledge: Further Essays in Interpretive Anthropology* (New York: Basic Books, 1983); and Charles Taylor, *Sources of the Self: The Making of Modern Identity* (Cambridge: Harvard University Press, 1989).
22. Scott, *Weapons of the Weak*, *op. cit.*, p. xix.

4 The Essence and Appearance of Globalization: The Rise of Finance Capital

John Weeks

THE CONVENTIONAL WISDOM

The pundits and ideologues of capital have a story to tell and repeat it early and often. The world economy has entered a new period, in which new rules apply derived from the economics of the pre-Keynesian period. Indeed, whatever insights Keynes might have had, they have been swept into the dustbin of history, along with those of others who argued for reforms of capitalism. Needless to say, the radical critics of capitalism are no more than an intellectual curiosity, rather like Ptolemaic astronomers and medieval alchemists.

The story derives from the premise that the countries of the world are now integrated through trade and capital flows to an extent that national economic policy is ineffective in so far as it does not follow a common set of highly restricted policies. Those who deviate from that set of policies can anticipate swift and terrible punishment by the impersonal discipline of *markets*, most notably the *financial markets*. This situation has occurred through an inevitable process which governments, and political actors in general, can no more change than the English monarch of the Dark Ages could prevent the tides of the North Sea from rolling in. It is fortunate, therefore, that the process is desirable as well as inevitable. The globalization of markets will increase the efficiency of resource allocation. As a result, growth will be more rapid throughout the world (and the more rapidly that governments accept the new policy rules the quicker will their countries gain).[1] Consumers will gain from cheaper prices (the welfare gains from realizing comparative advantage in trade); workers will gain from more rapidly rising wages;[2] and all, including the poor, will gain from faster growth.[3]

While it appears that the new policy rules restrict the options of governments to pursue economic and social goals, in fact they represent 'best-practice' policy which governments should undertake in any case. In other words, the new policy rules have the outstanding benefit of restricting governments to *sound* and *realistic* macroeconomic practice. Further, the rules are straightforward, and easily understood and implemented: near-zero fiscal deficits to reduce the crowding out of private investment; tight monetary policy to keep inflation in the low single digits and maintain strongly positive interest rates (to encourage saving and attract short-term capital flows); and a competitive exchange rate to bring about optimal *openness* of economies.[4]

In what follows, it is first argued that there is little evidence for the quantitative changes in international economic integration upon which the globalization thesis is based. This prompts the conclusion that the hypothesized process is not inevitable. Major changes have occurred in the international economic system over the last 20 years; they reflect changes in policy, not inexorable trends. There follows a critique of the theoretical arguments underlying the globalization thesis, especially with regard to the best-practice macro rules. Having made an empirical and theoretical critique, we present an alternative analytical framework for understanding the world economy. We argue that the last 20 years, as a result of conscious and purposeful policies, have fostered a growing hegemony of finance capital over productive capital. This change has accentuated the irrational and unproductive aspects of the circulation of capital. As a result, at the end of the twentieth century, capital can be considered to have run its course, not in a teleological sense, but in the sense that it is manifesting its most irrational and destructive tendencies. This process can be reversed, for it has resulted from policies which have liberated capital from controls by society.

MYTHS AND REALITIES OF GLOBALIZATION

The globalization thesis maintains that the world economy has entered a new era, which one can date roughly from the mid-1980s.[5] Several alleged mega-changes set this new era apart.[6] First, throughout the world economies are more open and trade is substantially more important than in previous eras. This has several consequences: consumption patterns are increasingly international, economic growth is increasingly *export-driven*, and national markets are linked. Second, foreign investment has dramatically increased in importance to become the vehicle of technology transfer and the engine of growth. Third, capital flows dominate trade flows such that the short-term movement of capital is an inexorable disciplining force on government economic policies. In this section the first two hypotheses are considered, while the third is treated in the analytical discussion of productive and financial capital.

Central to the globalization hypothesis is the allegation that international trade has expanded dramatically, such that the term *domestic* market has become almost an oxymoron. If true, this would be both evidence of the era and a major vehicle by which the benefits associated with the new era are realized. A casual inspection of international statistics reveals that international trade in the 1990s was a higher proportion of world output than in previous decades. However, this in itself does not support the 'new era' argument, since trade has grown faster than output in every decade since the end of World War II. This increased trade has been associated with concrete national and international policies, including the various agreements within the framework of the General Agreement on Tariffs and Trade (GATT) and the progressive economic integration of the western European countries. In support of the new era hypothesis, it must be shown that in the 1980s and 1990s this long-term trend accelerated significantly.

To empirically test this hypothesis, we inspect the behaviour of the export-GDP (gross domestic product) ratio for five country groups and the world as a whole: the sub-Sahara, South Asia, East Asia, Latin America, and the Organization for Economic Cooperation and Development (OECD) countries.[7] The hypothesis is tested by regressing the share of exports in GDP (logarithmic form) against a time trend, and dummy variables for five-year periods, with the first five-year period omitted. The results are presented in Table 4.1, with all non-significant coefficients omitted. Inspection of the last row of the table shows that for every country group there was a significant and positive trend in the export-GDP ratio over the 38 years, 1960 to 1997. As is to be expected, the highest trend is for the East Asian countries, for which the ratio increased at 7 per cent per annum.[8] However, the tests for differences across periods prompts the rejection of the new era hypothesis. For two country groups (South Asia and the OECD) and the World group, there was a significant *upward* shift in this measure of openness only in the pre-globalization period 1975–79. For the OECD countries, this was probably the result of the increase in intra-European trade. For the globalization periods, none of the shift-coefficients are significant, with the exception of the *negative*

Table 4.1 Exports as a proportion of GDP and long-term trend, by period, compared to 1970–74 (OLS method)

Periods	*Country groups* *Sub-Sahara*	*South Asia*	*East Asia*	*Latin America*	*OECD members*	*World*
Pre-globalization						
1965–69	No consistent	No consistent	No consistent	No consistent	No consistent	No consistent
1970–74	data for 1960s	data for 1960s	data for 1960s	data for 1960s	data for 1960s	data for 1960s
1975–79	nsgn	+1.1	nsgn	nsgn	+1.2	+1.1
Debt crisis						
1980–84	nsgn	nsgn	nsgn	nsgn	nsgn	nsgn
Globalization						
1985–89	nsgn	−1.3	nsgn	nsgn	nsgn	nsgn
1990–94	nsgn	nsgn	nsgn	nsgn	nsgn	nsgn
1995–97	nsgn	nsgn	nsgn	nsgn	nsgn	nsgn
Trend	+0.8	+3.0	+6.0	+1.3	+0.7	+1.2

Note: Only coefficients with a probability of .10 or less are considered significant. nsgn denotes non-significant. The period shift coefficients and the trend have been converted from logarithms to percentages.

Source: World Bank, *World Bank Stars 1996* [STARS = Socioecomomic Time-Series Access and Retrieval System: CD-ROM] (Washington, DC: World Bank, 1996, CD-ROM) (1960–69); World Bank, *World Development Indicators 1997* (Washington, DC: World Bank, 1997, CD-ROM) (1970–96); and United Nations, *The World Economy at the Beginning of 1998* (New York: Department of Economic and Social Affairs, 1997).

shift for South Asia. Thus, the share of exports in total production, for groups of countries and the world as a whole, was no different in the 1990s than what one would have expected on the basis of long-term trends. Further, if in 1985 one had calculated the trends for each group over the previous 25 years, then projected to 1997 the predicted value would not have been significantly different from the actual value.[9]

To pursue this point further, in Table 4.2 the growth rate of constant-price exports is subjected to a similar statistical test. In this case no trend is included, so the test is for differences in export growth across periods. Again, the new era hypothesis fails to gain support. Only for the countries of the sub-Saharan region is export growth consistently and significantly higher in the globalization periods, yet

Table 4.2 Rate of growth of exports, compared to 1970–74 (OLS method)

	Country groups					
Period	*Sub-Sahara*	*South Asia*	*East Asia*	*Latin America*	*OECD members*	*World*
Pre-globalization						
1965–69	No consistent	No consistent	No consistent	No consistent	No consistent	No consistent
1970–74	data for 1960s	data for 1960s	data for 1960s	data for 1960s	data for 1960s	data for 1960s
1975–79	+2.3	nsgn	nsgn	nsgn	nsgn	nsgn
Debt crisis						
1980–84	nsgn	nsgn	nsgn	nsgn	−1.9	−1.8
Globalization						
1985–89	+2.2	nsgn	nsgn	nsgn	nsgn	nsgn
1990–94	+3.6	+7.3	nsgn	nsgn	nsgn	nsgn
1995–97	+4.8	nsgn	nsgn	nsgn	nsgn	nsgn

Note: Only coefficients with a probability of .10 or less are considered significant. nsgn denotes non-significant. The period shift coefficients have been converted from logarithms to percentages.

Source: World Bank, *World Bank Stars 1996* (1960–69); World Bank, *World Development Indicators* 1997 (1970–96); and United Nations, The *World Economy at the Beginning of 1998*.

these countries, by general agreement among globalizationists, were the ones least integrated into the world economy.[10] South Asia displays one significantly higher coefficient (for 1990–94), and all the others are non-significant.

For direct foreign investment, the evidence is even stronger against the new era hypothesis (see Table 4.3). When one accounts for the trend of direct foreign investment in GDP (positive for each group), there are no significant globalization coefficients famous of the country groups.[11] Further, the level of foreign direct investment is less than 2 per cent of GDP for each region, or considerably less than a tenth of gross domestic investment. This small proportion implies that, except for unusual cases, it is not credible to assert that foreign direct investment could be the engine of growth or even technology transfer for most countries.

An alleged benefit of a more integrated world economy in the new era is that the increased efficiency associated with freer trade and capital flows would generate faster growth.[12] There is virtually no

Table 4.3 Foreign direct investment as a proportion of GDP and long-term trend, by period, compared to 1970–74 (OLS method)

Periods	*Country groups*				
	Sub-Sahara	*South Asia*	*East Asia*	*Latin America*	*OECD members*
Pre-globalization					
1965–69	No consistent	No consistent	No consistent	No consistent	No consistent
1970–74	data for 1960s	data for 1960s	data for 1960s	data for 1960s	data for 1960s
1975–79	nsgn	nsgn	nsgn	nsgn	No data
Debt crisis					
1980–84	nsgn	nsgn	nsgn	nsgn	(base period)
Globalization					
1985–89	nsgn	nsgn	nsgn	nsgn	nsgn
1990–94	nsgn	nsgn	nsgn	nsgn	nsgn
1995–97	nsgn	nsgn	nsgn	nsgn	nsgn
Trend	+0.2	+0.2	+0.6	+0.2	+0.8

Note: Only coefficients with a probability of .10 or less are considered significant. nsgn denotes non-significant. The period shift coefficients and the trend have been converted from logarithms to percentages.

Source: World Bank, *World Bank Stars 1996* (1960–69); World Bank, *World Development Indicators 1997* (1970–96); and United Nations, The *World Economy at the Beginning of 1998*.

rigorous empirical work which seeks to test this hypothesis, though it is the linchpin of the justification for liberalization and new era benefits. Indeed, if the new era has not brought faster growth, it has no justification at all. The mechanism by which faster growth is allegedly achieved is through a more efficient allocation of resources, via comparative advantage with freer trade, and a more efficient distribution of capital across countries. If there have been efficiency gains, then one would expect to find that for *more-integrated* countries the growth rate is higher for any rate of investment. This can be specified by use of a Harrod–Domar model:

$$g_{\mathrm{w}} = \alpha\beta + \phi P_{\mathrm{t}}$$

where g_{w} is the *warranted* rate of growth, α is the output – capital ratio, β the investment – GDP ratio, and P_{t} a shift variable associated with the new era. If allocative efficiency increased in the new era, then a time-series regression should produce a positive coefficient for ϕ. This hypothesis was tested, and the results are presented in Table 4.4. The hypothesis seeks to answer the question: Given the rate of investment for each group of countries, are there differences in growth rates among time periods? The answer is yes, but where differences appear they do not support the new era prediction. For South Asia and East Asia there are no significant differences. For the sub-Saharan region the growth rate for 1975–79 is significantly lower, and is also lower for 1980–84. Some support might be found for the new era hypothesis from the lower growth *discount* for 1985–89, were it not the case that the discount for 1990–94 is the highest of any period. For Latin America the result is similar: there is a decline in the growth discount for both periods in the 1980s, but a return to the debt-crisis level for 1995–97. For the OECD countries the discount is greater for both periods of the 1990s than for the 1970s, and for 1990–94 virtually the same as for the debt-crisis period. Thus, the evidence suggests that, at best, the globalization periods showed no improvement in growth.

Table 4.4 Growth rates by period, compared to 1960–64 (holding investment in GDP constant, OLS method)

	Country groups					
Periods	*Sub-Sahara*	*South Asia*	*East Asia*	*Latin America*	*OECD members*	*World*
Pre-globalization						
1965–69	nsgn	nsgn	nsgn	nsgn	nsgn	nsgn
1970–74	nsgn	nsgn	nsgn	nsgn	−2.5	nsgn
1975–79	−4.2	nsgn	nsgn	nsgn	−2.9	nsgn
Debt crisis						
1980–84	−4.8	nsgn	nsgn	−4.0	−3.4	−3.1
Globalization						
1985–89	−2.4	nsgn	nsgn	−2.5	−2.1	−1.7
1990–94	−5.2	nsgn	nsgn	−1.9	−3.5	−4.0
1995–97	nsgn	nsgn	nsgn	−3.9	−3.0	no data

Note: Only coefficients with a probability of .10 or less are considered significant. nsgn denotes non-significant. The period shift coefficients have been converted from logarithms to percentages.

Source: *World Bank, World Bank Stars 1996* (1960–69); World Bank, *World Development Indicators 1997* (1970–96); and United Nations, The *World Economy at the Beginning of 1998.*

With regard to the investment–GDP itself (see Table 4.5) there are no significant coefficients for the globalization periods, except for the OECD countries which show lower ratios for all three periods, 1985–97, adding to the long-term downward trend. In other words, in the advanced countries globalization was associated with a downward shift in the investment rate, even when one accounts for the negative trend. Figure 4.1 shows the behaviour of investment over 35 years. The figure is constructed with an ordinary least-squares (OLS) regression across the five country groups and over time, with dummy variables assigned to each year (with 1961 omitted). The vertical axis measures annual percentage variations from the average investment rate across groups and years. For over 25 years, from 1962 through 1978, there was a continuous increase in the investment rate relative to the 35–year average, with the exception of a downturn during 1965–68. This was followed by a continuous decline from 1978 through 1984 (1981 being the only increase), after which the investment rate again began to rise to a peak in 1990. This was followed by another

Table 4.5 Gross investment as a proportion of GDP and long-term trend, by period, compared to 1960–64 (OLS method)

Periods	*Country groups*					
	Sub-Sahara	*South Asia*	*East Asia*	*Latin America*	*OECD members*	*World*
Pre-globalization						
1965–69	+1.2	nsgn	+1.2	nsgn	nsgn	nsgn
1970–74	+1.5	nsgn	+1.4	nsgn	nsgn	nsgn
1975–79	+1.6	nsgn	+1.5	+1.3	nsgn	nsgn
Debt crisis						
1980–84	nsgn	nsgn	nsgn	nsgn	−1.2	nsgn
Globalization						
1985–89	nsgn	nsgn	nsgn	nsgn	−1.3	nsgn
1990–94	nsgn	nsgn	nsgn	nsgn	−1.4	nsgn
1995–97	nsgn	nsgn	nsgn	nsgn	−1.5	nsgn
Trend	nsgn	+1.4	+2.6	nsgn	−1.8	nsgn

Note: Only coefficients with a probability of .10 or less are considered significant. nsgn denotes non-significant. The period shift coefficients and the trend have been converted from logarithms to percentages.

Source: *World Bank, World Bank Stars 1996* (1960–69); World Bank, *World Development Indicators 1997* (1970-96); and United Nations, The *World Economy at the Beginning of 1998*.

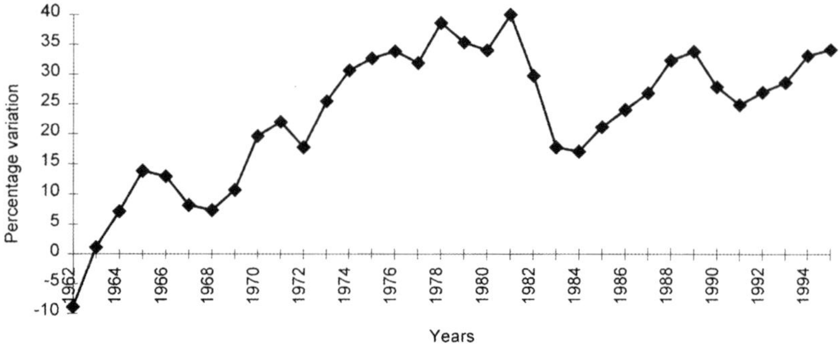

Figure 4.1 OLS annual variations of the investment to GDP ratio, across country groups, 1961–95 (from 1961 level)

Note: The following years are not significant at .10 or less: 1962–69 and 1984.

downward-and-upward cycle in the 1990s. The figure suggests that investment rates showed increasing instability in the globalization periods, a point pursued in a subsequent section.

Figure 4.2 brings together growth rates and investment ratios. As in Figure 4.1, annual growth variations are calculated by a regression across country groups. Dummy variables were assigned to years, using the Harrod–Domar equation (see discussion above).[13] The series with solid markers uses the actual investment rate, while the series with plain markers assumes the investment rate to be constant at the average for all years. Both series show pronounced cycles. If one excludes all single-year breaks in movements,[14] there are four complete cycles: 1964–69, 1969–77, 1977–84 and 1984–94, with durations of five, eight, seven and at least ten years.[15] This sequence suggests that something different did happen in the globalization period: beginning in 1984, world growth entered into a relative decline with a cycle duration considerably longer than those in the 1960s and 1970s.

More important from Figure 4.2 is the vertical difference between the two series and their relationship to the horizontal axis. During the pre-globalization period, 1962–79, the estimated annual growth variations were negative for 5 of 18 years (1962, 1967, 1972, 1975 and 1979), or 28 per cent. For the globalization period, 1985–95, they were negative in 8 of 11 years, *even though the investment rate was above average in each year*. For a given rate of investment (unshaded markers) growth was consistently lower after 1973 than before, and lower still after 1986. Inspection of the annual growth coefficients

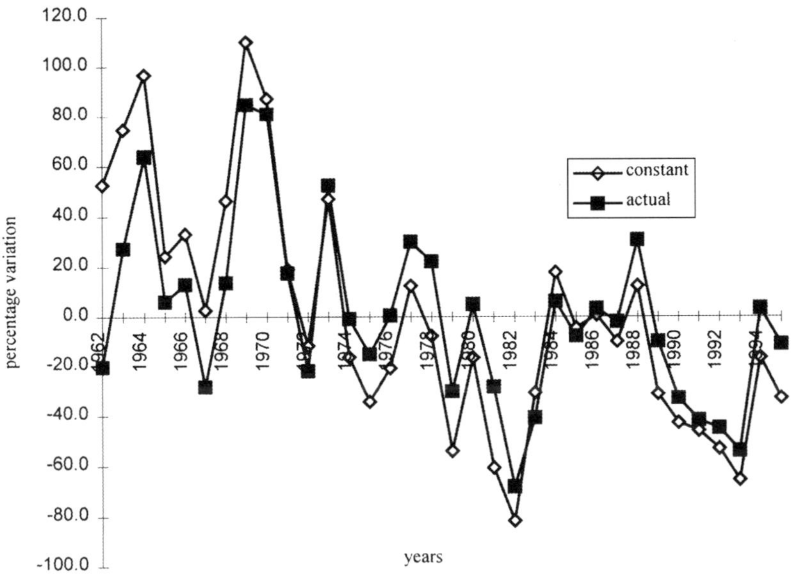

Figure 4.2 OLS annual variations in growth, actual and constant investment, 1961–95

Note: The following years are not significant at .10 or less: 1962, 1967, 1972, 1975, 1979, 1981–82 and 1989–92.

shows that during 1962–73, growth was almost 50 per cent above the 35-year average for the constant rate of investment, 23 per cent *lower* during 1974–86, and 32 per cent *lower* during 1987–95. In other words, *the output return to investment declined*, hardly consistent with increased allocative efficiency of either capital or resources as a whole.

We can conclude that the new era was not associated with significantly increased world trade, faster growth of exports, nor increased foreign investment (beyond long-term trend values); however, it does appear that globalization was associated with lower growth. We pursue these points analytically in the following section.

CRITIQUE OF THE CONVENTIONAL ANALYSIS

The discovery that growth rates have declined across countries during the globalization period should come as no surprise, for two reasons:

first, there is no compelling theoretical argument in orthodox theory that greater allocative efficiency (if such occurred) would increase growth rates; and, second, the macro Golden Rules of the new era can be shown by orthodox theory to be growth-depressing, or, at best, growth-neutral.

The first point can be demonstrated by use of the neoclassical 'production possibilities frontier', presented in Figure 4.3. The curve *PP′* is the familiar, first-year economics locus of all maximum production points in a two-product economy (full employment of resources). With no trade (autarky), consumption and production are at point *a*, with domestic relative prices p_d. In a neoclassical world, this is an inefficient allocation of resources. If the country eliminated all trade barriers it would face the relative prices of the world market, *p*w. This would result in a reallocation of resources to the production combination *b*, followed by trading along the world price line, to arrive at some point like *c*.[16] Thus, the distance along the line designated 'free trade', from *a* to *c*, measures the inefficiency of resource allocation under autarky. Assume that this inefficiency is quite high, say 5 per cent of national income. Assume further that in the general equilibrium at point *c*, the rate of saving and investment is 20 per cent of national income, with a capital output ratio of four. On these assumptions, the rate of growth *g* of the *efficient* economy is 5 per cent per annum.

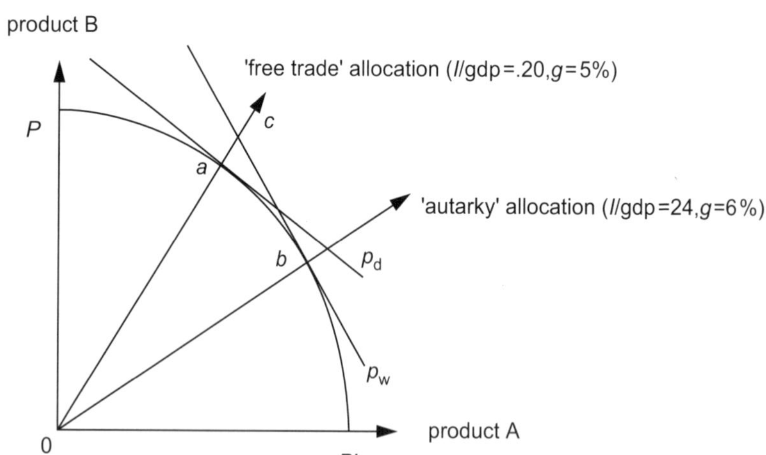

Figure 4.3 Hypothetical growth paths under 'efficient' and 'inefficient' resource allocation (neoclassical framework)

For purposes of argument, let the government of the country, in defiance of all neoclassical rationality, maintain autarky. At the same time, let the government further distort markets by introducing a forced saving scheme which raises the rate of saving to 24 per cent of national income. The increase in saving is then used by the government to invest, or allocated to the private sector for investment.[17] With the same capital–output ratio, the rate of growth g rises to 6 per cent per annum. After five years, national income is the same for the efficient and inefficient cases, and after ten years the latter has a national income 5 per cent higher than the former. If the inefficient case has a saving rate of 28 per cent (growth rate 7 per cent), national income is equalized to the efficient case in less than three years, and after ten years is 15 per cent higher.

Thus, examples in which *distorted* economies grow faster than *undistorted* economies are simple to construct. The orthodoxy must demonstrate that there is some mechanism by which the apparently growth-increasing distortion undermines itself, to produce slower growth.[18] And since no country is free of distortions, it must be demonstrated that each specific distortion is growth-reducing in its own specific manner, and that its growth-reducing effect overwhelms its growth-enhancing effect. In the absence of a theoretical framework to demonstrate this in general,[19] the effect of distortions on growth is an empirical question.

While no conclusion can be reached on the basis of neoclassical theory about the relationship between increased allocative efficiency and growth, the growth consequences of orthodoxy macro-policy is quite clear. As discussed above, the new era macro-rules call for low deficits, high real interest rates, and low inflation. Deficit reduction, other things equal, results in a fall in aggregate demand. This fall in demand would be offset if the deficit reduction led to a fall in real interest rates, which, in turn, increased private investment by more than the negative net fiscal stimulus (a reduction in 'crowding out'). As before, theory cannot demonstrate this; it is an empirical question whose outcome depends on the elasticity of the interest rate with respect to the deficit, and the elasticity of investment with respect to the interest rate. However, one need not investigate these elasticities to critique orthodox macro-policy, because in practice it calls for high real interest rates. If deficit reduction does not lead to lower real interest rates, then, whatever else it may or may not do, it reduces demand.[20]

Parallel to the 'crowding out' argument is that orthodox macro-policies foster growth by reducing inflation.[21] To produce a theoretical sequence by which a reduction in inflation would increase growth requires considerable imagination, as well as immunity to empirical evidence. A recent study, sponsored by the World Bank, reached the conclusion that for rates of price increase of less than 40 per cent per annum there is 'no evidence of a consistent relationship between growth and inflation, at any frequency'.[22] In the absence of an inflation–growth link, the new era macro-rules collapse under their own weight: if higher inflation does not reduce growth, then deficit reduction becomes a question of ideological preference rather than sound policy. Similarly, tight monetary policy (with high interest rates) is revealed for what it has always been recognized to be: deflationary and contractionary.

Neoclassical theory predicts that the new era macro-rules would be growth-reducing; the empirical evidence confirms that prediction. Yet, these rules are presented as if they were best practice, in defiance of clear theory and evidence. Twenty years ago no reputable economist would have endorsed such a patent absurdity, that demand-reduction stimulates growth. The theory has not changed; rather, the political and ideological context has changed and opportunistic arguments of convenience have become respectable. This change results from a shift in political and economic power from productive to financial capital.

AN ANALYTICAL FRAMEWORK

To understand the material and ideological changes that gave rise to globalization, it is necessary to consider the nature of capitalist social relations. By doing so, it will be possible to identify the essence of the changes in the world economy which are misleadingly summarized by this journalistic term. The changes arise from the contradictions of capitalist production and circulation, combined with concrete policy actions that realized the destructive potential of those contradictions. The essential contradiction that created the special character of the 1980s and 1990s is that profit arises from the production of commodities, but accrues to capital through exchange. As a result of conscious policies in the advanced countries, pioneered in the United States and the United Kingdom, financial capital asserted itself over productive capital such that the struggle over the distribution of profits between the elements of capital became dominant over the production of profit. In order to make this conclusion more than an assertion, it is necessary to develop in some detail the materialist (Marxist) theory of value.

In capitalist society, the products of labour appear as 'an immense accumulation of commodities'.[23] That commodities are the product of human labour in itself implies no particular value theory; it is a statement of the obvious. Equally obvious is that a commodity has a dual nature. For the seller it represents a quantity of value, which when realized in general-equivalent form can be used to acquire another commodity through further exchange. For the buyer a commodity represents a quality which is sought for a particular purposeful use (its use value). The distinction between the quantitative and qualitative aspect of a commodity is obvious and descriptive. It is the pursuit of this obvious dichotomy that yields the labour theory of value, the laws of capitalist development, and an understanding of the nature of globalization at the end of the twentieth century.

The exchange value and use value of a commodity are not in peace with each other. While the former can vary due to immediate and longer-term influences, the latter retains an intrinsic character; specifically, improvements in the methods of production can reduce exchange value for a given use value. On the basis of the tension caused by this real dichotomy arises the need for money, which is a general equivalent commodity of exchange. Out of the 'unpacking' of the commodity arises the need for a further concept. Since commodities do not exchange directly for each other, but through the intermediary form of money, the possibility arises that the exchange value of a commodity can vary as conditions of exchange vary. This raises the question of what determines the exchange value of a commodity – that is, the underlying determinant of exchange value as the money a commodity fetches fluctuates due to stochastic influences.

All theories of market prices posit the existence of an underlying determinant of exchange value which is hidden beneath the price form of exchange. In neoclassical political economy the underlying determinant is the *opportunity cost* of both producers and buyers; in materialist analysis it is socially necessary labour, a concept yet to unfold. For both schools, there is a *value* of commodities which lies beneath the surface of exchange. *Value* has a straightforward meaning: that which determines price, appearing in the form of quantities of money.

Like commodities, money has a contradictory nature. As the general equivalent it circulates with commodities, but, unlike other commodities, it need not be sold to realize its exchange value. With this characteristic it can serve as a general store and claim on value. As a claim on value, it can initiate exchange for commodities, commodities which can, in turn, be sold for money again. This process, exchanging money for commodities, then commodities for money, would only be done if the second quantity of money exceeds the initial quantity. In this way money serves as *capital*, and is self-expanding value; money which through its circulation yields more money. Exchange takes two forms: commodities via money to other commodities, and money via commodities to a greater quantity of money. The former, selling in order to buy (commodities – money – commodities, $C - M - C$), is the simpler. It is simple, because it requires little theoretical explanation. It involves disposing through exchange of a commodity whose use value is not desired, in order to obtain money, which can be employed to acquire a desired commodity. It is an equivalent exchange with no increase in values.[24] The second, buying in order to sell, is theoretically complex. It demands an explanation of the source of the increased quantity of money, the *surplus value*. As it appears, surplus value is a simple concept: the quantitative difference between the money at the end and beginning of a process of buying in order to sell. The theory of value arises from the need to explain its source.

We can rule out surplus value deriving *in the aggregate* from exchange itself.[25] It follows that capital (money) must exchange initially for a commodity whose value increases, or a commodity that is value increasing, between the moments of buying and selling. A commodity's value increases by entering into a process of production. The neoclassical school would agree that value arises in production,[26] though its treatment of production is essentially tautological.[27] Since an increase in value in the aggregate arises from production, it follows that capital passes through production to obtain surplus value. The full circuit of capital takes the form:

$$M - C \ldots P \ldots C' - M'$$

[Money > > Commodities, (Production), Commodities > > Money]

The next step in the analytical unfolding is also noncontroversial: the first purchase by the capitalist ($M - C$), must involve the acquisition of a commodity or commodities which, when used in production, add value. The elements of production can be divided between labourers (L) and the material means of production (MP). Including these, the full circuit becomes:

$$M - C\,(L, MP) \ldots C' - M'$$

[Money > > Elements of Production, (Production), Commodities > > Money]

The labour theory of value lies latent in this circuit. The fundamental difference between this analysis and that of neoclassical economics is that the former has recast the analysis of value as the movement of capital, while the latter treats value as the outcome of the desire by human beings for consumption.[28] However, our analysis cannot progress beyond description without an explanation of the origin of the surplus value arising from the circulation of capital.[29]

Even if one preferred to use the opportunity-cost theory of value, the framework

$$M - C \ldots P \ldots C' - M'$$

precludes it. In the neoclassical theory of value commodities are not produced in the real world sense. Stocks of *primary inputs* (labour and capital), when combined with a given technology, generate a flow of new value. In this stock-flow description of the economy an opportunity cost theory of value is consistent, albeit under highly restrictive conditions.[30] The materialist description of aggregate reproduction is not stock-flow, but involves the production of commodities by means of commodities (to use Sraffa's term[31]). In this description, the process of reproduction is considered through time, rather than in a timeless equilibrium period. In some arbitrarily selected initial time period (in principle one could go back to the Garden of Eden), there is produced a set of commodities which will be the input in the next time period. In the next time period those commodities are transformed into different material objects, during which value is added to them.[32] This view of production formally excludes marginal productivity analysis. It does so not because it allows no substitution between inputs,[33] but because formally there is no difference between material inputs that are consumed during one period of production and those used up over many time periods.[34] The commodity which can expand value is the labouring activity of human beings. This commodity which capitalists buy is the capacity to work, *labour power*.

It is a tautology that each commodity is the product of human labour.[35] When commodities exchange, they are rendered equal in practice. By definition, the labour that produced them is rendered equal through exchange: the concrete labour expended in production is converted to *abstract labour* in exchange (that is, into money). This purely formal conversion of concrete labour into its opposite becomes a real conversion through the process of competition. Competition among producers of a particular commodity establishes a standard input requirement, which Marx called *socially necessary labour*. This is rendered abstract through exchange, becoming *abstract* socially necessary labour. The labour theory of value is the explanation of the process by which abstract necessary labour is established through an integrated social process of production and exchange. Competition results from the general production of commodities when labour power is also a commodity; a common norm for the production of each commodity arises from the exchange of inputs and outputs. At each stage in the input–output process capitalists encounter the discipline of exchange.[36]

We can now summarize the theory of value or *law* of value: commodities are the products of human labour which are produced within the discipline of capitalist exchange, both for the output and the inputs that are used to create the output. Production is formally private, but essentially social.[37] Every capitalist producer participates in social interaction in which his/her commodity is but one part of an organic whole. This system of social reproduction arises from labour power being a commodity. The commodity status of labour power results from the separation of producers from the means by which production can be carried out. Workers are reunited with the means of production through the agency of capital. Having reunited workers and means of production through exchange, capitalists must transform commodities back into money.

The surplus value arises from the extraction of surplus labour in the process of production. This surplus labour is created as a result of the difference between the value of the commodity labour power and the value which labour power creates during a production period. Society's aggregate labour can be divided between that necessary to reproduce the working population, and the labour expended over and above that reproductive minimum, *necessary labour* and *surplus labour*.[38]

This discussion establishes two points that are the keystones of the analysis of globalization: profit (surplus value) arises in production; and it is distributed among the functional forms of capital through exchange. Productive (industrial) capital oversees the production of profit; unproductive (financial) capital oversees its distribution among the constituent parts of capital. For its unproductive distributional services, financial capital receives a return. The tension between productive and unproductive capital gives rise to the special character of the world economy in the 1980s and 1990s.

DOMINANCE OF FINANCE CAPITAL

From the simplest form of capital, $M - C - M'$, it appears that value can expand in the absence of production, requiring exchange alone. While this is impossible in the aggregate, capital seeks, when possible, to achieve the promise of profit without productive engagement. Prior to the full development of capitalist production relations (wage labour) in the advanced countries in the late-eighteenth and early-nineteenth centuries, this was achieved through the agency of merchants' capital. Merchants' capital devoted itself to trade, not production, achieving profit literally through buying cheap and selling dear. In those countries where capitalist relations came to dominate production, the importance of merchants' capital declined relatively to productive capital. Parallel to the development of productive capital emerged financial capital, which served as an intermediary for the concentration and centralization of productive capital.[39]

Between productive and financial capital there exists an inherent tension, with the former seeking to achieve profit via the appropriation of surplus value created under the domination of labour by productive capital. This tension arises from the functions of capital, rather than from a formal separation of productive enterprise from financial institutions. That is, the tension is systemic, residing within a capitalist enterprise which performs both functions, as well as between institutions separated by function. In the advanced capitalist countries between World War I and II, most notably in the United States, formal state regulations were legislated to separate financial from productive capital. As part of this process, financial capital was highly regulated into a compartmentalized system of commercial banks, investment banks and other specialized financial institutions.[40] The key aspect of this regulation was that each component part of the financial system was strictly regulated in the activities it could pursue. After World War II, a system of fixed exchange rates was introduced by the victorious powers, to be supervised by the International Monetary Fund. Thus, from 1945 until the mid-1970s, the scope for speculative action by financial capital was severely limited.

The dramatic expansion of lending by advanced country commercial banks to governments of underdeveloped countries was a direct result of financial regulations, especially the New Deal regulations in the United States. The accumulation of large deposits of 'petro dollars' in the major commercial banks created the possibility of a dramatic increase in lending. However, the particular form that lending took was the result of restrictions on commercial bank operations. When deregulation of financial institutions began in the second half of the 1970s, commercial lending to governments virtually ceased.[41] More important in the long run, the deregulation process eliminated the legal distinction between financial and productive capital, such that the merger of the two functions in the same institutions became increasingly prevalent.[42] Coinciding with this, the end of the system of fixed exchange rates created an entirely new arena for the intervention of unproductive capital. Further, deregulation of the process of corporate mergers and takeovers engendered a virtually unlimited field for financial speculation.

Thus, a series of concrete and purposeful state policies created a new environment for capital in which unproductive speculation could be pursued with limited oversight. The effect of these policy changes was to liberate capital from regulatory constraint. As a result of this liberation, the unproductive aspects of capital's circulation achieved dominance over the productive aspects. Therefore, it is not surprising that the new era is not characterized by significantly more trade, foreign direct investment or productive efficiency, but, rather, by currency speculation and financial takeovers. The dominance of the financial over the productive function explains the great emphasis in orthodox policies on liberalization of financial markets in underdeveloped countries, not withstanding the obvious disfunctionality of this deregulation.

CAPITAL RUNS ITS COURSE

With the current dominance of capital as finance, over capital as agency of production, capital as a social relation has run its course in that it manifests itself in its most socially dysfunctional form. While the ideologues of capital may produce mathematically elegant models to demonstrate that deregulated capital results in equilibrium, harmony and stable growth, quite the opposite is obvious for all to see, in Mexico and Indonesia to take two recent examples. As a beast taken from the wild and domesticated will return to a feral state when freed from restraints, capital undergoes a similar reversion when ineffectively regulated. However, what policy has created, policy can undo.

The argument that the present deregulated financial markets result from an inexorable and irreversible process of globalization is an ideological assertion that seeks to forestall policy changes that would limit the destructive tendencies of capital. Yet, a range of policy measures could be implemented, and have been implemented to constrain the movement of financial capital. Measures successfully used in underdeveloped countries include transaction taxes on foreign exchange dealings, restriction of foreign capital in dealing in futures markets, and reserve requirements for portfolio investments.[43] Like a river that runs wild and overflows its banks, financial capital can, to a certain extent, be channeled and tamed. The barrier to achieving this is not the inevitability of globalization, nor the impossibility of implementing controls, but, rather, the difficulty in constructing a political coalition in each country that would force the necessary policy changes.

The possibility of such a coalition has been weakened by a second major characteristic of the globalization era: along with the liberation of financial capital has gone a concerted and relentless attack upon trade union movements.[44] The rebuilding of the strength of organized labour, in advanced and underdeveloped countries, is the viable vehicle for creating the political conditions for re-regulation of capital. While organized labour's strength is weaker in the 1990s than it has been since the end of World War II, this weakness should not be exaggerated. In western Europe trade union movements retain considerable political power, and potentially so in Japan. In Latin America military dictatorships in the 1970s profoundly weakened organized labour, laying the ground work for liberalization in the 1980s to be carried out by nominally democratic governments. But these movements are again active, in opposition to the excesses of globalization. While in each country progressive coalitions can implement effective reforms to constrain capital, the key to a fundamental policy shift at the international level is the emergence of a progressive political movement in the United States.

The assertion that the present era of deregulation of finance capital is inevitable gains superficial credibility by the view of *progress* arising from the eighteenth-century Age of Reason, from which neoliberal ideology derives its origin. It this philosophy, history's development is essentially linear, and each period is the culmination of the changes that preceded it.[45] Thus, current policies are not alternatives which have been consciously chosen over others, but, rather, the synthesis and most advanced expression of what have gone before. Previous policies that constrained capital are seen as anachronistic, irrelevant to the new, more advanced stage of society. To the extent that materialist philosophy has also fostered such a linear view of history, it must be amended to treat history as a cyclical process in which policies reflect the balance of class power. At the end of the nineteenth century, in the context of an apparently triumphant imperialism and domination of capital over labour, the ideologues of capital proclaimed the dawn of a new era in which that triumph and domination would be eternal. Similarly, the current domination of finance capital is proclaimed as the inexorable outcome of irreversible market forces. However, the current policy framework is no more eternal than that of the late nineteenth century, which came to an abrupt end through a devastating European war and the Russian revolution. While one cannot predict the vehicle by which the dominance of finance capital will end, one can recognize it as but a moment in the life-cycle of capital, which can be altered through conscious political intervention.

Notes and References

1. See *Global Prospects and the Developing Economies 1996* (Washington, DC: World Bank, 1996), p. 26, especially the box entitled 'The faster and higher the integration, the greater the growth'.
2. This assertion is found in the World Bank report entitled 'Workers in a Changing World', *World Development Report 1995* (Oxford: Oxford University Press, 1995).
3. The argument that the new policy rules foster poverty reduction is made by Lionel Demery and Lyn Squire ('Macroeconomic Adjustment and Poverty in Africa: An Emerging Picture', *World Bank Research Observer*, vol. 11, no. 1 (February 1996), pp. 39–60, in defence of World Bank programmes.
4. These Golden Rules of macro-policy can be found in many publications of the international financial institutions. For a particularly clear statement see the 1992 World Bank report on structural adjustment lending, *World Bank Structural and Sectoral Adjustment Operations: The Second OED Overview* (Washington, DC: World Bank, 1992).
5. Like for all epochs, the dating of the globalization era is difficult to pin down. A reading of the literature indicates that no one dates it prior to 1980, and no one later than 1990. A compromise position is taken here by dating from 1985. This has the empirical advantage of excluding the most catastrophic years of the debt crisis.
6. Daniel Yergin and Joseph Stanislaw, *The Commanding Heights* (London: Simon & Schuster, 1998).

7. In Tables 4.1, 4.2, 4.4 and 4.5, World Bank categories are used. See *World Development Indicators 1997* (Washington, DC: World Bank, 1997, CD-ROM). The North Africa and the Middle East groups are not included because of missing data for some or all of the indicators. For political reasons, the World Bank excludes Taiwan (Republic of China), which would otherwise be in the East Asia group. *World Development Indicators 1997.*
8. This does not refer to percentage point increases, but the percentage rate of change (that is, the elasticity of *X*/GDP with respect to time).
9. This conclusion is implicitly suggested in a World Bank publication: 'Though developing countries in the aggregate kept pace with the world rate of trade integration, the ratio of trade to GDP actually *fell* in some 44 of 93 developing countries in the last ten years [that is, 1985-95]', *Global Prospects and the Developing Economies 1996* (Washington, DC: World Bank, 1996), rear cover, emphasis in original.
10. In a World Bank report, 24 of 36 sub-Saharan countries were defined as 'weak' or 'slow' integrators for the 'early 1980s to early 1990s', ten as 'moderate' and only two as 'fast'. No other group (East Asia, South Asia and Latin America) had close to two-thirds of the countries in the 'weak' and 'slow' categories. *Global Prospects*, table 2-2, p. 25. It can also be noted that for the periods when export growth was significantly *higher*, GDP growth was significantly *lower* for the sub-Saharan group.
11. The World Bank data base on CD-ROM (*World Development Indicators 1997*) does not give foreign direct investment aggregated by groups, but only by country. The statistics in Table 4.3 are simple averages across countries for the groups as defined by the World Bank. The database does not report foreign direct investment for OECD countries.
12. See, for example, 'Greater Openness Will Do the Most to Sustain East Asia's Rapid Economic Growth', *East Asia's Trade and Investment: Regional and Global Gains from Liberalization* (Washington, DC: World Bank, 1994), back book jacket.
13. That is, it is estimated from the equation:

$$ln\ (g_t) = a_o + a_1[ln\ (\text{inv/GDP})_t] + a_2 i\ (\text{5–year period}) + \ldots + a_3\text{j}\ (\text{Country group}) + \ldots$$

The periods are 1965–69 and so on, and the country groups are the sub-Sahara, South Asia, East Asia, Latin America and the OECD.

14. That is, if the following years are treated as random deviations from the surrounding trend: 1967, 1973, 1980, 1988.
15. Ten years for the latter duration assumes that the 1995 downturn would continue. If not, the cycle would be longer.
16. For simplicity, it is assumed that consumption remains in the same proportion as at point *a*. This highlights the increase in *welfare*, since more of both commodities are consumed after free trade is implemented.
17. The example corresponds to the policies of several East and Southeast Asian countries, which through social security schemes and other mechanisms raised savings rates. See Gabriel Palma, 'Whatever Hap-

pened to Latin America's Savings? Comparing Latin American and East Asian Savings Performances', *Project on East Asian Development: Lessons for a New Global Environment* (Geneva: United Nations Conference on Trade and Development, 1996).

18. An obvious neoclassical objection to our example would be that raising the saving and investment rate would have the effect of increasing the capital–output ratio. Even if this could be shown to be logically valid, whether the rise in the latter offset the rise in the former in any particular case would be an empirical question.
19. The famous Theory of the Second Best precludes any general argument: the impact of the efficiency of an economy of removing some but not all distortions cannot be predicted.
20. For a more detailed discussion of the Golden Rules of new era macropolicy, see Guy Standing, John Sender and John Weeks, *Restructuring the Labour Market: The South African Challenge* (Geneva: International Labour Office, 1996), ch. 2; and Paul Mosley, Turan Subasat and John Weeks, 'Assessing Adjustment in Africa', *World Development*, vol. 23, no. 9 (1995).
21. If something could be made true through repetition of assertion, this relationship would be incontrovertible. For a presentation of the benefits of inflation reduction refreshingly free of nuance or sophistication, see World Bank, *Adjustment in Africa: Reforms, Results, and the Road Ahead* (Oxford: Oxford University Press, 1994), where a regression purports to show that lower inflation leads to higher growth (refuted in Mosley, Subasat and Weeks, 'Assessing Adjustment in Africa', table 3).
22. The authors found that high inflation, or inflation crises, have a strong negative effect on growth.
23. Karl Marx, *Capital*, vol. 1 (London: Lawrence & Wishart, 1974), p. 43.
24. Marx called this process 'simple commodity circulation'.
25. Consider a two-commodity closed economy. The rise in the exchange value of one commodity implies a decline for the other. Thus, exchange redistributes rather than creates surplus value. A neoclassical would not contest this theoretical argument, but would insist that individual and social welfare is increased by exchange.
26. The neoclassical disagreement would come on two issues: (1) the process by which value is added in production (marginal productivity theory), and (2) what constitutes production (rejecting the distinction between productive and unproductive labour).
27. In neoclassical economies, market prices oscillate around long-run general equilibrium prices. If short-run and long-run average cost curves have a unique minimum point, and no *above- normal* profits are earned in any sector (perfect competition), then the general equilibrium set of relative prices is independent of demand. Demand determines the composition of output in general equilibrium, but not relative prices.
28. It is this recasting that eliminates the concept of *utility* from the analysis.
29. Even as pure description the foregoing is a considerable improvement upon neoclassical analysis, which treats a capitalist society as the exchange between individual agents, or even the Keynesian 'circular flow'. For a critique of the latter, see John Weeks (ed.), *Banks, Govern-*

ments, and Multilaterals Confront the Crisis (New York: New York University Press, 1989), ch. 1.

30. If production involves more than one output, neoclassical value theory is consistent only in general equilibrium. See Weeks, *Banks, Governments and Multilaterals*, ch. 10; and Ben Fine, *Economic Theory and Ideology* (London: Edward Arnold, 1980), ch. 3.
31. It would be more correct to write, 'production of products by means of products'. This indicates the generality of the framework; that is, it is not limited to a system of commodity (capitalist) production. When viewed in this way, production cannot logically be treated in terms of value-added categories alone, but must be analysed in terms of the total social product (value-added plus intermediate production). The Keynesian categories of consumption, investment and so on have their analogues in materialist theory, but are not the relevant categories of analysis. See John Weeks, 'On the Issue of Capitalist Circulation and the Concepts Appropriate to its Analysis', *Science and Society*, vol. 47, no. 2 (1983).
32. The essence of the production process is the material transformation of objects. The addition of value is a historically specific outcome. For example, a subsistence farmer who plants maize seed does not add value in production; he/she engages in specific and concrete labour which, if successful, results in more maize than was planted as seed.
33. Neoclassical marginal productivity theory is consistent with fixed coefficients of production, as demonstrated decades ago in R. Dorfman, P. Samuelson and R. Solow, *Linear Programming and Economic Analysis* (New York: McGraw-Hill, 1958), ch. 3.
34. At a more concrete level of analysis, the distinction between materials of production (circulating means of production) and tools of production (fixed means of production) is crucial. See John Weeks, *Capital and Exploitation* (Princeton, NJ: Princeton University Press, 1981), chs 7 and 8.
35. There is little controversy over whether units of labour time can be employed to *measure* value. Measurement is essentially a trivial exercise for which there are several possibilities. For example, if we consider only material commodities (excluding services), one could aggregate by weight. However useful this might be for certain purposes, such as planning the transport of commodities, it makes no sense as a theory of value. Similarly, labour time can be used as the unit of measure; the debate is over its significance for understanding aggregate reproduction.
36. John Weeks, 'Abstract Labour and Commodity Production', in P. Zarembka (ed.) *Research in Political Economy*, vol. 12 (Greenwich, Conn.: JAI Press, 1990). Marx referred to the disciplining effect of exchange when he wrote, 'a commodity is, in the first place, an object outside us', Marx, *Capital*, vol. 1, p. 43.
37. It is essentially social for two reasons. First, within units of production it involves cooperation among human beings, a social process. Second, no commodity is created within one production unit; every commodity is the result of the production of many commodities which serve directly and indirectly as inputs to it. Thus, the essence of production is production in the aggregate, with each individual commodity a constituent part.

38. This division implicitly assumes the division of society into classes, so that there is a dominant group which appropriates the surplus labour.
39. John Weeks, 'Epochs of Capitalism and the Progressiveness of Capital's Expansion', *Science and Society,* vol. 49, no. 4 (Winter 1985–86).
40. The Glass–Steagall Act during the first Franklin Roosevelt administration established the regulations limiting the activities of commercial banks in the United States. See Paul M. Sacks and Chris Canavan, 'Safe Passage Through Dire Straits: Managing an Orderly Exit from the Debt Crisis', in Weeks, *Banks, Governments and Multilaterals*, note 29 above.
41. Writing in 1989, Lissakers concludes, '[D]ebtor countries are in financial straits in part because commercial bank funds are no longer flowing. Foreign bank credit has dried up because the underlying macroeconomic, institutional, and regulatory conditions that drove banks heavily into cross-border lending in the 1970s are no longer present'. Karin Lissakers, 'Background to the Debt Crisis: Structural Adjustment in the Financial Markets', in Weeks, *Banks, Governments and Multilaterals*, *op.cit.*, p. 68.
42. Japan is the notable exception to the process of financial deregulation, and has come under pressure from the US government to initiate the process.
43. For example, 'Chile ... continued to expand the scope of measures designed to control the pace of its net capital inflows. Reserve requirements were extended to various portfolio investments ... Restrictions were placed on banks' use of the formal foreign-exchange market ... ', United Nations Conference on Trade and Development (UNCTAD), *Trade and Development Report 1996* (Geneva: UNCTAD, 1996), pp. 37–8.
44. John Weeks, *Economic Integration in Latin America: Impact on Labour* (London: SOAS, 1998), pp. 47–51.
45. I wish to thank Elizabeth Dore for pointing out this ideological treatment of history.

Part II
Case-Studies

5 Popular Resistance to Neoliberalism in Latin America

Richard Harris

INTRODUCTION

During the early 1980s, the inability of most of the Latin American countries to finance the huge foreign debts they were encouraged to assume during the preceding decade by the international financial community gave rise to what is known in Latin America as 'the debt crisis'. To stave off the complete collapse of their highly indebted and inflated economies, most of the Latin American governments were forced to devalue their currencies, refinance their foreign debts, drastically reduce government expenditures, and restructure their economies according to the terms set by the three major international financial institutions (IFIs) that operate in the region – that is, the International Monetary Fund, the World Bank, and the Inter-American Development Bank. This process of economic restructuring has taken place within the larger context of the increasing integration of national and regional economies into the global capitalist economic system and the resulting 'denationalization' of the Latin American economies.[1]

In response to the conditions set by these IFIs, most of the Latin American governments undertook structural reforms during the 1980s and early 1990s that involved the 'liberalization' of both their trade and financial regulations as well as the privatization of government-owned enterprises and public services. By pursuing these policies, they have diverted revenues from the public sector and from the incomes of the popular classes into the purses of Latin America's international creditors and upper classes.[2] Combined with the effects of the debt crisis of the early 1980s, the effects of these policies have drastically increased the number of Latin Americans living in poverty. For example, during the decade of the 1980s, the number of Latin Americans living in poverty increased from 118 million in 1980 to 196 million by 1990 – a 42 per cent increase or double the population growth rate of 22 per cent during the 1980s.[3]

These 'stabilization and structural adjustment policies' (to use the language of the IFIs) were piloted by the military dictatorship of General Augusto Pinochet in Chile during the 1970s.[4] Ironically, they have also become known as 'free-market reforms' even though they were developed by General Pinochet's dictatorial regime after the Chilean military had brutally overthrown the democratically elected socialist government of President Salvador Allende (1970–73). Once the military had demobilized and repressed the multiclass popular movement that had brought Allende and his democratic socialist government into office, they began to roll back the policy gains achieved by the popular classes during the preceding years. They introduced policies aimed at dismantling the welfare and income redistribution policies introduced in the preceding decades. At the same time, they set about the task of restructuring the Chilean economy and the state in favour of transnational capital and the Chilean upper class.

With the help of a team of US-educated Chilean economists called 'the Chicago Boys' and the assistance of the IFIs, the Pinochet regime introduced a combination of economic and social reforms. These reforms drastically reduced Chile's public-sector and social programmes, privatized a large number of the country's government-owned enterprises, deregulated the economy, removed most restrictions on foreign investment, eliminated price controls on basic necessities, dismantled Chile's progressive labour laws, and reduced or eliminated most of the government subsidies and services previously provided to the popular classes.[5]

Since the early 1980s, 'neoliberalism' has provided the ideological justification for this strategy of capitalist restructuring. In what is referred to as the 'Washington consensus',[6] this ideology was adopted by the IFIs (whose headquarters are in Washington, D.C.) and used by them to justify the so-called stabilization and structural adjustment programmes that they insisted governments in Latin America and other parts of the world should impose on their popular classes in order to pay off their debts, open up their economies to transnational capital, and 'integrate' them into the global market.

Since the late 1970s, most Latin American countries have adopted neoliberal economic reforms, at the insistence of the IFIs. Certain countries such as Chile, Uruguay, Colombia and Peru first introduced neoliberal policies in the 1970s, while others such as Argentina, Mexico, Bolivia, Costa Rica, Guatemala and Panama introduced them in the 1980s.[7] However, it was not until the 1990s that countries such as

Brazil, Venezuela, Honduras, Nicaragua, Ecuador and El Salvador adopted the neoliberal policy agenda. Although neoliberal policies were initially introduced by military or authoritarian regimes, it is important to note that the elected civilian governments that replaced these regimes in the late 1980s continued to carry out most of the same neoliberal policies as their authoritarian predecessors. In other words, they have won elections despite the fact that they have pursued policies that serve transnational capital and the local upper classes at the expense of the popular classes.

The continued electoral support for neoliberal regimes in Latin America 'has led conservative commentators to argue that neoliberalism has become the hegemonic ideology, or in less elegant terms, that it has become the accepted political discourse of the masses'.[8] It has even influenced leftist political parties and intellectuals throughout Latin America to accept as a *fait accompli* many of the neoliberal structural reforms that have been placed into effect in their countries over the last decade or more. However, while the centrist political regimes and the 'leftist pragmatists' in the opposition parties have accepted these neoliberal reforms as part of the current reality of Latin American politics and economics, there has been increasing popular resistance to these policies throughout the region. This resistance has elicited a variety of responses from the governments that pursue these neoliberal policies. This chapter examines both the increasing popular resistance to neoliberal policies in Latin America and the responses of the political regimes in the region to this resistance. I do not examine the political economy of change in either Mexico or Cuba since these cases are analysed in depth in this volume by Francis Adams and Susan Eckstein (in the next two chapters).

POPULAR RESISTANCE TO NEOLIBERAL REFORMS IN LATIN AMERICA

Since the introduction of the first neoliberal stabilization and structural reforms in Latin America, governments in the region have met with a wide range of popular resistance to these policies. At times, this resistance has taken relatively peaceful and *legal* forms of expression such as electoral opposition, law suits and court action, peaceful demonstrations, rallies, picketing, work stoppages and strikes. But there has also been an increasing incidence of *extralegal*, and at times violent, manifestations of popular resistance, ranging from the blockage of roads and highways to land occupations, urban riots, bombings, guerrilla warfare and even popular insurrections. Below, we shall examine representative examples of both types of popular resistance.

Since Chile was the first country in Latin America to introduce neoliberal structural reforms, Chile is a good place to begin our analysis of the popular resistance to these reforms. In the immediate years after the military coup, popular resistance to the neoliberal policies of the military regime was generally suppressed by force and intimidation. For example, most of the political parties and labour unions were dissolved by the military and many of their leaders were either murdered, imprisoned or exiled.[9] As a result, the only form of resistance possible was sporadic acts of sabotage and guerrilla warfare waged by leftist revolutionaries who were organized into clandestine groups. However, by the late 1970s, internal and international pressures forced the military regime into permitting the resumption of union activity. In spite of the restrictions imposed on them, the reconstituted unions almost immediately set to work organizing popular opposition to the regime and its policies.[10] As a result, the military launched another wave of repression and jailed or exiled many of the union leaders and activists.

However, in late 1981 and 1982, Chile suffered the worst economic crisis since the Great Depression of the 1930s, thanks to the military dictatorship's neoliberal 'free-market' policies. These policies left the Chilean economy wide open to the effects both of the economic recession in the United States during the early 1980s, and the worldwide rise in interest rates stemming from the tightening of international credit.[11] As a result, by 1983, more than one-third of Chile's workforce was unemployed and the gross domestic product had dropped by 14 per cent. With this 'crash' of Chile's neoliberal 'economic miracle', the military regime 'witnessed an unprecedented wave of anti- government protests by unions, shantytown dwellers, and even some middle-class and professional groups that had supported the military's seizure of power ten years earlier'.[12]

Over the next couple of years, the military government bailed out the near-bankrupt and heavily indebted private sector by assuming approximately $16 billion of the private sector's foreign debt.[13] And with considerable financial help from the IFIs, a drop in world oil prices and a rise in the price of Chile's copper on the international market, the economy experienced strong growth after 1985. This recovery of the economy made it possible for the supporters of the regime's so-called free-market policies to claim that Chile's 'economic miracle' had survived. Nevertheless, Chile's unions continued to protest the military regime's economic and social policies. The main targets of their protests were both the 'reforms' in the labour laws imposed by the dictatorship on the workforce and the wholesale privatization of Chile's numerous public enterprises. The unions not only protested against the labour law reforms and privatization measures of the government, they also played a fundamental role in mobilizing popular support for the increasing number of anti-government demonstrations and strikes that took place throughout the country during the remainder of the 1980s.[14] This popular resistance, as well as international pressures on the military to relinquish control over the government and permit a redemocratization of Chilean politics, pressured the military into returning the country to civilian rule in 1990.

However, the new civilian governments that have been elected to office since the withdrawal of the military from the centre-stage of Chilean political life have continued to carry out many of the neoliberal policies introduced by the military dictatorship. As a result, popular protests and other acts of popular resistance against the neoliberal policies of the civilian regime in Chile, as well as the civilian regimes in other Latin American countries, have become a common occurrence. This continuing popular resistance to neoliberalism, however, has not succeeded in stopping or replacing the neoliberal agenda. As Duncan Green has noted in his insightful study of the effects of neoliberal policies on Latin America,[15] the popular resistance to neoliberal policies in the region has failed to produce a viable alternative to these policies. Green analyses what he characterizes as the 'austerity protests' in Latin America during the last two decades. These austerity protests, sometimes called 'IMF riots' because they have tended to be associated with the economic austerity measures recommended to the Latin American governments by the International Monetary Fund (IMF), have occurred in response to the stabilization and structural adjustment policies undertaken by civilian governments throughout the region.

Since the mid-1990s, there has been a notable upsurge in popular resistance to the neoliberal policies of the Latin American governments. The privatization of public enterprises, worker layoffs, the dismantling of agrarian reform laws, the reform of the labour laws to permit a more 'flexible' deployment of the workforce, rising prices on basic commodities, falling real wages, and widespread unemployment and underemployment have provoked wave after wave of protests.

During 1994, there was also a wave of mass land invasions in Brazil organized by the *Movimento dos Sem Terra* (the Landless Movement or the MST). The MST launched a major offensive of land invasions and threw its support behind the electoral campaign of Brazil's popular Workers Party.[16] Among the critical issues addressed by the MST's offensive were the government's neoliberal economic policies that support narrow agro-export interests rather than the small producers, the landless peasants and the unemployed.

In Ecuador, mass mobilizations organized by the country's indigenous communities totally shut down the country for two weeks in 1994.[17] These popular protests were directed at the government's new Agrarian Development Law, which sought to eliminate communal lands and institute measures that would favour large landowners and commercial agricultural enterprises over the indigenous communities and the peasantry. The protests mobilized the country's large indigenous population, peasants and small farmers, and drew widespread popular support from the population as a whole. Despite the repressive measures taken by the government to break the nationwide protests and general strike, they did not succeed in forcing the mass movement to back down. The government was forced to negotiate with the leaders of the indigenous organizations and modify the agrarian law, which was a key element of the government's larger neoliberal agenda.

During 1995, a wave of protests and strikes against neoliberal economic reforms swept across Latin America.[18] There were general strikes in Bolivia and Panama, a month-long strike of public employees in Brazil who were opposed to the government's plans for privatization, regional protests in Argentina, clashes between demonstrators and the government in Nicaragua, and mass mobilizations in Mexico and Venezuela. In Bolivia, the labour federation declared a general strike and organized public demonstrations around the country in opposition to the neoliberal policies of President Gonzalo Sánchez de Lozada. The latter responded with a 90–day state of siege, a ban on all demonstrations and strikes, and the detention of more than 400 people. However, the protests continued and were discontinued only when the government agreed to negotiate with the leader of the labour federation. In Brazil, the workers from the state-owned petroleum, electrical power, telecommunications and public transportation sectors went on strike, as well as the university, health and social-service employees. They closed nine of the country's 11 oil refineries and paralysed public transportation. Their demands included pay increases and opposition to the government's plans to privatize important public enterprises. President Fernando Henrique Cardoso ended the strike by ordering the military to occupy the country's oil refineries, and by setting up a special commission of labour, business and government leaders to debate the government's proposed reforms to open up the economy and privatize the country's state-owned industries. In Mexico, the annual May Day celebrations brought out the largest labour demonstrations in Mexican history. These demonstrations attacked the government's neoliberal policies as the cause of the country's economic crisis and the increased suffering of the popular classes.

At the outset of 1996, the *Central Obrera Boliviana* (Bolivian Workers Confederation or COB) called a general strike in Bolivia to protest the government's neoliberal economic policies, which in this case involved increasing fuel prices, holding down wages, and allowing food and public transportation prices to rise.[19] Public-sector employees, peasants, students and miners set up road blocks and held marches in Bolivia's three largest cities to protest the government's policies. About the same time, there were strikes and protest marches in Ecuador and Peru in reaction to the plans of the governments in these two countries to privatize the state-owned power and petroleum companies.[20]

A similar pattern of development can be observed in various parts of Latin America. For example, in Bolivia by the end of 1996 street demonstrations and the occupation of government offices became an almost daily occurrence as the Bolivian union confederation, the COB, led a wave of popular protests against the government's neoliberal economic model, particularly its plans for privatizing the state oil company and the government pension system.[21] There was also an upsurge of strikes, protests and court action in Argentina that signalled an important increase in popular resistance to President Carlos Menem's neoliberal policies. On 2 January 1997, in response to union legal action, an Argentine court ruled that the decrees Menem had issued to 'liberalize' the country's labour laws 'had transgressed, violated, and overriden [the constitutional provisions which establish that] the unions are charged, as representatives of the workers, with the negotiation of collective agreements'.[22] When Menem made it clear that he intended to continue issuing decrees to make labour contracts 'more flexible', the leader of Argentina's central labour confederation warned that 'if there are more decrees, there will be more strikes'. There were more decrees and more strikes, and by mid-

1997 the country was engulfed by a rolling wave of road and highway blockades in the provinces most affected by that country's high unemployment rate.

These *puebladas* (popular uprisings) spread from one end of the country to the other, and resulted in riots that damaged public buildings in Buenos Aires. In response, the national and provincial governments introduced low-paying, temporary job programmes, and President Menem accused two small extreme leftist groups of being behind the disturbances. The opposition parties in turn accused the Menem government of fabricating the 'resurgence of subversion' as a political maneuver designed to discredit the popular protests and justify the use of repressive measures to stop them from continuing.

The central government responded to this increasingly more violent wave of protests by threatening to imprison anyone caught blockading the highways and by indicating it was willing to commit funds for temporary jobs and assistance for the areas hardest hit by unemployment.[23] During the midst of the protests, the head of the IMF, Michael Camdesus, visited Argentina. He said that the Menem administration was combating the country's high unemployment correctly, and urged the government to continue with its plans to reform the labour laws. Camdesus asserted that if business had greater flexibility in its dealings with labour, this would encourage economic growth and create more employment. In contrast, the head of Caritas (the Catholic relief organization) in Argentina accused the government of 'lacking social sensitivity,' and argued that the wave of protests indicated 'the people have rebelled because the only chance they have of being heard is to block the highways'.[24]

Strikes and public protests against government austerity measures in Ecuador and Venezuela were also commonplace in 1997.[25] At the beginning of the year, there was a wave of strikes and demonstrations by unions, students, teachers and Indian organizations in Ecuador to protest President Abdalá Bucaram's Argentine-style currency convertibility and austerity plan. The strikes and mass protests received widespread public support and convinced the Congress to remove President Bucaram on the grounds of his 'mental incapacity' to govern. His replacement, Fabián Alarcón, took office 'making conciliatory noises, criticizing convertibility and speaking of measures that would not hammer the poor'.[26] The Ecuadorian union movement, which organized the strikes and mass protests that toppled Bucaram, gave Alarcón until 1 May to make good on his promises to the people. They also called for a moratorium on Ecuador's foreign debt payments and the establishment of a constituent assembly to reform the constitution.[27]

However, the new president found himself caught between the conflicting pressures of the unions and the international financial community. For example, the IMF announced that it was going to send a team to Ecuador to analyse the government's economic policies before deciding whether to support their request for rescheduling their debts with the so-called Paris Club of government creditors.[28] In addition, the World Bank offered assistance to Alarcón in developing a set of acceptable economic policies. Since Bucaram's unpopular convertibility plan was an orthodox neoliberal reform that was consistent with IMF guidelines, Alarcón was faced with the impossible task of coming up with a new economic programme that could still meet the approval of the IMF, the World Bank and the country's foreign creditors, but also gain the approval of the unions who were calling for a moratorium on Ecuador's debt payments.

In Venezuela, a strike by the country's 27 000 public-sector doctors began a wave of strikes in that country and prompted former President Luis Herrera Campins to warn that the doctors' strike signalled that 'a middle-class rebellion' was developing against the government's neoliberal economic policies.[29] The strikes, work stoppages and protests took on a more violent character as bloody clashes erupted between the police and students who were protesting against the government's economic policies. After several months of protests and strikes, the government took steps to quell the growing opposition by offering to increase the country's minimum wage as well as the wages of certain sectors of the work force.[30] Despite these and other concessions made by the government of President Rafael Caldera, more strikes and anti-government protests took place. A public opinion poll taken in mid-1997 revealed that there was general dissatisfaction with the government's IMF-style stabilization programme.[31]

In the Dominican Republic, the left-wing coalition *Fuerza de la Revolución* (Force of the Revolution) began the year by promising the government of President Leonel Fernandez that it would face a 'hot year' of strikes, protests and mass demonstrations unless the government reversed its neoliberal economic policies, particularly the increases in fuel prices and taxes it announced at the end of December.[32] The leader of *Fuerza de la Revolución*, Narciso Isa Conde, accused the government of letting big business dictate the government's economic policies. Isa Conde also charged the government with being responsible for the fact that he and other leaders of

Fuerza de la Revolución had been subjected to police harassment and death threats. President Fernandez assured Isa Conde that the harassment against him and the other leaders of the left-wing coalition would be stopped. He upheld the opposition's right to protest and criticized the actions of the police as 'unnecessary and fraught with risk'.

In Brazil, President Cardoso's neoliberal programme faced a broad range of popular protests in 1997.[33] These protests were initiated by the MST, which organized a march of landless peasants to the Brazilian capital on the first anniversary of the massacre by state police of protesting peasants who had been occupying a highway in the state of Pará. The march attracted metalworkers from São Paulo who were protesting unemployment, opponents of the privatization of Brazil's giant federal mining company, public employees opposed to reforms in the public sector, pension holders who were opposed to the government's plans to privatize the social security programme, dockworkers from the country's largest port in Santos who were protesting plans to privatize the docks, and a broad spectrum of opposition political leaders and elected officials. The leadership of the MST declared that they wanted Cardoso to make changes in his economic policy to deal with the country's problems of agrarian reform, unemployment, the globalization of the economy, high interest rates, and privatization of important state-owned companies. The MST promised to organize, in association with the national union confederation, more mass protests in the capital against the government's neoliberal economic policies.

In June 1997, the 'contagion' of protests against neoliberalism which had been developing in Argentina since April crossed the border into Uruguay. The first protest took place in the town of Paysandú which has one of the highest rates of unemployment in the country. Workers from the public and private sectors were joined in the streets by local traders in a peaceful demonstration calling for government action.[34] A few days later, another protest took place in the town of Durazno where the townspeople took to the streets to protest the lack of jobs. In contrast to Argentina, there were no highway blockades and no police repression. However, President Julio María Sanguinetti tried to discredit the protests on the grounds that they were politically motivated and he mimicked his Argentine counterpart President Carlos Menem by charging that the protests were organized by former communists and radical elements within the leftist coalition *Frente Amplio* (Broad Front or FA). The leader of the FA, Liber Seregni, acknowledged that the government of President Sanguinetti was not pursuing an orthodox neoliberal programme, and he said that the protests indicated the government should abandon its plans to privatize and downsize the state.

Opposition to privatization was also an important issue in protests that took place in Guatemala, Panama, Nicaragua, Chile and Peru during 1997. In Guatemala, the privatization of the government-owned telecommunications company, GUATEL, and the increasing cost of living united the unions in a series of protest marches through the streets of Guatemala City.[35] In Panama, public-sector workers staged a series of protests in opposition to the passage of a new law by the national legislature that provides for the privatization of the public employees' retirement fund.[36] These protests culminated in a national protest that was directed at the government's economic policies, especially privatization. In Nicaragua, a wave of protests rocked the country during 1997 in opposition to the economic austerity measures undertaken by the government of President Arnoldo Alemán.[37] Alemán was under pressure from the IMF to meet the terms of a new Enhanced Structural Adjustment Facility (ESAF). He responded by adopting classic neoliberal measures: deep cuts in public spending, reducing the size of the public workforce, increasing government revenues through new taxes and higher utility rates, and privatizing government-owned companies. To oppose these government austerity measures, the opposition Sandinista National Liberation Front organized a series of popular protests.

What the foregoing cases of popular resistance to neoliberal reforms indicate is that there is widespread and growing organized resistance to the measures taken by the Latin American governments to open up their economies to transnational capital and to privatize both public enterprises and public services (particularly health care and social security). In the following pages, we shall analyse the measures taken by the current neoliberal regimes and the IFIs to counter this increasing wave of popular resistance throughout the region.

REGIME RESPONSES TO POPULAR RESISTANCE

The neoliberal regimes in Latin America have responded to increasing popular resistance by relying on two broad types of measures: (1) tactical measures aimed at suppressing eruptions of popular resistance; and (2) more strategic measures aimed at preventing or maintaining within manageable limits popular resistance to the neoliberal agenda. The following chapter by Francis Adams provides a detailed analysis of how the Mexican government has combined both tactical and strategic measures to counter popular resistance to neoliberalism. It is important to note that the IFIs have played a major role in both developing the second type of measures and assisting the neoliberal regimes to implement these measures.

The previously mentioned examples of popular resistance to the policies of neoliberal regimes in Latin America illustrate the range of tactical measures that have been taken by these regimes to suppress or control the resistance to their policies coming from the popular classes. Generally speaking, a continuum of tactical measures have been used – starting first with what can be called 'police methods' and, if these methods are inadequate, the use of a 'state of emergency' or 'military methods' in which the armed forces are used to suppress further popular protests and strikes. In certain cases, anti-protest legislation is passed to forestall further expressions of popular resistance.

If these measures do not succeed in repressing popular protests, they are usually followed by negotiations with the leaders of the resistance and by concessions to some of their demands. In certain cases, negotiations and minor concessions are combined at the outset with police and military methods in a combined 'carrot and stick' approach. The most frequent type of concession is the promise of a government 'make-work' programme that provides low- wage, temporary jobs for unemployed workers and youths in infrastructure and public works projects. Other common concessions are modest pay increases for striking workers or temporary relief of one kind or another for the price increases in basic goods and services that have given rise to popular protests.

The most frequent response on the part of neoliberal regimes throughout the region has been to use 'police methods' as an immediate tactical response aimed at suppressing the outbreak and spread of popular resistance. These methods are aimed at immediately suppressing, by the use of force or the threat of force, both organized and unorganized, legal as well as illegal, forms of popular resistance; and if the resistance cannot be suppressed in the first instance, then these methods are often combined with military methods to control and contain the resistance so that it does not gain increasing popular support.

For example, these methods were the immediate response of the government authorities in Argentina to the wave of popular protests or *puebladas* that took place throughout the country in 1997. The provincial and central governments used the local police and the national *gendarmes* to break up the road blockades and the public demonstrations organized by protesters in the various provincial cities and towns where these protests took place.[38] The police and *gendarmes* used tear gas, beatings, rubber bullets, arrests, various types of police intimidation, and the imprisonment of some of the protesters to quell the protests. And in an attempt to avoid further protests and bloody confrontations with the police, temporary 'make-work programmes' were offered by the provincial governments in several of the provinces following negotiations with the protesters.

Police methods have been used in Brazil, Bolivia, the Dominican Republic, Ecuador, Honduras, Mexico, Nicaragua, Peru and Venezuela to suppress popular resistance to the neoliberal policies of the governments in these countries. In addition to these measures, either the threat or the declaration of a 'state of emergency' and anti-protest legislation have been used in certain countries to prevent popular resistance from gaining momentum and gathering widespread popular support. For instance, in Ecuador the government declared a 'state of mobilization' in response to the popular mobilizations led by the country's indigenous communities that shut down that country for two weeks in 1994. This measure provided the legal cover for using the armed forces to violently repress peaceful rallies, break up road blockades, occupy indigenous communities, beat and arrest their leaders, and destroy their crops and homes.[39] But this measure failed to repress the popular mobilizations in Ecuador, so the government entered into negotiations with the main indigenous organizations and made some concessions to them. This tactic succeeded and the regime went ahead with its neoliberal agrarian policies.

These tactical measures have been used by Latin American governments to suppress and control popular resistance to neoliberal policies. However, these measures are only effective at suppressing and controlling outbreaks of popular resistance after they have already erupted. They have not prevented nor have they reduced the increasing incidence and intensity of popular resistance in Latin America.

To prevent the emergence of widespread popular resistance, both the Latin American governments and the IFIs have developed and implemented more strategic measures. In recent years, the World Bank, the Inter-American Development Bank and the IMF have, in varying degrees, advocated that Latin American governments should complement their neoliberal structural adjustment and austerity programmes with 'poverty alleviation' programmes. The introduction of these 'anti-poverty' programmes into the picture has added a 'neostructuralist' element to the neoliberal package of policies and programmes.

According to Fernando Leiva, a radical Chilean economist,[40] 'neostructuralism comes onto the scene once the dirty work has been done by the neoliberals' and in place of the 'savage capitalism of the Pinochet school', the state is now asked to take a more activist role in combating poverty and promoting a more equitable form of economic growth. While the World Bank, the IMF and the Inter-American Development Bank have begun to advocate and provide limited funding to the Latin American governments for 'poverty alleviation' programmes targeted at those sectors of the population hardest hit by the neoliberal reforms of the 1980s and 1990s, they have not been very enthusiastic advocates of this 'neostructuralist' approach. The main advocate of this approach has been the United Nations Economic Commission for Latin America and the Caribbean (ECLAC or as it is known in Latin America, CEPAL).

In the 1960s, CEPAL promoted a 'structuralist' model of economic development that was centred on state-supported strategies of import-substitution industrialization combined with income redistribution measures. This model is now considered an anathema in current economic thinking because of the dominance of neoliberal ideology. As a result, 'neostructuralism' or '*Cepalismo*' now embraces much of the neoliberal creed. Contrary to the view of the hard-line neoliberals, however, the CEPAL economists argue that economic growth and social equity can be complementary if the state assists the private sector by helping it create jobs, develop human capital (through education, job training, health care and housing), undertake a modernizing agrarian reform, and use tax reforms to achieve a modest amount of income redistribution.[41]

To make its case, CEPAL has released a series of studies on the social inequities, skewed income distribution, and macroeconomic imbalances in Latin America that are the result of neoliberal adjustment policies that CEPAL has criticized for being poorly designed and carried out too rapidly by the neoliberal regimes. For example, one recent CEPAL study on income distribution in the five largest countries in Latin America (Argentina, Brazil, Chile, Colombia and Mexico) reveals that the richest 10 per cent of the population earn 69.5

times more than the poorest 10 per cent of the population in Brazil, 49.7 in Mexico, 41.7 in Colombia, 36.4 in Chile and 25.6 in Argentina.[42] The study concludes that the most important factors associated with low income and unemployment are lack of education, job training and an adequate social safety net. Thus, CEPAL wants the IFIs and the Latin American governments to place more emphasis on education, job training and social services.

To prevent popular resistance from giving rise to increasing levels of political instability that would threaten the neoliberal agenda in Latin America, the IFIs and Latin American governments have incorporated some of the 'neostructuralist' policy recommendations of CEPAL into their more strategic responses to popular resistance. These more strategic responses involve measures aimed at 'alleviating poverty' and 'developing human capital'. Since it is estimated that by the year 2000, as many as seven out of every ten Latin Americans may live below the poverty line,[43] it is not surprising that the IFIs and the neoliberal regimes in Latin America have been forced to develop a set of social policies that is aimed at preventing the most politically destabilizing consequences of the neoliberal project.

These social policies are largely 'targeted' at the new poor who have been created by the structural adjustment measures undertaken by the neoliberal regimes. They are not, however, aimed at eliminating the structural conditions underlying poverty in Latin America, since according to neoliberal ideology poverty is considered to be a social pathology rather than a consequence of the capitalist economic system. Thus, Carlos Vilas has noted in his critique of neoliberal social polices in Latin America that these policies operate more like charity than anything else. Vilas's analysis reveals that neoliberal social policies emphasize three basic elements: (1) privatization, (2) targeting, and (3) decentralization.[44] The privatization of social programmes involves the extensive use of NGOs and private contractors to provide relief and social services to the lower classes rather than regular government agencies. This is consistent with the ideological importance that is given to privatization within the neoliberal agenda. The targeting of these social programmes primarily at the hardest hit sectors of the urban and rural poor as well as the large informal sector of the working population is consistent with both the neoliberal critique of the ineffectiveness associated with government administered universal social services and the limited funds which the IFIs and the Latin American government are willing to commit to these social programmes. Finally, decentralization of the implementation of these programmes to the local level sounds good but in practice tends to result in the use of these programmes for the purpose of providing political patronage and resources to local officials, groups, and communities in return for their support of the government. In sum, the privatization, targeting, and decentralization of these social programmes help to give them more legitimacy and make them more effective as strategic measures for controlling popular resistance and opposition to the neoliberal regimes.

The policy mechanism that has all three of these elements and seems to best fit the neoliberal strategy for alleviating poverty and preventing popular resistance to neoliberal structural adjustment policies is the social investment fund (SIF). The first SIF was established in Bolivia with funds provided by the World Bank, other international organizations and European aid agencies. Called the *Fondo Social de Emergencia* (Emergency Social Fund or FSE), it was created to ameliorate the worst effects of Bolivia's structural adjustment programme on that country's impoverished lower classes.[45] The FSE provided funds and technical assistance to a large number of NGOs, state agencies, local governments and private contractors who were supposed to provide either short-term employment in public works projects or various types of social assistance to the sectors of the population most affected by the government's neoliberal structural adjustment and austerity programme. However, while the FSE improved the ability of the NGOs and state agencies to deliver short-term employment and social assistance to the population, the major benefits derived from the FSE had 'nothing to do with improving the welfare of poor people, but with overcoming opposition to structural adjustment.'[46] Moreover, the FSE has given rise to a proliferation of SIF- financed NGOs in Bolivia which 'have demonstrated a notable lack of enthusiasm for participating in the political mobilization of poor people', and which have 'with the assistance of the international donors, usurped political space that once belonged to grassroots organizations'. Thus, the NGOs engaged in delivering neoliberal poverty programmes have become an instrument for 'the generation of support for, and removal of, opposition to structural adjustment policies'.[47]

Since the FSE was established in Bolivia, similar social investment funds or SIFs have been established in most of the Latin American countries where neoliberal policies have been implemented.[48] Nowhere has this strategy been more successful than in Chile. A Chilean SIF was established in 1990 to combat the 100 per cent increase in poverty that took place between 1970 and 1990 in that country. Unlike the governments of most of the other Latin American countries, the civilian governments in Chile have taken a more long-term approach to combating poverty and they have given priority to self-help, credit, training and technical assistance programmes for small producers and poor communities.[49] However, despite the fact that the social policies of the first civilian government under President Patricio Aylwin reduced the percentage of Chileans living in poverty from 44.6 per cent in 1989 to 28 per cent in 1994,[50] the gap in income between the richest and poorest Chileans has increased and the current government of President Eduardo Frei has not been able to improve on Aylwin's record. The limited funds available for improving the conditions of the poorest sectors of the population and the privatization of Chile's social services have left the government with very little strategic capacity to achieve 'growth with equity' by reducing either the level of poverty or the increasing income gap between the upper and lower classes.

Because they have privatized many social services and they are unwilling to commit more than a very limited amount of funding for social programmes, the Latin American governments have been forced to rely heavily upon the use of NGOs to implement short- term employment and social assistance programmes instead of programmes that generate long-term employment and address the underlying structural causes of poverty. As a result, they have seriously undermined their strategic capacity to forestall popular resistance to their economic policies and their social programmes look more like tactical responses to popular resistance than strategic responses aimed at preventing this resistance over the long run.

For example, a SIF was created in 1990 by the United Nations Development Programme to ameliorate the effects of the neoliberal structural adjustment reforms in Honduras. Between 1990 and 1994, almost 5500 projects were funded by this social investment fund. However, 70 per cent of these projects were short-term public works projects, and only 7 per cent were projects that created any long-term productive employment.[51] In addition, close to 60 per cent of the projects were carried out in the five richest departments of Honduras, and only 10 per cent were targeted at the six poorest departments of the country. In this case, the central government's use of SIF funds and projects as tools of political patronage and electioneering 'was so blatant that it alienated many NGOs that had initially collaborated with the fund' and led many of them to accuse the Honduran government 'of using the fund to assert state control over the NGOs and social movements' in Honduras.[52] This case reflects a relatively common tendency on the part of the Latin American governments to use SIFs and other poverty alleviation programmes as resources for political patronage and graft. Used in this manner, they lose the potential they might have to eliminate some of the conditions that give rise to the frequent popular protests and increasing popular resistance that take place in their countries.

The effectiveness of these poverty alleviation measures with regard to ameliorating the worst effects of the neoliberal reforms and counteracting popular resistance to these reforms is dependent upon both the mediating role played by NGOs (often international NGOs) and the external funding supplied by the IFIs and other foreign donors. In general, this dependency on external resources has led to the 'denationalization' of the social programmes of the Latin American governments, an emphasis on short-term as opposed to medium- or long-term poverty alleviation projects (due to the unpredictable nature of external funding), and an increase in the foreign debt of the Latin American governments due to the increase in external loans for the SIFs.[53] These conditions have also limited the effectiveness of these measures and reduced their strategic capacity to contain the rising wave of popular resistance to neoliberal policies in the region. As a result, the poverty alleviation programmes carried out by the Latin American governments with the backing of the IFIs have failed to prevent or reduce the increasing incidence of popular resistance to neoliberal policies in Latin America.

THE NEED FOR A VIABLE POPULAR ALTERNATIVE TO NEOLIBERALISM

In view of the patent failure of the neoliberal project to combat effectively either the poverty suffered by the majority of Latin Americans or the extreme social and economic inequities that characterize the Latin American societies, it is clear that there is need for a viable alternative project that will genuinely serve the needs of the majority of the population by creating the sustaining conditions for greater social, economic and political democracy. The strength of the neoliberal regimes is that they have presented a coherent strategy that appears to be in step with the times, but the 'unending series of adjustments, each implemented with the promise that it would be the final one' has begun to erode the credibility of these regimes and has led to 'downward social mobility for key supporters of the neoliberal model – not only the poor and public employees, but sectors of the professional and business class who [have been] badly hit' by these adjustments, so much so that even 'sectors of the military and church hierarchy' have begun to question the viability of the neoliberal agenda.[54]

The Centre–Left opposition parties and movements in most of the Latin American countries have failed to take full advantage of this situation. They have failed to win major electoral victories over the neoliberals because they have been unable to offer the electorate a viable alternative to the neoliberal agenda. Moreover, the neoliberal political forces in power have successfully exploited the authoritarian legacy of fear and insecurity in the political culture of these countries that stems from the recent era of military rule. They have also used their privileged access to the elite-controlled mass media and the extensive campaign funds of the upper classes to their advantage.[55]

The Centre–Left parties have abandoned their previous social democratic reform agenda for a more pragmatic 'social liberal' agenda which is hardly distinguishable from that of the neoliberals, except that they advocate more state expenditures on social programmes to ease the effects of the neoliberal reforms. They have also tended to shy away from mobilizing the popular classes through general strikes and mass demonstrations. Instead, they have focused on parliamentary and electoral politics, even though popular resistance to these regimes has continued to erupt in the streets, factories, universities and countryside while they have sat in their offices and parliamentary chambers.

To displace the neoliberals from power, the parties of the Left and other organized progressive political forces in Latin America will need to overcome their internal differences, join together in a broad political front, and mobilize popular support for a genuinely alternative project of social and economic development that responds to the needs and interests of the diverse, multi- class spectrum of social movements and grassroots organizations that have arisen in opposition to the neoliberal regimes.[56] In the past, Centre–Left and leftist political movements have won electoral victories in Latin America 'when the elections were the *culmination* of mass mobilizations and struggles, of land occupations, and urban movements', and when these political movements have polarized the population in a manner favourable to an electoral victory by these forces.[57] However, in addition to adopting this kind of mobilizing strategy for the purposes of gaining political power, the opponents of neoliberalism need to develop and promote an alternative project of social and economic development that is both politically and economically viable.

To date, leftist and progressive forces in Latin America have not been able to put forward either a *viable* social democratic or a *credible* democratic socialist project as an effective *alternative* to the neoliberal agenda. However, the basic elements of these two alternatives to neoliberalism would appear to be needed in any alternative project that provides a viable course of sustainable economic development based upon social justice, equity, and popular democracy.

If popular resistance to the ills of neoliberal globalization continues to grow in Latin America as it has over the last decade, then broad-based popular movements may arise that not only succeed in creating an alternative project of inward-oriented, sustainable development, *but also a state capable of exercising democratic control at the national level over both domestic and transnational capital.* The next few years will reveal whether or not the conditions for this course of development emerge, but in the meantime it is at least safe to predict that there will be continuing popular resistance to the neoliberal regimes in Latin America due to the inherently inequitable and unpopular nature of the policies they pursue as well as the widespread suffering they impose upon the majority of the population.

Notes and References

1. Richard L. Harris, 'The Global Context of Contemporary Latin American Affairs', in S. Halebsky and R. L. Harris (eds), *Capital, Power, and Inequality in Latin America* (Boulder, Col.: Westview, 1995), pp. 279–394.
2. John Weeks, 'The Contemporary Latin American Economies: Neoliberal Reconstruction', in *Capital, Power, and Inequality in Latin America, ibid.,* pp. 126–7.
3. Carlos Vilas, 'Neoliberal Social Policy: Managing Poverty (Somehow)', *NACLA Report on the Americas*, vol. 29, no. 6 (May/June 1996), p. 16.
4. Joseph Collins and John Lear, *Chile's Free-Market Miracle: A Second Look* (Oakland, Cal.: Food First, 1995).
5. *Ibid.*
6. V. Bulmer-Thomas, 'Introduction', in V. Bulmer-Thomas (ed.), *The New Economic Model in Latin America and its Impact on Income Distribution and Poverty* (New York: St Martin's Press, 1996), p. 10; and Duncan Green, *Silent Revolution: The Rise of Market Economics in Latin America* (London: Cassell, 1995), p. 204.

7. John Weeks, 'The Contemporary Latin American Economies', *op.cit.*, pp. 117–18.
8. H. Veltmeyer, J. Petras and S. Vieux, *Neoliberalism and Class Conflict in Latin America* (New York: St Martin's Press, 1997), p. 213.
9. Collins and Lear, *Chile's Free-Market Miracle*, *op.cit.*, pp. 70–1.
10. *Ibid.*, p. 71.
11. *Ibid.*, pp. 32–3.
12. *Ibid.*, p. 33.
13. *Ibid.*
14. *Ibid.*, p. 80.
15. D. Green, *Silent Revolution*, *op.cit.*
16. H. Veltmeyer, J. Petras and S. Vieux, *Neoliberalism and Class Conflict in Latin America*, *op.cit.*, pp. 192–4.
17. N. Pacari, 'Taking on the Neoliberal Agenda', *NACLA Report on the Americas*, vol. 29, no. 5 (March/April 1996), pp. 23–32.
18. 'New Waves of Protests Across Region Sparked by Neoliberal Reforms', *NACLA Report on the Americas*, vol. 29, no. 4 (July/August 1995), pp. 1–2.
19. 'Bolivia: Protests Greet Fuel Price Increases', *Latin American Weekly Report* (*LAWR*), 8 February 1996, p. 53.
20. 'Peru: Fujimori Unyielding on Petroperú', and 'Ecuador: Public Sector Strike Wins Big Pay Rises', *LAWR*, 22 February 1996, p. 83.
21. 'Argentina: Menem's Decrees "Unconstitutional"', *LAWR*, 7 January 1997, p. 15.
22. *Ibid.*, 16.
23. 'Church and IMF Provide Contrasting Views of Unrest in Argentina', *LAWR*, 27 May 1997, p. 244.
24. *Ibid.*, p. 241.
25. 'Venezuela: Strikers Call Seven-Day Truce', *LAWR*, 14 January 1997, p. 35.
26. 'Ecuador: Convertibility Plan Now in Doubt', *LAWR*, 11 February 1997, p. 77.
27. 'Ecuador: Alarcón Faces Union Ultimatum', *LAWR*, 25 February 1997, p. 101.
28. *Ibid.*
29. 'Venezuela: Strikers Call Seven-Day Truce', *LAWR*, 14 January 1997, p. 35.
30. 'Venezuela: Peace Deal Struck with Public Sector', *LAWR*, 18 February 1997, p. 93.
31. 'Venezuela: Agenda Venezuela Stabilization Programme', *LAWR*, 8 July 1997, p. 33.
32. 'Dominican Republic: Fernandez Upholds Right to Protest', *LAWR*, 21 January 1997, p. 41.
33. 'Brazil: The MST Opens the Floodgates', *LAWR*, p. 181.
34. 'Uruguayans Join Wave of Protests', *LAWR*, 24 June 1997, pp. 294–5.
35. 'Guatemala: Opposition to Privatization', *Central American Report* (*CAR*), 20 March 1997, p. 4.
36. 'Panama: New State Pension Law Continues to Worry Workers', *CAR*, 22 May 1997, p. 8.

37. 'Nicaragua: New ESAF Approaches', *CAR*, 16 October 1997, p. 3.
38. 'Argentina: Menem's Decrees "Unconstitutional"' *LAWR*, 7 January 1997, p. 15.
39. N. Pacari, 'Taking on the Neoliberal Agenda', *op.cit.*, p. 24.
40. D. Green, *Silent Revolution*, *op.cit.*, p. 189.
41. *Ibid.*, pp. 88–9 and 244–5.
42. 'Ecuador: Back to Harsh Reality', *LAWR*, 4 March 1997, pp. 114–15.
43. K. Stahl, 'Anti-poverty Programmes: Making Structural Adjustment More Palatable', *NACLA Report on the Americas*, vol. 29, no. 6 (May/June 1996), p. 32.
44. C. Vilas, 'Neoliberal Social Policy', *op.cit.*, p. 19.
45. H. Veltmeyer, J. Petras and S. Vieux, *Neoliberalism and Class Conflict in Latin America*, *op.cit.*, pp. 172–3.
46. *Ibid.*, p. 174.
47. *Ibid.*, p. 177.
48. K. Stahl, 'Anti-poverty Programmes', *op.cit.*, p. 32.
49. *Ibid.*, p. 36.
50. P. Vergara, 'In Pursuit of Growth with Equity: The Limits of Chile's Free-Market Social Reforms', *NACLA Report on the Americas*, vol. 29, no. 6 (May/June 1996), p. 37.
51. K. Stahl, 'Anti-poverty Programmes', *op.cit.*, pp. 33–4.
52. *Ibid.*, p. 35.
53. K. Stahl, 'Anti-poverty Programmes', *op.cit.*, p. 36; and H. Veltmeyer, J. Petras and S. Vieux, *Neoliberalism and Class Conflict in Latin America*, *op.cit.*, pp. 176–7.
54. H. Veltmeyer, J. Petras and S. Vieux, *Neoliberalism and Class Conflict in Latin America*, *op.cit.*, p. 221.
55. *Ibid.*, pp. 214–15.
56. D. Green, *Silent Revolution*, *op.cit.*, p. 195.
57. H. Veltmeyer, J. Petras and S. Vieux, *Neoliberalism and Class Conflict in Latin America*, *op.cit.*, p. 218.

6 Economic Reform and Political Turmoil in Mexico

Francis Adams

Mexico offers a striking example of the political challenges posed by globalization. While there are compelling pressures to undertake free market reforms, these reforms threaten the economic well-being of various social groups and provoke popular resistance. State elites have scrambled to devise strategies which *preserve* neoliberal adjustment *without jeopardizing* regime stability.

Mexico's market-oriented reforms, first introduced in the mid-1980s, are among the most comprehensive in the developing world. During the past decade successive Mexican governments have sold off most public corporations, deregulated local markets, slashed public spending and dismantled foreign trade and investment controls. Although this 'neoliberal revolution' has produced a windfall for some Mexicans, the benefits of market reform have been poorly distributed. In fact, unemployment has increased and living standards declined since these measures were first introduced. Social protest and organized resistance was thus predictable. The scope and intensity of popular discontent, however, has surprised even the most astute observers of Mexican affairs. *During the past decade, the nation's political elite have faced some of the greatest challenges to state authority and control in the modern era.*

This chapter reviews Mexico's experience with economic adjustment since the mid-1980s. The first section outlines the specific domestic and foreign economic reforms which have been adopted. I then turn to the distributional effects of these reforms, placing special focus on those groups most adversely affected by neoliberalism. The third and fourth sections explore the various ways in which poor and working-class Mexicans have resisted market reform and the political strategies which state elites have deployed in response to these grassroots challenges. While coercion has sometimes been used to deactivate popular sectors, Mexico's leaders have not relied exclusively on a military solution. As Richard Harris notes in the preceding chapter, *repression alone would simply undermine the government's domestic legitimacy and strengthen the major opposition groups.* Rather, state elites have frequently negotiated with their most vocal opponents, adopting compromise measures which lessen the social costs of adjustment. The delicate balance between *coercion* and *compromise* is the central focus of this chapter.

NEOLIBERAL REFORMS

The state has long played a dominant role in Mexico's economy. In the half-century between 1935 and 1985 the state owned and controlled the largest industries, tightly regulated wages, prices and interest rates and assumed primary responsibility for the provision of basic goods and services. Successive Mexican governments also maintained highly restrictive foreign trade and investment regimes in an attempt to protect domestic industries from external competition. Foreign goods were subject to steep tariffs and a wide array of import permits and licenses. Foreign investment was not permitted in key sectors of the economy (most notably banking, communications, steel, electricity and petroleum) and rarely exceeded 49 per cent of capital stock in any single industry.[1]

Mexico's state-led import-substitution strategy was moderately successful. Between 1950 and 1970, the Mexican economy grew about 6 per cent per year, the job market expanded and, although poverty remained widespread, basic living conditions improved. Profits from state industries helped finance expanded public services, particularly primary education and basic health care and consumer subsidies for basic foods and transportation. Between 1930 and 1980 life expectancy for the average Mexican rose from 40 to 65 years.

The Mexican political system was also *remarkably* stable during this period. Mexico was the only major Latin American country which did not experience a military coup between 1950 and 1980. Mexico's political stability derives, to a considerable extent, from the hegemonic position of the ruling Institutional Revolutionary Party (PRI).[2] The PRI has won every presidential election since the 1930s and, until just recently, controlled both the national legislature and state governments.[3] The PRI's extraordinary political success has been studied elsewhere.[4] For the purposes of this chapter, it is suffice to note that the PRI has managed to incorporate most of the major social and economic interest groups into its party structure. Government-allied unions loyally support the PRI's candidates and are in turn rewarded with state patronage, higher wages and political influence.[5]

Mexico's economic success began to unravel toward the end of the 1970s. Although protectionism had spurred considerable domestic industrialization, the lack of foreign competition created few incentives to modernize production or conserve resources. State corporations became increasingly inefficient and a considerable drain on public budgets. By 1979 Mexico's public sector deficit had reached 17 per cent of total gross domestic product.

Mexico's import substitution strategy was also problematic in another respect. Domestic industries were increasingly dependent on importing raw materials, capital goods and technology. However, because these industries were primarily producing for the captive market at home, the country was not earning enough from exports to meet its foreign exchange needs. The government responded by borrowing heavily from abroad, since credit was abundant, interest rates relatively low at the time and new-found petroleum reserves could be used as collateral. By the early 1980s Mexico's foreign debt had mushroomed to $85 billion and a sudden drop in global petroleum prices made it increasingly difficult to service these loans. At this point, foreign banks refused to provide new resources to help the Mexican government meet its interest payments. In order to avoid defaulting, Mexico's leaders turned to the International Monetary Fund (IMF) for support. Foreign exchange support from the IMF was extended only after the government agreed to undertake dramatic market-oriented restructuring. Similar agreements were then reached with the World Bank, the Paris Club and the United States.

Mexico's neoliberal reforms were first instituted during the presidency of Miguel de la Madrid.[6] Between 1982 and 1988 the government sold 750 small and medium-size state-owned corporations, substantially deregulated domestic markets and slashed public sector expenditures. The de la Madrid administration also began dismantling protectionist trade and investment regimes. Tariffs, quotas and other trade barriers were simplified and reduced and official reference prices for imports were eliminated.[7] Various sectors of the Mexican economy were also opened to foreign investment and local ownership requirements were relaxed. The 1986 decision to join the General Agreement on Tariffs and Trade (GATT) underscored Mexico's new outward orientation.

Neoliberal adjustment in Mexico was accelerated under President Carlos Salinas de Gotari (1988–94). Salinas privatized many of the largest government enterprises, including the telephone and banking systems, airlines and steel production,[8] and slashed tariffs and import licences. Some of the major domestic service industries were also opened to foreign investors for the first time.[9] The Salinas administration also introduced market reforms in the countryside.[10] For generations, Article 27 of the Mexican constitution had preserved communally-held land for rural peasants. Under the *ejido* system, peasant farmers received use-right titles from their local villages to work tracts of land collectively. They were not permitted to sell or rent the land. In 1992 the *ejido* system was reformed to give members rights more like private ownership including the ability to sell their land. These reforms opened the door to domestic and foreign investments in agriculture. The government argued that subsistence peasants would now be able to modernize their agricultural practices and become more competitive. The government also phased out crop subsidies and reduced its role in agricultural credit and marketing.

Salinas also sought expanded trade with the United States and Canada. Under the North American Free Trade Agreement (NAFTA), which took effect in 1994, customs duties on nearly 10 000 products are being phased out over a 15–year period. The Mexican government is also required to reduce restrictions on foreign investment in most sectors of its economy, including banking, insurance and securities, investment services, transportation and telecommunications. Because the agreement calls for equal treatment for both foreign and national investors, virtually all limits on foreign investment will be removed by the end of the century.[11]

Since taking office in 1994, President Ernesto Zedillo has remained faithful to the neoliberal agenda of his two immediate predecessors. The Zedillo administration completed the sale of government-owned railroads and airports and expanded opportunities for foreign investment in PEMEX, the state-owned oil monopoly. Foreign investment is now allowed in secondary petrochemical and natural gas distribution operations.

After a decade of neoliberal reform, the private sector has largely replaced the state, exports have become the driving force of the economy and foreign investment is considered a key source of capital and advanced technology. For Mexico's political elite, a market economy, driven by exports and private capital, is the best hope for modernization of the nation's industries, expanded employment and rising living standards.

SOCIAL IMPACT OF NEO-LIBERALISM

The neoliberal reforms outlined above have touched the lives of most Mexicans. Clearly, some people have benefited tremendously from these reforms. The privatization of state-owned industries, for example, produced an extraordinary windfall for some Mexican entrepreneurs. As Andrew Reding notes '[p]rivatization in Mexico has meant basically transferring enterprises from the country's political elite to its economic elite instead of seeking to decentralize ownership'.[12] Moreover, domestic industries and agribusinesses have gained enhanced access to external markets and secured joint arrangements with foreign firms. There have also been expanded employment opportunities for professional and skilled labourers with transnational corporations. Workers in corporations with transnational ties have seen their wages rise by as much as 30 per cent in recent years.[13]

Neoliberal reform has certainly *intensified* the concentration of wealth in Mexico. A 1994 study by the Economic Research Institute of Mexico's National Autonomous University found that privatization had resulted in 50 per cent of the country's assets being held by just five conglomerates.[14] In addition, the combined wealth of Mexico's 15 richest individuals was $25.6 billion, the equivalent of 10 per cent of the country's gross domestic product.[15] The richest 10 per cent of the population now control 41 per cent of the country's wealth, and the 35 richest families have as much wealth as the *15 million* poorest Mexicans. *Mexico is now home to the fourth largest number of billionaires in the world.*

Of course, neoliberalism has not produced the same windfall for Mexico's rural and urban poor. These groups have experienced a relative decline in their living standards. In the countryside, changes in the *ejido* system have led to increased concentrations of land holdings, as peasant farmers are displaced by both domestic and foreign investors.[16] Traditional corn and bean farmers have also lost price supports and other subsidies. Moreover, because Mexican farmers are often unable to afford improvements like tractors, fertilizers or hybrid seeds, they have not been able to compete with US-based agribusinesses. Between 1984 and 1993 employment in the agricultural sector declined of 4.5 per cent per year.[17]

Neoliberal reforms have also undermined small and medium-size businesses throughout Mexico. The drop in domestic demand and the influx of cheap goods from abroad have contributed to the collapse of thousands of family-owned enterprises, restaurants and repair shops. According to a study jointly released by the Mexican Confederation of Chambers of Commerce and the government statistics agency, NAFTA has adversely affected 60 per cent of commercial establishments in Mexico, with traditional manufacturing industries, such as textiles, apparel and footwear, experiencing the greatest setbacks.[18]

Mexico's 1994–95 currency crisis can also be traced, at least in part, to its new outward orientation strategy. The crisis began when foreign investors started withdrawing capital from the country. The government responded by buying billions of pesos on the open market. While these purchases temporarily stabilized the peso, they could not continue indefinitely. As foreign reserves dwindled, the government was forced to let the peso float freely on currency markets. This sent the peso into a free fall, losing roughly a third of its value against the dollar in January 1995. The Mexican stock market also went into a tailspin, plunging by about 25 per cent. Within a year the nation's unemployment rate had doubled, with one million Mexicans losing their jobs and inflation jumped from 7 per cent to 52 per cent as prices on basic items like electricity, gasoline and tortillas surged. Mexico's gross domestic product (GDP) declined 6.9 per cent in 1994 and another 6.2 per cent in 1995.[19]

Mexico's declining living standards have been well-documented. The World Bank estimates that the number of Mexicans living in poverty grew by an average of 660 000 during each of the past 15 years while the United Nations Population Fund puts this number at 1.2 million.[20] More than a quarter of the workforce remains unemployed or underemployed and manufacturing wages, adjusted for inflation, are below 1981 levels. Since the early 1980s the minimum wage has fallen 39 per cent and average wages in manufacturing by one-fourth.[21] The income of the poorest 20 per cent of the population fell from 5 per cent of national income in 1984, to 4.3 per cent in 1992.[22]

OPPOSITION TO REFORM

Market-oriented reforms have clearly contributed to greater poverty and inequality in Mexico. As living conditions have deteriorated, organized resistance to neoliberalism has intensified. This section reviews the most prominent forms of resistance, including armed insurrection, civil disobedience, labour strikes and independent political activity.

The most dramatic example of popular resistance to neoliberalism occurred in the Mexican countryside. On 1 January 1994, a thousand Mayan peasants in the southern state of Chiapas rose up under the banner of legendary revolutionary Emeliano Zapata. The Zapatista National Liberation Army (EZLN) seized the highland city of San Cristóbal de las Casas, three other towns and several villages along the Guatemalan border. Their uprising was deliberately timed to coincide with the implementation of NAFTA which the insurgents labeled a 'death certificate for the ethnic people of Mexico'. The EZLN demanded land, housing, food, health care, education, freedom, democracy, justice and peace. They have since called for an 'intercontinental network of resistance to neoliberalism'.[23]

This scenario was repeated in August 1996 when a second revolutionary group, the Popular Revolutionary Army (EPR), carried out 18 coordinated attacks in and around the state of Guerrero. Skirmishes took place in Tlaxiaco, where guerrillas opened fire on a municipal palace and a police barracks and in Michoacan, where armed groups ambushed military convoys. The EPR 'Manifesto of Aguas Blancas' called for 'revolutionary armed struggle to oust the unpopular, nondemocratic, demagogic and illegitimate government that serves the interest of national and foreign capital'.

Resistance to neoliberalism has also been reflected in various forms of civil disobedience. The Mexican Action Network on Free Trade (RMALC) formulated an 'Alternative Economic Strategy for Mexico's Development' and advocated disrupting the government's economic programmes. A debtors cartel, *El Barzón*, emerged in response to the country's skyrocketing interest rates and currency devaluations. The group has its origins in a 1993 protest by a small number of deeply indebted farmers in the western state of Jalisco who used their tractors to block highways. The cartel now includes artisans, shopkeepers and credit card holders who are demanding temporary suspension of legal action against debtors. *El Barzón* has also called for restructuring overdue loans, renegotiating the foreign debt, creating an equitable tax policy, suspending the privatization of state industries, increasing the minimum wage and reorientating public spending.

Various segments of organized labour have also campaigned against neoliberalism. The PRI-affiliated Confederation of Mexican Workers (CTM), which is made up of 32 state federations and five national unions, has long enjoyed a virtual monopoly over unionized workplaces. The CTM has frequently been criticized for failing to advance the interests of average workers. In fact, the CTM has consistently signed collective bargaining agreements or 'pacts' with the government and business over the past ten years which have cut wages and made labour contracts more flexible.[24]

Popular indignation with the CTM leadership has led to the formation of dissident groups or 'democratic currents' within the official unions. Democratic currents have emerged within the National Electricians Union and Telephone Workers Union. The National Teachers Union held a series of marches in which they demanded better wages and working conditions and the Petroleum Workers Union blocked oil wells in the gulf state of Tabasco to protest the government's decision to privatize part of the petrochemical industry. There have also been a growing number of unauthorized strikes in the eastern and central parts of the country. Moreover, politically autonomous labour organizations have emerged in recent years. The Union Movement of the Nation, May 1 Inter-Union Coordinating Committee and Authentic Labour Front have eroded the power and influence of the CTM.[25]

The government's neoliberal agenda has also led to divisions within the PRI. In the summer of 1986 the Movement for Democratic Renovation was formed within the ruling party to protest the government's economic policies. This movement advocated returning to the populist redistributional policies of the past, suspending foreign debt payments and ending the privatizations. It was led by Cuauhtémoc Cárdenas Solózano, the former governor of Michoacan and son of Lázaro Cárdenas, the populist president of Mexico from 1934 to 1940 and by Porfirio Muñoz Ledo, former Secretary-General of the PRI.

In 1988, Cárdenas split from the PRI to contest the presidential elections as part of a centre-left coalition of four parties and several non-parties under the banner Democratic Front for National Reconstruction (FDN).[26] The FDN argued that the privatization of state enterprises limited the government's ability to manage the economy. The FDN also criticized the government's 'subservience' to the IMF and 'sell-out' to foreign interests. It called for a suspension in debt- service payments, a commitment to a mixed economy and the 'assumption by the state of its full responsibilities towards public and social enterprises'.[27] The FDN was later transformed into the centre-left Party of the Democratic Revolution (PRD).[28] The PRD platform calls for 'renegotiation' of NAFTA, taxes on short-term capital flows, controls on bank interest margins, partial renegotiation of the foreign debt and re-examination of some privatizations.

Splits within the PRI have eroded its privileged position with the Mexican electorate. This was reflected in the 1997 mid-term elections in which 500 Chamber of Deputies seats were contested. The PRI lost its absolute majority in the Chamber of Deputies for the first time in seven decades,[29] and President Zedillo is now obligated to negotiate with opposition members of the legislature. Cárdenas was also elected mayor of Mexico City with 47 per cent of the vote (20 points ahead of the PRI candidate), while the PRD took 38 of 66 seats on the City Council.

COERCION AND COMPROMISE

As noted above, the PRI's remarkable political success stems largely from its ability to channel social demands within its *corporatist* structure and use *patronage* to coopt its most vocal opponents. *Popular resistance to neoliberalism, however, has severely tested this system of elite control.* Since the mid–1980s, Mexico's leaders have grappled simultan eously with peasant rebellions, civil disobedience, labour unrest and divisions within the ruling party. In an attempt to preserve free market reforms without further jeopardizing political stability, the government has relied upon a combination of coercion and compromise. While military and police force has been deployed in response to direct challenges to state authority, the government has also made significant concessions to opposition groups in an attempt to lessen the social costs of adjustment.

The use of force was most evident in response to the Chiapas rebellion. Through the combination of numerical superiority, air power and sophisticated weapons, the government retook control of the four towns held by the EZLN. Military airplanes and helicopter gunships bombed villages suspected of being rebel strongholds. Over 15 000 soldiers were mobilized to block roads and highways. After 12 days of fighting, the government reported 145 people had been killed while local residents placed this number at more than 400. Human rights groups also documented hundreds of illegal detentions and house searches. Some of those detained were threatened and beaten.[30] The region continues to be militarized with soldiers permanently stationed in nearly every town and village. The army has also completed a major road project to facilitate troop movements and has built permanent installations in a dozen communities.[31] Zapatista leaders have frequently complained that followers have been subject to intimidation, harassment, arbitrary arrest and detention. There have also been attacks on EZLN sympathizers by paramilitary groups which are thought to be linked to local PRI officials.

The military presence is also on the rise in other areas of the country.[32] President Zedillo dismissed the EPR guerrillas as 'terrorists', 'delinquents' and 'unimportant criminals' and vowed to use 'all the force of the state' to crush their uprising. The army mobilized thousands of troops in a counter-insurgency campaign throughout Guerrero. Once again, human rights groups have documented the selective use of detention and torture.

The government's military crackdown met widespread opposition throughout Mexico. Two weeks after the fighting began in Chiapas, 100 000 people gathered in Mexico City to protest the military attacks and demand a negotiated settlement.[33] The Salinas administration quickly reversed course, announcing a unilateral cease-fire, granting amnesty to anyone who had participated in the uprising and agreeing to peace talks with the EZLN. A specially designated Commission for Peace and Reconciliation was established to coordinate the talks. The government also increased public sector expenditures on schools, roads, housing, health clinics, farm credits and crop subsidies in the region.

In February 1996 the Zedillo administration and the Zapatistas signed a temporary agreement entitled 'Indigenous Rights and Culture'. The accord laid the groundwork for significant changes in indigenous rights, political participation and cultural autonomy.[34] It called for new laws to outlaw discrimination against indigenous communities and for the creation of a special office to respond to human rights violations and land disputes.[35] However, peace talks have since broken down and there seems to be little prospect for reaching a final accord in the near future.[36]

The Mexican government has also balanced coercion and compromise in response to civil protest. The Inter-Church Committee on Human Rights in Latin America has documented a systematic campaign of political persecution, including death threats and surveillance of homes. Campesino leaders who have attempted to defend *ejido* lands have been subject to intimidation and harassment.[37] Americas Watch has also criticized the Mexican government for human rights abuses, including torture, disappearances, extra-judicial killings by police and security forces and violence against unions.

At the same time, the government has introduced new compensatory programmes to cushion the social costs of market reform.[38] The government began providing property titles for families living in the illegal housing areas that surround many of the nation's cities. In addition, after the formation of *El Barzón* the government launched a programme to aid poor and medium-income debtors.[39] As Ann Varley notes, these programmes have helped maintain political stability by demobilizing independent organizations in low-income areas.[40]

Possibly the best example of a politically-motivated compensatory programme was the National Solidarity Programme (PRONASOL) which President Salinas launched in 1989. PRONASOL was a community- based welfare and public works programme specifically designed to lessen the hardships posed by economic restructuring. Funds were used for the construction of health clinics, hospitals, schools, water supply systems, sewage systems, electrical generators and food distribution stores.[41] Between 1989 and 1993 the government allocated $12 billion for various PRONASOL projects throughout the country.[42] During the last two years of the programme, PRONASOL accounted for 35 per cent of non-debt government spending. As Miguel Ángel Centeno notes, PRONASOL was the ‘perfect example’ of classic PRI tactics, whereby opposition and discontent could be diffused and co-opted through patronage.[43]

The PRONASOL programme diverged from the traditional patterns of patronage in one important respect. Through a process called ‘co-participation’, PRONASOL resources were managed by neighbourhood ‘Solidarity Committees’. One hundred and fifty thousand solidarity committees were registered in 1993. The Salinas administration felt that simply spending money on a particular group did not guarantee their loyalty. Political allegiance could be maximized if recipients of government funds helped design and implement the projects. People receiving assistance were thus required to contribute their own time, work and money to the various public works projects.[44]

It is also important to note that PRONASOL funds did not go to the poorest neighbourhoods in Mexico. Rather, resources generally went to communities and groups deemed politically crucial to rebuilding the PRI. PRONASOL funds were especially directed towards those regions where competing parties were strongest.[45] As Riordan Roett notes, the government hoped to win over opposition leaders who would replenish the PRI’s political cadres at the precinct and district level.[46] Kathleen Bruhn describes the National Solidarity Programme as ‘an innovative social spending programme designed to win back popular support for the government in the context of neoliberal policies’.[47] When inaugurating PRONASOL projects, Salinas personally visited small towns across the country to make sure the PRI was associated with the benefits of the programme.

The government also developed a compensatory programme for rural peasants. The Programme of Direct Support of the Countryside (PROCAMPO), announced in the fall of 1993, gave direct subsidies to peasant producers of corn, beans, wheat, rice, soya, sorghum and cotton.[48] These subsidies were designed to offset losses due to the decline in agricultural prices. PROCAMPO also appealed to local desires for autonomy, giving peasants greater control over production programmes.[49] A Permanent Agrarian Congress (CAP) was established to extend government ties with campesino movements and reincorporate opposition grassroots movements into the ruling party, while various 'cooperation agreements' were signed with independent peasant organizations.

Since assuming power in 1994, Ernesto Zedillo has established his own antipoverty initiative. *Progressa* funds programmes in health care, education and nutrition and is expected to serve 400 000 families by the end of 1998. Families chosen to participate in the programme receive free health care, mothers receive a monthly stipend and children receive free nutritional supplements. Scholarships are also awarded for primary and secondary schools.[50] The programme places a priority on channeling resources to women.

Mexico's political elite also hoped to forge an accommodation with opposition political parties.[51] The Zedillo administration entered into negotiations over political reform which eventually led to a July 1996 agreement. The agreement separated the Federal Electoral Institute (IFE) from control of the Interior Ministry, and included provisions for public financing of elections and equitable access for all political parties to the state-controlled media. Measures were also established to give greater powers to judicial and legislative branches, decentralize power from the federal government to state and local governments and combat public-sector corruption.[52]

CONCLUSION

Clearly Mexico's transition from a state-led to a free market economy and from import-substitution to export liberalism, has deepened social polarization and shaken the country's political order. State elites have attempted to undercut resistance without jeopardizing the overall reform programme, and this has sometimes involved the use of force to repress direct challenges to state authority. At the same time, Mexico's political leaders realize excessive force would simply undermine the government's already precarious political legitimacy and stability. Both the Salinas and Zedillo administrations were consistently willing to negotiate with opposition groups and enact compensatory programmes designed to lessen the social costs of structural adjustment. By integrating the Mexican economy in global markets, the government is increasingly at the mercy of international financial speculators. Since the influx of both direct and portfolio investment is a key component of its current strategy, it is important to guarantee a stable and profitable investment climate. *Compensatory programmes help purchase social peace.*

However, Mexico's system of elite control and co-optation rests on a shaky foundation. Because compensatory programmes have been funded almost entirely by the proceeds from privatization, they can only be considered a short-term solution. Once these revenues are exhausted, the government's capacity to buy off opposition groups will be severely weakened.

Mexico has clearly reached a critical juncture in its economic and political development. Neoliberal economic reforms could not have been adopted without tremendous political costs. Whether the traditional structures of power can absorb these costs over the long run and whether the PRI can maintain its hegemonic position over Mexican politics, appears increasingly doubtful.

Notes and References

1. It should be noted that transnational corporations sometimes circumvented these restrictions by forming wholly-owned subsidiaries within Mexico.
2. Mexico's political stability also derives from a high concentration of power in the presidency. Until recently, the Mexican president enjoyed extraordinary decision-making authority, able to issue executive decrees, introduce legislative proposals, handpick governors and judges and even choose his own successor.
3. Forerunners to the PRI include the National Revolutionary Party between 1929 and 1938, and the Mexican Revolutionary Party between 1938 and 1945.
4. Dan Cothran, *Political Stability and Democracy in Mexico: The 'Perfect Dictatorship'?* (Westport, Conn.: Praeger, 1994); George Grayson, *Mexico: From Corporatism to Pluralism* (Fort Worth: Harcourt Brace, 1998); Howard Handelman, *Mexican Politics: The Dynamics of Change* (New

York: St Martin's Press, 1997); Kevin Middlebrook, *The Paradox of Revolution: Labor, the State and Authoritarianism in Mexico* (Baltimore: Johns Hopkins, 1995); Andrew Reding, 'Mexico: The Crumbling of the Perfect Democracy', *World Policy Journal*, vol. 8 (Spring 1991) pp. 255–84.

5. Within the PRI's structure, the CTM officially represents workers in the formal sector, the National Peasants Confederation (CNC) represents campesinos and the National Confederation of Popular Organizations (CNOP) represents small business-people, professionals and government employees.
6. See Robert Kaufman, 'Economic Orthodoxy and Political Change in Mexico: The Stabilization and Adjustment Policies of the de la Madrid Administration', in B. Stallings and R. Kaufman (eds), *Debt and Democracy in Latin America* (Boulder: Westview, 1989), pp. 109–29; Gerardo Otero (ed.), *Neoliberalism Revisited: Economic Restructuring and Mexico's Political Future* (Boulder: Westview, 1996); Manuel Pastor and Carol Wise, 'Origins and Sustainability of Mexico's Free Trade Policy', *International Organization*, vol. 48 (Summer 1994), 459–89.
7. In 1985 more than 90 per cent of domestic production was protected by a system of import licenses and tariffs with a maximum tariff of 100 per cent. By 1988, all tariff levels were reduced by 50 per cent and the highest tariff was just 20 per cent.
8. Pedro Aspe, *El Camino Mexicano de la Transformación Economica* (Mexico: Fondo de Cultural Económica, 1993); Jesus Silva–Herzog, 'México Hoy, en el Nuevo Entorno Internacional', *Revista del Instituto de Estudios Economicos*, vol. 4 (1992), pp. 245–53, Adrianna Ten Kate, 'El Ajuste Estructural de México: Dos Historias Diferentes', *Pensamiento Iberoamericano*, vol. 21 (January–June, 1992), pp. 57–78.
9. Foreign investment of up to 30 per cent was allowed in stock brokerage houses and financial groups. The government also relaxed restrictions on foreign participation in the insurance industry, raising maximum allowable foreign participation from 15 per cent to 49 per cent.
10. Roderick Camp, *Politics in Mexico* (Oxford: Oxford University Press, 1996); Riordan Roett, *Political and Economic Liberalization in Mexico: At a Critical Juncture?* (Boulder: Lynne Rienner, 1993).
11. A significant percentage of new investments have been in Mexico's maquiladora industries. These industries import raw materials and component parts. The product is then assembled and re-exported, usually to the United States, where tax is paid only on the value added in Mexico.
12. A. Reding, 'Mexico', *op.cit.*, p. 274.
13. Wayne Cornelius, 'Designing Social Policy for Mexico's Liberalized Economy', in R. Roett (ed.), *The Challenge of Institutional Reform in Mexico* (Boulder: Lynne Rienner, 1995), p. 141.
14. *Ibid.*
15. Carlos Heredia, 'Downward Mobility: Mexican Workers After NAFTA', *NACLA: Report on the Americans*, vol. 30, no. 3 (November–December 1996), p. 35.

16. David Barkin, 'Mexico's Disappearing Countryside', in F. Rosen and D. McFadyen (eds), *Free Trade and Economic Restructuring in Latin America* (New York: Monthly Review, 1995), pp. 197–208.
17. Inter-Church Committee on Human Rights in Latin America, *Systematic Human Rights Violations in Mexico: January 1995– March 1996* (Toronto: ICCHRLA, 1996), p. 13.
18. C. Heredia, 'Downward Mobility', *op.cit.*, p. 35.
19. David Barkin, Irene Ortiz and Fred Rosen, 'Globalization and Resistance: The Remaking of Mexico', *NACLA: Report on the Americas*, vol. 30, no. 4 (January–February 1997), pp. 14–27; see also Francisco Alba, 'El Mercado de Trabajo: Cambios en el Modelo de Absorción de la Fuerza Laboral', in *C. Bazdresch, N. Bucay, S. Loaeza and N. Lustig México: Auge, Crisis y Ajuste* (eds), (Mexico: Fondo de Cultural Económica, 1993), pp. 179–200.
20. Carlos Heredia and May Purcell, *Structural Adjustment in Mexico: The Roots of the Crisis* (Washington, DC: The Development Gap, 1995), p. 5.
21. John Sheahan, 'Effects of Liberalization Programs on Poverty and Inequality', *Latin American Research Review*, vol. 32, no. 3 (1997), pp. 7–37; Rosa Albina Garavito and Augusto Bolivar, *México en la Decada de los Ochenta: La Modernizacion en Cifras* (Mexico: UAM–Azcapotzalco, 1990).
22. C. Heredia and M. Purcell, *Structural Adjustment in Mexico*, *op.cit.*, p. 5.23.
23. The EZLN has since formed the Zapatista National Liberation Front (FZLN) as its civilian political arm, and Zapatista Civil Dialog Committees have been formed in villages and towns throughout Mexico.
24. This process was referred to as the Economic Solidarity Pact during the de la Madrid administration, the Pact for Stability and Economic Growth during the Salinas administration and the Pact for Well-Being, Stability and Growth during the Zedillo administration. The pacts combined orthodox fiscal and monetary restraint with controls on wages and prices. The process of negotiated pacts is response to social problems became known as 'concertación social' (social cooperation). See Nora Lustig, *Mexico: The Remaking of an Economy* (Washington, DC: The Brookings Institution, 1992); John Sheahan, *Conflict and Change in Mexican Economic Strategy* (La Jolla: Centre for US–Mexican Studies, University of California at San Diego, 1991); Sergio Zermeño, 'Intellectuals and the State in the "Lost Decade"', in N. Harvey (ed.), *Mexico: Dilemmas of Transition* (London: University of London, Institute of Latin American Studies, 1993); Paul Haber, 'Cárdenas, Salinas and the Urban Popular Movement,' in *Mexico: Dilemmas of Transition*, *ibid.*, pp. 218–48; and Hector de la Cueva, 'Cracks in PRI Unionism', *NACLA Report on the Americas*, vol. 30, no. 4 (January–February 1997), pp. 16–17.
25. Kevin Middlebrook, 'Labor Politics and Democratization in Mexico', *LASA Forum*, vol. 28, no. 3 (Fall 1997), pp. 12–15.
26. Although Cárdenas officially lost this election, there was considerable evidence of electoral fraud and many informed observers believe he actually out-polled Salinas.

27. Judith Teichman, *Privatization and Political Change in Mexico* (Pittsburgh: University of Pittsburgh Press, 1995), pp. 172–3.
28. For a detailed review of the evolution of the Party of the Democratic Revolution see Kathleen Bruhn, *Taking on Goliath: The Emergence of a New Left Party and the Struggle for Democracy in Mexico* (University Park, Penn.: Pennsylvania State University, 1997).
29. Four opposition parties won a total of 261 seats while the PRI retained 239 seats.
30. Dan LaBotz, *Democracy in Mexico: Peasant Rebellion and Political Reform* (Boston: South End, 1995), pp. 6–7, 26.
31. Lynn Stephen, 'Election Day in Chiapas: A Low–Intensity War', *NACLA Report on the Americas*, vol. 31, no. 2 (September/October 1997), pp. 10–11.
32. Nora Lustig, 'Mexico: The Slippery Road to Stability', *The Brookings Review* (Spring 1996), pp. 4–9.
33. Since this time, two new groups, the Citizens Network of Support for the Zapatista Cause and the Coordinating Group of Nongovernmental Organizations for Peace (CONPAZ), have also called on the government to withdraw its troops.
34. L. Stephen, 'Election Day in Chiapas, *op.cit.*
35. At the same time, the government rejected demands for autonomous regions under indigenous rule, local control of natural resources and preservation of the *ejido* system.
36. The government refused to enter into a similar dialogue with the Popular Revolutionary Army, but has also stepped up the provision of basic services, including free medical care, to those areas where the guerrillas are most active.
37. The Inter-Church Committee on Human Rights in Latin America, *Systematic Human Rights Violations in Mexico*, *op.cit.*, p. 23. The government responded by establishing a National Human Rights Commission to investigate alleged human rights violations.
38. Agustin Escobar Latapi and Mercedes Gonzales de la Rocha, *Social Responses to Mexico's Economic Crisis of the 1980s* (La Jolla: Centre for US–Mexican Studies, University of California at San Diego, 1991).
39. N. Lustig, 'Mexico: The Slippery Road to Stability', *op.cit.*,
40. Ann Varley, 'Clientelism or Technocracy? The Politics of Urban Land Regulation', in *Mexico: Dilemmas of Transition*, *op.cit.*, p. 268.
41. A small number of PRONASOL programmes took the form of direct transfers, such as scholarships to primary schools children, nutritional supplements and health care programmes. Nora Lustig, 'The 1982 Debt Crisis, Chiapas, NAFTA and Mexico's Poor', *Challenge* (March–April 1995), p. 48; Consejo Consultivo del Programa Nacional de Solidaridad, *El Programa Nacional de Solidaridad* (México D.F.: Fondo de Cultura Economico, 1994).
42. D. LaBotz, *Democracy in Mexico*, *op.cit.*, p. 109.
43. Miguel Angel Centeno, *Democracy Within Reason: Technocratic Revolution in Mexico* (University Park: Pennsylvania State University Press, 1994), p. 66.
44. D. LaBotz, *Democracy in Mexico*, *op.cit.*,p. 106.

45. Ibid., p. 108. Most areas targeted for assistance through PRONASOL have been those where the PRI lost in the July 1988 elections: La Laguna, Michoacán and Chalco. See Neil Harvey, 'The Limits of Concetation in Rural Mexico', in *Mexico: Dilemmas of Transitionop.cit.*, p. 209; and J. Teichman, *Privatization and Political Change in Mexico, op.cit.*, p. 178. For Bruhn, PRONASOL funding seemed to reflect political priorities, especially 'a desire to undermine the vote that supported critics of neoliberalism in the 1988 presidential election', Kathleen Bruhn, 'Social Spending and Political Support: The ''Lessons'' of the National Solidarity Program in Mexico', *Comparative Politics* (January 1996), p. 152.
46. R. Roett, *Political and Economic Liberalization in Mexico, op.cit.*, p. 60. For Roett, PRONASOL helped reconstruct the grand multiclass alliance between labour and capital which characterized pre-crisis Mexico (p. 58). As Paul Haber notes, PRONASOL agreements were sometimes signed with groups highly critical of the state. This reflected the government's desire to coopt and reincorporate social groups which were outside the system. P. Haber, 'Cárdenas, Salinas and the Urban Popular Movement', *op.cit.*, p. 219. See also Dan LaBotz, who argues that PRONASOL succeeded in capturing many of the independent groups which had emerged in the 1970s and 1980s. D. LaBotz, *Democracy in Mexico, op.cit.*, pp. 108–9. See also Denise Dresser, *Neopopulist Solutions to Neoliberal Problems: Mexico's National Solidarity Program* (La Jolla: Centre for US–Mexican Studies, University of California at San Diego, 1991); Julio Moguel, 'Salinas's Failed War on Poverty', in *Free Trade and Economic Restructuring in Latin America op.cit.*; Wayne Cornelius, Ann Craig and Jonathan Fox (eds), *Transforming State–Society Relations in Mexico: The National Solidarity Strategy* (La Jolla: Centre for US–Mexican Studies, University of California at San Diego, 1994).
47. K. Bruhn, 'Social Spending and Political Support', *op.cit.*, p. 152.
48. A more detailed description of PROCAMPO can be found in J. Teichman, *Privatization and Political Change in Mexico, op.cit.*, p. 95; and Riordan Roett, *The Challenge of Institutional Reform in Mexico* (Boulder: Lynne Rienner, 1995), p. 144.
49. N. Harvey, 'The Limits of Concetation in Rural Mexico', *op.cit.*, p. 205.
50. *Progressa* differs from PRONASOL in one important respect. Because Zedillo's programme is administered by the state governments, rather than the central government, local officials have been able to exercise a higher degree of control over how the resources are allocated.
51. It should be noted that the government has been accused of deploying political violence against opposition parties. The PDR claims that hundreds of its members were killed by the policc, the army or PRI-officials during the Salinas administration. D. LaBotz, *Democracy in Mexico, op.cit.*, p. 16.
52. Roura Gonzáles, Dieter Nohlen Felipe and Daniel Zavatto, 'Análisis del Sistema Electoral Méxicano: Informe de un Grupo de Expertos', Mexico City, United Nations Development Program, 1997; Susan Kaufman Purcell, 'Interdependence of Political and Economic Reforms in Mexico', *SAIS Review*, vol. 15 (Winter–Spring 1995), pp. 1–13.

7 Reforming Cuban Socialism: State–Society Dynamics

Susan Eckstein

At the close of the twentieth century Cuba was an anomaly. It was one of only a few remaining Communist 'vanguard party' systems without relations with the United States, the sole global hegemon since the precipitous collapse of the Soviet Union. Indeed, in the 1990s the United States tightened the embargo.

US policy notwithstanding, Fidel Castro's Cuba always had economic relations with Western countries. But in the 1990s it became almost entirely dependent on market economy-based trade and investment. Even economic relations with China became conducted on a hard currency basis. While Castro's economic policies have always been partially grounded in pragmatic considerations, even when legitimated ideologically in the name of Marxism–Leninism,[1] he faced few options in the 1990s.

Constraints on Cuban state policy, however, were domestic as well as international. Despite formal political concentration of power in the Cuban Communist party and in Castro, I will describe how and explain why a domestic market opening evolved, including unwittingly, in response to domestic pressures. Yet, the populace has been selective in the aspects of a market economy they aspired to and tolerated.

BASES OF NON-COMPLIANCE UNDER STATE SOCIALISM

Under ideal-typical state socialism the state owns the means of production and society is dominated by 'vanguard party' rule. Such a political system does not provide institutional means for a populace to press for policies of their own choosing. Yet, people do not necessarily passively acquiesce to conditions they dislike. What people think and what they do are shaped by their positions in institutional hierarchies, and the broader context in which the institutions are embedded. Potentially conflicting viewpoints and interests are rooted in positions of domination and subordination. While elites may try to obscure disparities of interests by emphasizing shared commitments, subordinates do not necessarily believe what they are told, even when outwardly submissive.

Power relations, in turn, influence how people respond to conditions they dislike. Aggrieved individuals in principle have four options, which may vary in how coordinated or individuated the response assumes. They may 'exit', that is, opt out, or overtly express their disquietude, what Hirschman calls 'voice'.[2] But if the articulation of grievance is illegal or personally risky, people may be more inclined to privatize their grievances or turn to informal covert modes of defiance. Depending on what displeases them, and their perceived options, they may turn to covert forms of rule-breaking.[3] The weaker and more repressed the autonomous formally-sanctioned organizational fabric of society is, that is, the weaker the civil society, the more likely people are to defy covertly rather than overtly conditions they dislike.

Rule-breakers may not fully understand the ramifications of their non-compliance, irrespective of the form it takes. They may generate consequences they had not intended. The impact they have depends on their material and organizational resources,[4] and the scale and scope of their non-compliance. But, most importantly, the impact hinges on the effects their actions have on undermining institutional performance and legitimacy, and on how persons in authoritative positions respond. Persons in dominant positions may respond with indifference, reform, cooptation or repression. Their responses, in turn, will be tempered by the resources they command, their personal and institutional priorities, and the broader context in which their institutions are embedded.

In the economic domain, the focus of this chapter, tensions between persons in dominant and subordinate positions may be rooted in social relations of work and reward for work. Acts of defiance may vary from strikes and work stoppages to less risky work slowdowns, arson, pilfering and absenteeism. They may also include rejection of the work situation altogether, such as leaving the state sector for private economic activity, and in extreme cases emigration, rejecting the economy (as well as the polity) altogether.

Economic tensions may centre on the system of distribution as well – in particular, on access to goods and services. When the state regulates distribution, these matters can easily be politicized. People who feel prices are unjust may loot stores or protest the cost of living. Yet, if the state keeps prices artificially low, precisely to avoid such politicization, it runs the risk of creating conditions conducive to black marketeering. The more scarce coveted goods are, the greater the profits to be made from diverting goods from the official distributive system. And once black marketeering becomes rampant, it can contribute to a 'culture of illegality' that makes a range of individual and organized illegal economic activity the more probable.

In the political domain, the other focus of this study, grievances may be grounded in dissatisfaction with existing political and administrative arrangements, or specific state policies. Political institutions and processes may be sources and targets of discord, independently of economically rooted tensions. The fewer the sanctioned opportunities for the articulation of grievance and the less tolerant a regime is of opposition, the more likely people will turn to covert means of 'expressing' their disquietude – for example, to political 'footdragging', refusal to partake in political activity expected of them, and electoral sabotage such as ballot destruction. The absence of politically articulated defiance does not necessarily signify satisfaction with existing political arrangements, however. People may merely acquiesce until they perceive conditions to 'go public' to be propitious.

Below, economic and political non-compliance and state responses in Cuba in the 1990s are examined. The focus is on how institutional arrangements have patterned disobedience and tempered state responses. Both what people in authority and in subordinate positions do will be shown to be structurally patterned but not predetermined. The analysis is historically grounded, with conclusions inductively derived. I rely mainly on primary and some secondary source materials. However, published information on non-compliance is incomplete. The government does not wish to publicize how ineffective its authority is and how unpopular its policies are, and perpetrators of covert activity often do not want to draw attention to themselves for fear of reprisal. Accordingly, the incidences described below should be considered a sampling of those that have actually transpired.

DISQUIETUDE

No available data fully documents Cuban discontent since the collapse of Soviet aid and trade. However, the evidence available suggests that it has been considerable, at least in certain domains. A 1990 party-conducted survey, for one, revealed certain disquietude among ordinary people already before the full impact of the collapse of Soviet bloc relations. Only half of the people interviewed said that they were satisfied with their material situation.[5] Despite free education, free health care, inexpensive if not free housing, and food subsidies, two-thirds of the interviewees said that they felt the cost of living to be high and about one-third felt that their salaries were unjustifiably low.[6] Dissatisfaction revealed in the 1990 survey, however, was as much a function of expectations and aspirations as of income, for higher-income respondents voiced the most complaints.[7] They were the most inclined to feel that their salaries were unjust and to feel that people working hardest were entitled to earn more.[8] Such findings suggest that government support may be weakest among the more privileged stratum and that discontent is rooted at least as much in subjective as in objective conditions.

The same survey reported complaints with governance. One of every seven complaints centred on bureaucratism: on red tape, excessive numbers of meetings, *sociolismo* (buddy socialism), abuse of office, private use of government vehicles, corruption, and the like.[9] People also attacked Popular Power, the official politico-administrative system. They claimed it was insufficiently responsive to their needs, in part because delegates lacked adequate authority. In addition, they criticized the Cuban Women's Federation (the FMC), a mass organization closely identified with Castro's rule for three decades.[10] The dissatisfaction with Popular Power recorded in the survey confirmed findings of a poll published in the summer of 1990 in the weekly magazine *Bohemia*.[11] More than half the people interviewed in the *Bohemia* study said that Popular Power needed to change, less than a third said they were prepared to serve as a Popular Power assembly delegate, and two out of five respondents felt that they were not participating fully in the governing of the country.

Another non-random survey of 400 adults found Castro no longer the nearly ubiquitously esteemed hero he once had been. He was referred to as 'the most important TV artist' and 'a dictator'.[12] Gallup, in turn, interviewed 1000 islanders in late 1994, around the time that the economy hit rock bottom. Nearly half of all interviewees complained of subsistence concerns. At the same time, though, most of them reported satisfaction with health care and education, believed that the achievements of the revolution outweighed its failures, saw the US-imposed embargo, not internal factors, as the main cause of island problems, and expected Cuba's situation to improve in the near future. Almost no one identified politics as the country's main problem. Compared to Nicaraguans and Guatemalans who Gallup also polled, Cubans were more satisfied with their lot.[13]

None of the surveys were based on representative samples, and the findings may be biased by self-censorship. Nonetheless, they suggest that disquietude about economic conditions, about such fundamental issues as food, and certain aspects of the political system, is widespread. At the same time the surveys do not convey a sense that islanders are ready to tear down the state and insist on a democratic-market transition.

DISOBEDIENCE

How people feel is not necessarily reflected in what they do. People may fear reprisal if they outwardly oppose conditions they dislike. They may feel fatalistic and powerless, incapable of bringing about change. Or they may feel that their personal grievances are not collectively shared. Under the circumstances, what people do, quite independently of how they feel, is likely to vary by institutional domain. And the greater the risks of outward defiance, the more probable aggrieved individuals are to oppose covertly conditions they dislike.

Political Disobedience

While Cubans did not take to the streets and directly challenge their government, as did their East European and Soviet counterparts, they defied the regime, occasionally overtly but more typically covertly. Overt defiance has included the formation of groups that function independently of the state. The nominal purpose of such groups has varied from non-political to political, from concern with family reunification with emigres, artistic freedom, support of *perestroika* (before the Soviet Union dissolved) and freedom of religious worship, to democracy. A party chief of ideology acknowledged there to be about 50 such 'counter-revolutionary' groups in 1992, involving some one thousand people.[14] Four years later an umbrella group, Concilio Cubano, claimed some 140 dissident human-rights and unofficial professional and trade unionist group affiliates.[15]

In the course of the early 1990s other groups were formed not in opposition to the state, but despite the state. Groups addressed concerns with food, medical assistance, housing rehabilitation and community self-help.[16] And writers formed small groupings, including to publish their work informally when the government cut back paper imports.

Political defiance was also covert, and islanders quietly sabotaged the electoral process. Although the government prohibited opposition candidates and parties to run for office in the 1993 elections and although it turned the elections into a plebiscite, into a 'yes for Cuba', officially 7 per cent of all islanders, and 15 per cent of Havana voters, registered protest votes – they either spoiled their ballot or cast a blank ballot.[17] In addition, 12 per cent of voters refused to comply with the government's call for a 'show of unity', by refusing to vote for the entire slate of candidates. In the elections two and one-half years later the rate of voter dissidence was, according to official sources, (suspiciously) similar. Electoral dissatisfaction reportedly rose a mere 0.6 per cent. Whether the government honestly reported the electoral results is unknown, but the figures can minimally be assumed to be a conservative estimate of electoral opposition.

Political non-conformity took a more overt but seemingly unorganized form on 5 August 1994, when central Havana became the scene of a brief anti-Castro protest by some one to two thousand people. Never before had such a public riot occurred under Castro. The riot was not entirely spontaneous, for protesters appeared on the scene with placards saying 'down with Fidel'. And in looting stores they simultaneously showed anger with material conditions.[18] Repression, and Castro's appearance on the scene, kept potential 'contagion' at bay; so too did Castro's immediate announcement of a lifting of restrictions on emigration. He let it be known that he would tolerate 'exit' but not 'voice'.

Some 33 000 islanders responded to the opportunity to leave without risk of arrest, life threatening as the voyage to the United States in makeshift rafts was. Cubans typically left in small groups, though on occasion 30, 60 and even 250 islanders coordinated their exodus. The numbers opting for 'exit' had been on the rise since the latter 1980s, despite the risks of arrest, but in the summer of 1994 the exodus took the form of a mass movement. Most typically rafters were young men, both because the trip across the straits of Florida was physically demanding and because young men found themselves with little to lose, as island employment opportunities massively contracted with the economic crisis. Interviews with Cuban arrivals revealed islanders to be fleeing a crumbling economy more than a political system they despised (in contrast to earlier emigrés). They dwelled on existence without food, underwear, soap, shampoo and medicines.[19] At the same time, though, that Cubans reported leaving for economic reasons, US law – until September 1995 – turned them into political refugees, victims of Communism; in that manner escapees gained immigration rights denied to most other Third World entrants. The line between economic and political protest, of regime rejection altogether, was here blurred.

The *balsero* (rafter) movement lasted a mere month, but not because the conditions that had precipitated the exodus had been resolved. Rather, the movement dissipated because the 'opportunity structure' changed – a Cuban–US bilateral agreement led both government parties involved to prohibit such emigration (although the United States agreed to admit more legal emigration). Cuban civil disobedience had here brought about a change not merely in Cuban but US policy.

Still other islanders left inconspicuously. Cubans who successfully attained US travel visas took vacations abroad from which they, in growing and undocumented numbers, never returned. The 1980 mass exodus from the port of Mariel democratized access to this semilegal route. Air tickets for travel abroad had to be paid in hard currency. Since the *marielitos* included a broader socioeconomic range than earlier waves of defectors, a broader range of islanders came to have contacts abroad who could help pay their tickets. Here, access to an emigré network influenced who left and who stayed. However, the option to 'exit' in this manner also drew to a halt in 1996 with the US passage of the Helms–Burton bill.

Economic Disobedience

Publicly coordinated labour protests have been rare. Decades of government and party control over union leadership and union activity at the national level made strike activity improbable. However, that control did not prevent covert labour defiance, and the government periodically provided institutionalized means for workers to channel grievances.

Labour defiance included quiet non-compliance with state calls to do farmwork. The demand for farm labour had picked up with import cutbacks following the collapse of Soviet aid and trade – food imports and inputs for mechanized capital-intensive farming at the time precipitously subsided. The massive schooling under Castro induced disdain for manual work in the fields. Since the agrarian labour shortages coincided with widespread and growing unemployment and underemployment in the cities, rural labour shortages were not the result of a general labour shortage. The refusal to do farmwork contributed to a near-subsistence crisis and to a 50 per cent contraction in sugar production, the country's main source of export earnings until then.

Faced with an unfulfilled need for farm labour, the government turned to the urban population for seasonal assistance. Some 500 000 Havana residents responded to the official calling in 1992.[20] Yet, here too the government met with quiet labour resistance. About half of the volunteers were party cadre, even though a minority of the population were card-carrying Communists. And in at least one instance city dwellers outrightly protested the agrarian mobilizations. Some city high school students, angry about being sent to the fields, organized a march back to Havana.[21] Because the mobilizations were costly and inefficient, and unpopular (though not as unpopular as in the 1960s,[22] the government phased them out by the middle of the decade. In light of its continued unmet need for labour it turned to the armed forces for assistance. Raul Castro, Fidel's brother in charge of the Armed Forces Ministry, spoke to the military's new role: 'We've defined beans as more important than cannons at this moment'.[23] While recruits had no agricultural training, hierarchical controls within the armed forces made for compliance.

The government's ability to regulate the civilian labour force outside of agriculture concomitantly eroded. Absenteeism reached a record high, though there is no publicly available data to verify how pervasive it became. People absented themselves from work to tend to what came to be time-consuming daily chores (for example, to stand in shopping and bus queues). However, their motivation to work also subsided as peso earnings became nearly worthless. There was little to buy legally, and the government provided most social needs at little or no cost.

Even while remaining on the state payroll, islanders increasingly pursued private economic activity, much of which, especially at the start of the decade, was illegal. In 1991 a high level government official estimated that about 20 per cent of the labour force pursued private lines of work, only one-fourth with official licenses.[24] They did so not because of commitment to capitalism but because they perceived it to be in their own immediate economic interests to do so. By mid-decade people in the informal economy earned seven times as much, on average, as those on official salaries.[25]

As the value of state earnings caved in, the government came to have difficulty delivering the very services that made the revolution distinctive and that were central to its legitimacy: education and health care. Teachers and nurses increasingly absented themselves from work and abandoned their jobs for hard currency- earning work in tourism. Some took early retirement and used their pensions to set up businesses. They, in essence, opted to 'exit' the state for the private sector, defying a law that barred them from so doing. Desertion rates were so high that teacher shortages arose in key subjects.[26]

Workers, meanwhile, resisted government efforts to end guaranteed employment and generous unemployment compensation – state initiatives designed to put its fiscal needs ahead of its longstanding social commitment to labour. Faced with a deficit that had increased sixfold in the 1980s, the government sought to reduce its expenditures by ending all but short-term rational unemployment compensation. Fiscally rational as the 1991 labour measure might have been, the government never implemented the reform. It opted instead to keep an estimated one-third of the labour force underemployed on its payroll.[27] It quickly came to consider the political risks of massive unemployment more important than deficit reduction. Responsive as the government then was to popular pressure, four years later, after the deficit had increased another threefold, it considered politics a luxury it could no longer afford. It once again announced plans for massive layoffs.

Islanders, in turn, sabotaged government efforts to regulate distribution. The government tried to 'equalize sacrifice' by regulating access to goods through rationing, at affordable prices. However, scarcities drove up the 'real', market value of goods, contributing to a runaway black market. The black market led to the near-collapse of the official distribution system, as people at every stage from the point of production in the countryside to final distribution in the city siphoned things off for black-market profiteering. Illicit dealings involved durables as well as food, manufactured goods becoming almost impossible to acquire legally; the government prohibited their sales once domestic industrial production collapsed and it could afford to import little other than essentials.

The value of black-market transactions rose from an estimated two billion pesos in 1989 to 14.5 billion pesos in mid-1993. It came to exceed the value of official retail trade.[28] Nearly everyone came to participate in the black market, as buyer and seller, and people spent most of their disposable income on black- market purchases. Black-market consumption hinges less on islanders' morality than their pocketbooks. With demand so in excess of supply, prices of goods on the black market skyrocketed. Chicken, for example, came to cost nearly the equivalent of state workers' official average monthly earnings, and jeans and shoes even more.

Government control over the distributive system caved in just when it officially increased. Rationing, because of its black-market effect, became part of the problem of consumption, not its solution. Reflecting the scale of black marketeering, in 1992, 19 people allegedly privately sold 32 tons of chicken meat stolen from state stores,[29] a gasoline coupon ring distributed bogus coupons for an estimated 265 000 gallons of gasoline and a 25–person truck driver ring delivered foods to black marketeers. By the latter 1990s, theft of building materials was so extensive that it contributed to the emergence of an informal home improvements industry.[30]

Fueling the black market in goods was a runaway black market in dollars, the illegal dollar economy estimated to be on the order of $200 million in mid-1993.[31] Increasingly the dollar became Cubans' currency of choice, as the black-market value of the dollar soared. The illicit exchange rate for the dollar rose from about six times the official rate in 1989 to over 100 times the official rate in the mid-1990s. Officially the two currencies were on par. Goods that came to be unaffordable to Cubans dependent on peso earnings were affordable to the fifth of the population with access to dollars (through emigré remittances, tourism and other illegal domestic sources).

While off-the-books sales of foodstuffs became the most widespread illicit activity, theft, pilfering and corruption reached record levels as well. Given that most of the economy was state-owned, the illegal activities entailed crimes against the state, and the appropriation of state monies for private ends. And because hard currency activities became the key loci of illicit dealings, government efforts to address its own institutional concerns, for foreign debt repayment and trade, were thereby sabotaged. In the first half of 1990, 25 million pesos in government funds went unaccounted for. The following year officials arrested 500 people, including catering and tourism workers, police officers and interior ministry staff, up to quite high levels, for theft, embezzlement, speculation, bribery and hard currency trafficking.[32] Two large crime rings were uncovered that involved illegal currency dealings, appropriation of foreign currency from plane landing fees, illegal buying and selling of televisions and other items taken from tourist stores, and dealings in stolen goods. One of the crime rings centred around Havana's port, the other around Varadero international airport, led by the customs chief there.[33]

Crime involved ordinary citizens as well as high-level state employees, and the peso as well as the dollar economy. In April 1991, for example, the government halted its railway parcel delivery service because too many food parcels sent by city dwellers to relatives in the provinces were stolen en route.[34] And crop theft became so rampant as food shortages arose (and the profitability of black marketeering accordingly picked up) that rural authorities handed out weapons in 1991 to 'peasant vigilance detachments' on cooperatives.[35] *Campesinos* lost control over the fruits of their labour. Moreover, nearly half the farm output sold to the state never reached official urban outlets, and even when the government placed armed guards on lorries food deliveries earmarked for official outlets were diverted to private channels.[36]

In sum, Cubans, unhappy with the dramatic and sudden decline in their living standards, covertly defied official rules and regulations. They sought to make the best of a bad situation. Participation in the expanding informal economy fueled a range of economic crimes that sabotaged state control over production, distribution and revenue accumulation.

IMPACT OF DEFIANCE

Official responses to civilian disobedience have ranged from indifference to reform, cooptation and repression. They have varied at least as much by institutional domain as with the intensity of defiance and how directly the socialist order was challenged. Dissidents have accomplished little. They have been arrested and imprisoned, though in the 1990s typically not for extended periods of time. They have gained no formal political representation. There was a moment prior to the 1993 elections when the national leadership hinted that opposition candidates would be allowed to run for office, but that possibility never materialized.

Of great significance is that when the government was most directly challenged, en masse, with the 1994 riot, it responded with minimal force. It relied on Rapid Reaction Brigades, goon-type squads closely associated with the Ministry of Interior. But it mainly sought to defuse the volatile situation, by opening up the option to exit, to emigrate by sea, and then by initiating economic reforms to improve the food supply, as detailed below.

The government initiated a number of political reforms, only some of which directly addressed demands 'from below'. The measures extended formal democratization. Firstly, as of 1992 the government allowed for direct elections for all levels of the Popular Power political-administrative system and it incorporated People's Councils into the Popular Power system. The changes democratized the system slightly, but only within the contours of a Leninist party-state. And the changes had not been demanded by politically defiant groups. Second, the government periodically called mass meetings to discuss grievances, and it responded to some of the articulated concerns (for example, removal of certain unpopular officials, deferred implementation of taxation). Third, the government oversaw a circulation of elites. It replaced most top-level functionaries in the key political institutions: the National Assembly (sanctioned by the populace in the elections), the Central Committee, the Political Bureau and the Council of State. A younger generation was brought into office to appeal to increasingly apathetic and disaffected youth. But the shakeup was largely symbolic. It resulted in no major policy shift, and no shift demanded specifically 'from below'. Within the party, rank- and-file members, in addition, gained the right for the first time to select committee officers by secret ballot.

But the government 'took with one hand what it gave with another'. It harassed, arrested and imprisoned outspoken dissident and human rights activists, it banned the 1996 conference called by Concilio Cubano, and it dismissed reformist researchers affiliated with two party-linked research groups.[37]

Official responses extended to discourse. Castro quite remarkably coopted symbolically the 5 August protest. State reformism included a redefinition of culturally sanctioned politics. On the one-year anniversary of the event he claimed 5 August a 'great revolutionary victory' in that it re-established order so quickly and without force. To further appropriate and redefine the symbolism of the 1994 protest, and transform it into a patriotic cause, he had the government organize a 'Cuba Vive' manifestation, involving half a million islanders:[38] Castro even joined the march. For the second anniversary the government sponsored another mass festivity. In so doing Castro deprived the disaffected of a key symbol of resistance that might have served as a rallying point for anti-regime riots.

Covert and overt disobedience did more to undermine the functioning of the ideal-typical socialist economy than polity. With efforts to enforce socialist organizational and distributional principles proving to no avail, the government attempted to regain economic control through market reforms.

Periodic draconian arrests of people committing economic crimes – theft, embezzlement, speculation, bribery and black marketeering – may have halted illicit acts by individual perpetrators. However, the illegal activity persisted because it was rooted in socioeconomic conditions – for example, in the paucity of coveted goods available through the ration system, the undervaluation of the peso in an increasingly dollarized economy, and excess pesos in circulation – not in the crime-prone character of individuals. Broad-based and varied in form, the illicit activity undermined state authority, independent of rule breakers' intent.

To address the production and distribution crisis, as well as to restore its moral authority and reduce its fiscal deficit, the government initiated a number of market reforms. While islanders typically did not defy aspects of the socialist economy with this end in view, they had such an effect. Market reforms included increased official use of material incentives to attract labour to agriculture (for example, wage hikes, the introduction of yield-related earnings and privileged access to housing). In 1991 the government also conceded to relegalize categories of self-employment (which it subsequently expanded); the government had outlawed such employment in the mid-1980s, purportedly because people had grown rich through robbing, bribing and corrupting others.[39]

In 1993 the government officially allowed a 'parallel dollar economy'. It decriminalized dollar possession, established hard currency stores where islanders could shop with foreign currency, and legalized tip retention. The same year it transformed most state farms into cooperatives (with members entitled to profits generated) in 1993.

The following year the government (re)introduced markets where vendors could sell goods and services at prices customers were willing to pay. It also introduced a new (domestically) convertible peso (intended to gradually replace the dollar in the national economy). In 1995 and 1996 the government set up currency exchange booths near the markets and centres of tourism, to crowd out the black market in dollars in a manner that enhanced its ability to appropriate the hard currency in circulation. But it pegged the official exchange rate to the informal 'street' rate, reflecting the power of the informal economy. In essence, the government legalized much of what had been transpiring illegally, and it did so while still committed officially to socialism. In the process the island came to have an officially sanctioned private, informal or 'second economy', which especially in commerce came to exceed the formal economy in importance. The government accommodated to the widespread economic disobedience by reducing its own formal role in the economy.

The government tried to adopt market features in a manner that addressed its own institutional needs. Accordingly, not all measures had the populace's interests at heart. An imposition of taxes on private economic activity (other than the income tax, mentioned above, that it deferred implementing) and the licensing (for a fee) of private employment, together with the establishment of hard currency stores and toleration of hard currency remittances, were intended to raise state revenue (especially hard currency revenue). And the transformation of subsidized state farms into cooperatives and the plans to dismiss 'unnecessary workers' were designed to lower state expenditures and increase productivity.

The reforms followed no economic blueprint or state plan. They were introduced piecemeal because the leadership was reluctant to abandon socialism, internally divided about the economic strategy to be pursued, and uncertain about the effects policies would have. On innumerable occasions Castro continued to claim that he found capitalism repugnant, and that the reforms were 'born of special needs', not desire.[40] Indeed, he argued that the reforms were designed to defend rather than transform socialism, but they transformed the meaning of Cuban socialism.

The reform process deepened in the course of the decade to redress problems that earlier measures had either left unresolved or created. In implementing reforms the government was not uniformly subservient to society. Some measures, such as the 1994 fiscal reforms, advanced state interests at the populace's expense. The measures were designed to reduce state expenditures, increase state revenue, and 'mop up' money in circulation. Islanders, on their part, selectively accepted the reforms. New state initiatives prompted new modes of non-compliance as well as compliance. Members of cooperatives concentrated on production of food for the domestic economy rather than sugar for export; the former was more profitable for farmers, the latter more profitable (and hard currency generating) for the state. People also resisted taxation, and continued to purchase certain goods in the black market when they were cheaper than at officially approved outlets.

The government's response to economic non-compliance included repression as well as reform. The government, for example, periodically sponsored draconian arrests of people engaged in theft, embezzlement, speculation, bribery and large-scale black marketing. The arrests may have halted illicit acts by individual perpetrators. However, they did not put a stop to the crimes because the socioeconomic roots of the problems persisted.

CONCLUSION

While rarely attacking the state 'frontally', Cubans of all walks of life have covertly defied rules and regulations associated with the ideal-typical socialist state Castro once imposed. How they defied the state has varied in good part with their structure of opportunities. That is, defiance has been socially patterned, though not predetermined. This is similar to the form of defiance outlined by Manochehr Dorraj and Mustapha Pasha elsewhere in this volume.

The effects of individual and coordinated acts of defiance have been much greater than the perpetrators intended. Outcomes have not been confined to the specific motives and sentiments that prompted nonconformity with official rules and regulations. People typically tried to modify concrete conditions they disliked, but the sum effect of their individual and coordinated acts in some instances has been to transform institutions, first illegally, then legally.

Market features were not merely a post-1989 phenomenon, introduced to survive in the new world order and to accommodate to emergent domestic social pressures. Over the years Castro's government has relied on different mixes of state/market features.[41] What changed in the 1990s was the magnitude of first illegal and then increasingly legal market permeation. And the changes complemented other market reforms rooted in the external sector, beyond the scope of this chapter. The role of market features under state socialism, of course, is not unique to Cuba. Informal and formal market features were important in Soviet bloc countries before their demise, the form they took varying somewhat by country, with historical traditions, the broader context in which the state socialist economies were embedded, specific state policies, and formal and informal social dynamics. Forces rooted in market features contributed to the undoing of those regimes, though the examples of post-Mao China and Vietnam suggest that they need not have such an effect, at least in the short and medium term.

Whether market dynamics set in motion 'from below' ultimately contribute to a political as well as economic transformation in Cuba remains to be seen. However, Cuba's future is contingent in no small part also on US foreign policy, global market opportunities and the politics of the exile community, that is, on conditions emanating from abroad, as well as domestically.

Concealed behind the continued formal veneer of an orthodox 'vanguard party' regime is a state functioning very differently than the ideal-typical socialist state it once approximated. And as state institutions and policies have changed, *de facto* and *de jure*, they have set in motion new conditions to which people in all walks of life respond. *The Cuban experience demonstrates that people need to be incorporated into the analysis of state socialism.* And state socialism needs to be understood as a set of institutional arrangements that may change over time, in form and function.

Notes and References

1. Susan Eckstein, *Back from the Future: Cuba under Castro* (Princeton, NJ: Princeton University Press, 1994), esp. chs 2–4.
2. Albert Hirschman, *Exit, Voice, and Loyalty* (Cambridge: Harvard University Press, 1970).
3. James Scott, *Weapons of the Weak: Everyday Forms of Peasant Resistance* (New Haven: Yale University Press, 1985).
4. Doug McAdam, John McCarthy and Mayer Zald, 'Social Movements and Collective Behavior: Building Macro–Micro Bridges', in N. Smelser and R. Burt (eds), *Handbook of Sociology* (Beverly Hills, Cal.: Sage, 1988).
5. Dario Machado Rodríguez. *Cuba: Participación social en los años 90* (Havana: Centro de Estudios Sociopolíticos y de Opinión Ajunto al Comité del PCC, May 1990), p. 54.
6. *Ibid.*, p. 40.
7. *Ibid.*, pp. 28, 29.
8. *Ibid.*, pp. 28, 47.
9. *Ibid.*, p. 58.
10. *Ibid.*, p. 57.
11. Economist Intelligence Unit (EIU), *Cuban Country Profile*, no. 4 (1990), p. 15.
12. A.R.M. Ritter, 'Prospects for Economic and Political Change in Cuba in the 1990s', paper presented at the Latin American Studies Association, Washington, DC, April 1991, p. 24.
13. *Miami Herald*, 18 December 1994, 39A.
14. *Granma Weekly Review* (*GWR*), 8 March 1990, p. 1; *Granma International* (*GI*), 19 January 1992, p. 4.
15. *Caribbean and Central American Report/Latin American Regional Reports*, 4 April 1996, p. 7. The Cuban government claimed that Concilio

Cubano was funded by the United States and that it had links with violent exile groups. *GI*, 28 June 1995, p. 2; and 5 July 1995, p. 1.
16. Gillian Gunn, 'Cuba's NGOs: Government Puppets or Seeds of Civil Society?' *Cuba Briefing Paper Series*, no. 7 (February 1995), pp. 1–11.
17. *GI*, 28 March 1993, p. 8; and 7 July 1993, p. 15. About 30 US-based radio stations broadcast an appeal to voters to either cast blank votes or spoil their ballot. According to some accounts, 20 per cent of voters protested in this way in the municipal elections, 30 to 35 per cent in Havana and Santiago. EIU, *Cuba Country Report*, no. 1 (1993), p. 11, and *Latin American Weekly Report*, 4 March 1993, p. 6.
18. *Latin American Weekly Report*, 11 September 1994, p. 386.
19. *New York Times*, 2 June 1991, p. 24.
20. *GI*, 20 September 1992, p. 5.
21. *Cuba Business* (October 1990), p. 3.
22. S. Eckstein, *Back from the Future*, *op.cit.*
23. EIU, *Cuban Country Profile* (1992–93), p. 7; *GI*, 5 May 1993, p. 4.
24. Jorge Pérez–López, *Cuba's Second Economy* (New Brunswick, NJ: Transaction Books, 1994).
25. Angela Ferriol Muruaga, *Situación social en el ajuste económico* (Havana: Instituto Nacional de Investigaciones Económicas, 1995), p. 22.
26. *Cuba Business* (September 1994), p. 6. In Cienfuegos in 1993, for example, 9 per cent of all teachers abandoned their jobs.
27. Personal interview with a Cuban economist in Havana, June 1993.
28. *Ibid.*
29. EIU, *Cuban Country Report*, no. 2 (1992), p. 16; *Cuba Business* (June 1992), p. 6.
30. EIU, *Cuban Country Profile* (1996–97), p. 28.
31. Personal interview, Havana, June 1993. According to *The Economist* (24 June 1993, p. 46), exiles in Miami sent an estimated $300 million yearly to their families in Cuba.
32. EIU, *Cuban Country Report*, no. 1 (1991), p. 17.
33. *Cuba Business* (February 1991), p. 12; *GWR*, 20 January 1991, p. 3.
34. EIU, *Cuban Country Report*, no. 3 (1991), p. 8.
35. EIU, *Cuban Country Report*, no. 4 (1991), p. 18.
36. EIU, *Cuban Country Profile* (1994–95), p. 20.
37. *Cuban Country Report*, 16 May 1996; *Latin American Monitor*, vol. 13, no. 5 (May 1996), p. 7.
38. *GI*, 19 July 1995, p. 9; and 16 August 1995, p. 2; *Cuba Business* (September 1995), p. 6.
39. S. Eckstein, *Back from the Future*, *op.cit.*, p. 78.
40. See, for example, *GI*, 23 August 1995, p. 10.
41. S. Eckstein, *Back from the Future*, *op.cit.*

8 Globalization and South Africa's Transition through a Consociational Arrangement

Kidane Mengisteab

INTRODUCTION

As many of the chapters in this volume have demonstrated, globalization imposes a serious dilemma on the state in developing countries. This dilemma is perhaps more visible in South Africa than anywhere else. South Africa's transition from apartheid was originally founded on a *consociational* arrangement, which is a mechanism that attempts to unify different race and ethnic groups and social classes under a shared political and economic system on the basis of carefully *negotiated* terms that are acceptable to all groups.

According to Arend Lijphart, one of the architects of consociationalism, South Africa put in place the essential characteristics of a consociational arrangement following the downfall of the apartheid system.[1] These characteristics include grand coalitions, a mutual veto among ethnic and race groups, proportional representation and segmental group autonomy. Political parties representing different races, ethnic groups and social classes are represented in a coalition government with cabinet positions. Proportional representation is prescribed for elections for the National Assembly and the provincial legislatures, and a two-thirds majority requirement for adopting the constitution also gives some degree of veto for minorities. Decentralization and autonomy in areas such as education are also provided although some groups, including the Inkatha Freedom Party (IFP), find these levels of decentralization insufficient.

In addition to these formal arrangements in the political arena, South Africa's transition involved significant economic compromises between the forces of change and the power-holders under the old regime. The Reconstruction and Development Programme (RDP) of the African National Congress (ANC), for example, espouses a social democratic economic strategy which effects compromises between the interests of different social classes and between the benefactors and the victims of apartheid. A consociational arrangement is thus a strategy of state building which involves some negotiated form of sharing of political and economic power among the different segments of society. The levels of centralization/decentralization of power, the questions of how to manage the relations between minority and majority ethnic groups, what electoral systems to adopt, the demarcation between the spheres of private and public decisions and how much state intervention in economic activity is acceptable and what development strategy is adopted are among the highly contentious issues that are subject to the outcomes of negotiated compromises among the disparate groups.

South Africa's transition is taking place in an era when capitalism has entered a new phase of globalization. Being in a formative stage, globalization is a moving target and thus difficult to conceptualize. Nevertheless, its most critical distinguishing aspects include a flexible and globally more integrated system of production, changing power relations between capital and labour in favour of capital, a process of worldwide convergence towards a less regulated market system, especially in the area of financial mobility and a considerably reconfigured and diminished level of state involvement in economic activity. Corresponding with these changes is the rise to prominence of a neoliberal ideology.

It is the contention of this chapter that this new phase of capitalism imposes serious constraints on autonomous policy-making by individual countries, especially the less powerful ones, and as a result undermines consociational arrangements. Implementation of a consociational arrangement in South Africa has already been seriously hamstrung. The government of South Africa is increasingly facing the dilemma of having to choose between adhering to its consociational strategy of transformation, and succumbing to the pressures of globalization. The principal objective of this chapter is to examine the nature of the relations between globalization and consociationalism. The rest of the chapter is divided into four parts: the first briefly outlines the internal dynamics and limitations of a consociational arrangement; the second part describes the most critical aspects of globalization; the third analyses the conflicts between globalization and consociationalism; and the last part discusses how the ANC-led South African government has so far responded to the dilemma globalization imposes on its consociational arrangement of transition.

INTERNAL DYNAMICS OF CONSOCIATIONALISM

The appropriateness of a consociational arrangement as a strategy of state building has provoked considerable debate. Proponents claim that the arrangement is indispensable in developing societies that suffer from serious ethnic cleavages.[2] There is also little doubt that the arrangement has contributed to mitigating conflict in South Africa. Given apartheid's impact on race and ethnic relations in the country, it was difficult to conceive an end to the country's chronic violence and a beginning of a peaceful state building process without some kind of consociational arrangement. This negotiated pact is generally credited for making a peaceful transition possible in the country by promising to safeguard the key interests of the conflicting parties. White minorities were given assurances that their interests would not be subverted by majorities. The deprived majorities were also promised the uprooting of the mechanisms that denied them access to political and economic resources and the redistribution of resources to address past injustices.

Critics, on the other hand, raise a number of doubts. One major concern is that a consociational arrangement tends to preserve communal differences leading to risks of disintegration in the long run.[3] There is no doubt that a consociational arrangement affirms the rights of groups, establishes permanent institutions that enable ethnic and racial groups to safeguard their interests and preserve their group loyalties. However, the same institutions also mitigate intergroup conflicts by allowing peaceful reconciliation of differences. It is unclear why establishing mechanisms that ensure diversity is regarded as undesirable unless it is assumed that building a nation state out of multinations through assimilation is possible and superior to diversity. Building a nation state out of a multination state is increasingly proving to be an unrealistic goal. The countries that were believed to have succeeded in this process have not been all that successful. The United Kingdom, France and Spain, for example, can hardly be regarded as nation states.[4] State building through consociational arrangements does not aim to build a nation state. Rather, it has a less ambitious goal of integrating different nations (ethnonational groups) to form a workable and peaceful multination state. Its aim, at least in the short and intermediate terms, is not to transfer the loyalties of citizens from the nation, ethnic or race group to the state but to minimize conflict between the groups and the state and among groups.

Ethnic, national and racial identities are dear to human beings but they are not the only identities. The relative importance of different identities may also change over time. It is conceivable that the focus of consociationalism also shifts to other identities over time. In any case, state building requires that existing tensions between groups need to be resolved even when the long-run implications of the solutions are unclear and consociationalism appears to be the most promising arrangement to mitigate intergroup conflicts.

Another concern about consociational arrangements is that they lack a system of opposition institutions that any healthy democratic system requires.[5] This concern also has some validity since political parties entering into coalition with the majority party may cease to mount effective opposition. Yet once the consociational framework is charted and the rules of the game are established, consociationalism does not necessarily require continued coalitions of parties. The withdrawal of the Nationalist Party from a coalition with the ANC in South Africa has not, for example, shattered the consociational arrangement. In other words, a consequential arrangement requires coalitions initially but not in perpetuity.

There are also contentions that the consociational arrangement is not workable. Jacques-Mariel Nzouankeu, for example, contends that 'consensual democracy, which is a variant of a consociational power-sharing arrangement, does not recognize the conflict between private and public interests and as a result, can only exist in a society of gods or among slaves'.[6] Moreover, he claims that it has already failed in Africa. There are two problems with these contentions. First, contrary to Nzouankeu's claim, no post-independence African state seriously adopted a genuine consensus democracy. South Africa is among the first African countries to chart a consociational approach. In fact, failure to embrace it beyond the level of rhetoric is regarded by some as Africa's neglect of its cultural heritage.[7] Secondly, consensus democracy does not require negation of self-interest in favour of that of the community in an unfree and submissive manner as Nzouankeu claims. On the contrary, it implies negotiations and concessions between different social groups with competing interests in order to obtain consensus by blurring differences. In many African villages decisions are still made along these lines with minorities enjoying a virtual power of veto. Those communities do not have police forces and jails to enforce majority decisions. The only means available to them for ensuring general observance of village decisions is by basing them on consensus. This makes the villagers neither gods nor slaves.

The village-type consensus system may not be practical at the national level; however, there is no compelling reason why consociationalism with consensus on key issues is not possible.

Another major concern over a consociational arrangement is that it is essentially an elite pact that consolidates elite domination over society by mitigating intra-elite competition. This is a critical concern because if the economically deprived segments of society, such as the African population in South Africa, continue to be neglected under a consociational arrangement, it is likely that the arrangement would fail to promote state building and democratization and conflicts may be reignited. Consociationalism is unlikely to succeed unless it is socially democratic because ethnic based divisions, tensions and conflicts are often accompanied by inter-ethnic inequalities in terms of access to economic resources and political power. This is particularly true in South Africa due to the country's legacy of apartheid and the gross inequalities between racial groups.

As in South Africa, the elite clearly play the key role in negotiating and designing consociational arrangements. It is thus entirely possible that the outcome could be merely a compromise among the elites that does not take into account popular interest. On the other hand, depending on the amount of pressure the masses are able to mount on the elite, consociational arrangements can take a social democratic form that compromises not only among the elites but also between the elites and the masses. As already noted, South Africa's consociational arrangement, as reflected in the RDP, was initially designed along social democratic lines with political, economic and ideological compromises.

From the forgoing analysis, it is clear that consociationalism is by no means a perfect system. It is also rather difficult to implement. Serious imbalances in the relative power of the different entities and the dominance of the elite over the masses can rather easily undermine it. These difficulties are not insurmountable and consociationalism is not necessarily static; however, given its internal weaknesses consociationalism is likely to be highly vulnerable to unfavourable exogenous conditions.

THE ESSENCE OF GLOBALIZATION

As noted earlier, there is little agreement as to what globalization is, or if it is taking place. Both Samir Amin and John Weeks have outlined the broad parameters of globalization earlier in this volume, althrough their analyses diverge in important respects. There is, however, little doubt that some fundamental changes are taking place in the global socioeconomic system. Among the most notable changes in the global system are the coming to an end of the welfare state and the transformation of market–state relations. Roughly between the third decade of the twentieth century and the end of the cold war, the growing strength of labour movements and the threat of communism induced the rise of the welfare state, in which capital made notable concessions to labour to ensure the survival of capitalism. By the end of the cold war, however, the concessions of capital have begun to be rolled back and a global convergence of policy is underway. A host of factors have contributed to this shift in market–state relations, including the crisis of socialism and the dissipation of its threat, the economic crisis of statism and rising budgetary problems of the welfare state, the fading away of the memory of the depression of the 1930s and the soaring power of capital over labour and society at large.

A neoliberal ideology of *laissez faire* that attributes most economic ills to 'excessive' state intervention in economic activity (deviation from the market system) has accompanied the changes in market–state relations. The following statement from the World Bank's World Development Report epitomizes the antistate ideology of the unfolding global order:

> The state has to move from doing many things badly to doing its fewer core tasks well. This means government must at once shrink and change its nature.[8]

This neoliberal ideology has rapidly risen to a hegemonic position, and countries all over the world are pressured to adhere to it. This ideological convergence, which has become synonymous with globalization, aspires to limit the role of the state to its 'most fundamental' functions, including defence, maintaining peace and order, enforcing private contracts, adjudicating conflicts, providing stable currency, infrastructure development and provision of primary education.[9]

State disengagement from economic activity has not yet reached the level advocated by the staunch advocates of the neoliberal orthodoxy. Nevertheless, a trend has been set and the state in most countries has significantly disengaged in a number of areas. Privatization of state-owned assets, deregulation of private business activity, deregulation of the financial sector and reducing public expenditures and taxes are among the examples. Disengagement has, in fact, become an area of competition among states. It is now generally believed that the more the state disengages, the more it would be able to lure capital. In the words of James Rinehart:

> [c]ompetitiveness now means not cheap prices but which workers, which taxpayers, which provinces and which countries can give the most to the corporation in exchange for new investment or to insure that work does not move elsewhere.[10]

The Heritage Foundation's index of 'Economic Freedom' gives a good indication of the compliance (non-compliance) of countries with deregulations.[11]

The widespread disengagement of the state from economic activity has led many observers to view the state as a victim of globalization. It has become fashionable to assert that the era of the nation state is over and that national-level governance is ineffective in the face of globalized economic and social processes.[12] Others have argued that the state has facilitated if not authored globalization.[13] Undoubtedly, globalization has undercut the conventional national economic as well as political authority of the state. Yet the role of the state in globalization and globalization's impact on the state need to be reexamined since not all states play the same role.

The state is an overarching organization of citizens and different segments of citizens expect it to do different things. The role the state plays is thus largely determined by the balance of social forces which varies from country to country. There is little doubt that at the present time the most powerful capital advocates for less regulations, while labour, environmentalists, less-competitive firms, the poor and many other groups generally prefer a more engaged state. But the state is often more influenced by the most powerful segments of society. The domination of domestic capital over the rest of society is not firmly established in many developing countries. As a result, capital-driven globalization poses a dilemma for the state in these countries. There is ample evidence that in most developing countries the state promotes globalization through adherence to structural adjustment programmes largely under considerable pressure from the International Monetary Fund (IMF), the World Bank, foreign capital and donor countries. In contrast, the state in the powerful countries of the North, where the hegemony of capital over other social classes is well-established, has largely joined hands with multinational corporations and the multilateral financial institutions in promoting globalization. This explains why most states in the North have joined powerful capital in promoting globalization and have not resisted their disengagement even when they appear to have the power to do so. The liberal economic order which was championed by the hegemonic state in previous phases of capitalism is now projected by the collective consensus of the states of the North.

Disengagement of the state from economic activity is certainly not new. Classical liberalism of the nineteenth century had similar features. However, it represents a significant departure from the rapidly fading order of the Keynesian welfare state that predominated over the last 50 years or so.

Another important aspect of globalization that is related to the transformation of market–state relations is the metamorphosis of the production system. The Fordist system of mass production, which was predominant in the post-World War II era, is now largely replaced by what is referred to as the flexible and lean production system.[14] The Fordist system had been based on large-scale mass production with fixed location, rather inflexible technologies and a workforce that was reasonably protected by collective bargaining and redistributive policies of the welfare state which regulated capital mobility. By contrast, lean production is flexible in terms of technologies and product lines. Deregulation of capital mobility has also enhanced its flexibility in terms of location. More importantly, it requires a smaller and more flexible workforce.

The flexibility of the new production system, in tandem with declining state regulation on financial mobility, has increasingly integrated global production. It has also given capital the power of exit and enormous leverage over labour. As Ruigrok and van Tulder note, corporations are not yet 'footloose' or 'borderless'.[15] A trend, which has already markedly changed the relations between capital and labour has, nevertheless, been established. The threat of relocation has often been used to tame the demands of labour unions and workers at large. Unions have largely failed to cope with the flexibility and decentralization of enterprises and the power of exit of capital. As a result, wage rates, which under the Fordist production system were largely determined by collective bargaining between management and unions, are now increasingly brought under the market mechanism. Growth rates of wages have shown a tendency to decline as a result. In the OECD countries, for example, a marked decline in the growth rates of real wages has occurred since the first oil shock.[16] Another outcome of the changing capital–labour relations is the growing ability of firms to hire and fire workers and to destandardize employment.

Part-time employment, temporary work and fixed-term contracts are now more common.[17] Job security has also been severely eroded, and the weakness of unions has undermined the ability of labour to influence overall policy-making of governments. Even traditionally labour-friendly political parties have increasingly modified their platforms towards the right.

State disengagement, in conjunction with de-unionization of workers, deregulation of the labour market and decentralization of wage bargaining has led to enormous growth in inequality both between and within countries.[18] Income distribution has increasingly become uneven, especially since the early 1980s.

IMPACTS OF GLOBALIZATION ON CONSOCIATIONAL ARRANGEMENTS

With this rather sketchy description of the characteristics of globalization and consociational arrangements, we now examine the areas of conflict between the two. One area in which the two are clearly incompatible is in the role the state plays in economic activity. With globalization states are competing to curtail their regulatory, redistributive and resource allocation roles partly to enhance the efficiency and competitiveness of their economies, and partly to conform with the prevailing dominant ideology. Narrowing the scope of state involvement is celebrated by many from the liberal tradition for a variety of reasons. Some even argue that it promotes democracy. Samuel Brittan, for example, contends that limiting the state reverses the Keynesian economic system, which in his view represented the most self- destructive tendencies of democracy.[19] W.H. Hutt also claims that state involvement in economic activity constitutes the transfer of control from the people and market democracy to politicians and coercive interest groups.[20] As a result, he views state disengagement as restoring democracy.

F.A. Hayek, who is arguably the most notable critic of the welfare collectivist system, also views state disengagement as enhancing democracy. In Hayek's view, it is 'outright impossible' for a government which has unlimited powers to confine itself to serving the agreed view of the majority of the electorate or to promote the general interest since it buys its authority by handing out special favours to particular groups.[21]

Undoubtedly state involvement is not a sufficient condition for democracy. Governments often are either self-serving or reward the most powerful interest groups. Needless to say, the market mechanism can impose certain restraints upon the abuses of the political elite. However, the claims that the market system is democratic and that the domination of powerful interest groups over social (general) interest would be less under a *laissez-faire* market system than under a welfare state are unfounded. The reality in market-dominated societies is a hierarchical system in which the majority of individuals are subordinated to the power of giant transnational corporations and the affluent.

Under the one-person-one-vote system of existing democracies, the masses obtain some power from their numbers. Self-serving politicians can also be recalled. The market system provides no mechanism for such a recall of self-serving dominant elites. The masses also lose any advantage from their size in a 'market democracy' where voting is on the basis of purchasing power. Existing democracies are by no means real expressions of the general population. Citizens have unequal amounts of political power and have unequal influence on decisions. Democracy, where the general populace controls decision-making, thus largely remains an ideal but progress towards increasing popular influence is possible. Despite the limitations of existing democracies, only the sphere of public decisions can limit the dictatorship of an elite, be it political or economic. In other words, the solution to the undemocratic state lies in democratizing it, not in merely subordinating it to market forces. The more the role of the state is retrenched, the more the sphere of public decisions is narrowed without creating any viable democratic alternative.

Another reason for celebrating state disengagement is that it conforms with the moral order of a free society and a market system.[22] For Hayek, for example, redistributive state activity and social justice are opposed to the moral order of a free society which is based on efficiency, growth and individual freedom. It is possible that a market system devoid of state regulation might increase efficiency, but such a social order strips capitalism of much of the 'human face' and social justice it had obtained in the era of the welfare state and returns it to the worst excesses of the early industrial revolution. It also destroys the framework of a mixed economic system in which the market and the state restrain each other's tendencies to degenerate to dictatorships. Moreover, as Barber notes, in the absence of state regulations the market tends to self-destruct as it leads to the rise of monopoly or anarchy.[23]

In any case, inadequate state engagement in economic activity is clearly detrimental to the success of a consociational system. As already noted, a social democratic consociational arrangement is essentially a system of compromise between different ethnic groups and social classes. In the case of South Africa, consociationalism is designed to be a compromise between races and among ethnic groups, between labour and capital and between the landed elite and the landless. The contending positions in regards to the role of the state in the country are roughly that the privileged groups advocate a free market system with a limited state, and the victims of apartheid endorse an engaged state expecting that the state would help them obtain access to land, housing and educational and health facilities and expand employment opportunities. There is little doubt that the progressive disengagement of the state imposed by globalization nullifies the social democratic aspects of consociationalism. In the absence of an actively engaged state that implements and safeguards the compromises, consociationalism is likely to be reduced to a merely elite pact. Globalization, thus, by disarming the state, tends to dictate a certain social order that invalidates the negotiated terms of consociationalism.

From another angle, with a reduced role for the state and a freer and globally more integrated economic system that is based on global competitiveness, the country loses autonomy in formulating policies that address its specific problems. Under globalization, welfare policies and concessions to labour are seen as hindrances to competitiveness. Even autonomous policies on tax, employment, income distribution, environmental and safety regulations, are all restrained by the logic of global competitiveness. To the extent that policies on these key issues are not made autonomously, a locally negotiated consociational system largely becomes irrelevant.

Scope of Democracy

Another related critical area of conflict between globalization and consociationalism is the scope of democracy. With the rise of the new phase of capitalism, liberal democracy has eclipsed all other forms of democracy. Some, in fact, have argued that non-liberal forms of democracy are non-democratic,[24] and that their decline has also been accompanied by a progressive gravitation of liberal democracy towards its minimalist form.[25] With disengagement of the state and the freeing of economic process from the political process, economic issues have increasingly been removed from the sphere of public decisions. As a result, democracy is increasingly limited to the ability of citizens to elect their political leaders.

Demarcating the spheres of private and public decisions is a serious problem of democracy. Since different social classes advance different socioeconomic arrangements, the relative size of the spheres of public and private decisions are related to the balance of power among social classes. As capital becomes more dominant over other classes, the sphere of private decision expands and the sphere of public decision shrinks. Conversely, as the power of labour relative to that of capital increases, the sphere of public decision expands. A number of studies establish the relationship between the strength of unions and the development of the welfare state and the parliamentary fortunes of social democratic parties.[26]

The unfolding era of globalization has ushered in an enormous surge in the power of capital and a decline in the organization and influence of labour.[27] The growing disorganization of labour has led to parliamentary defeats of social democratic and other labour-friendly political parties that advocate an expanded sphere of public decisions. The surge in its relative power has allowed capital, especially financial capital, to impose its own discipline on governments and to narrow the sphere of public decisions. Fear of loss of competitiveness in attracting capital has increasingly forced governments to make their policies increasingly capital-friendly rather than responding to popular will or broad social interest. The general population has increasingly lost the ability to influence economic policy.

The marked increase in the role of international and regional (supranational) organizations in the global system has also contributed to the narrowing of the scope of democracy. Increasing global integration and growing state disengagement have allowed transnational and regional organizations to increasingly assume major roles in coordinating economic, political and environmental convergence. Organizations such as the World Trade Organization (WTO), the IMF, the World Bank, the European Union (EU) and the North American Free Trade Agreement (NAFTA), have become major players in the new global system. These arrangements, which are designed to supplement market discipline, have become authors of international rules that hold together the unfolding global system. In so doing they increasingly encroach on what used to be decided by individual states.[28] The Multilateral Agreement on Investment which was being negotiated by the OECD countries is a case in point. This initiative was designed to protect foreign investment capital from any governmental discrimination and had the potential to institute a transnational regulatory framework of private corporate ownership and trade as a sovereign order overriding national, regional and municipal jurisdictions. Under this regime, states, especially those of developing countries, would be unable to promote local firms and financial institutions.

Often international organizations have also given elected officials the justification to lower corporate taxes, eliminate or reduce public and social expenditures and lax regulatory measures against the wishes of their populations. Government officials frequently claim that competitiveness and international obligations restrict their policy options. In any case, the more policy decisions are transferred from the state to these organizations and their technocrats, the more they are removed from the influence of the general population.

Globalization and Development

Globalization has also dictated a development strategy that corresponds with state disengagement and the narrowing of the scope of democracy. The new development strategy emphasizes efficiency, growth and competitiveness over social justice and redistribution. It also advances openness and export promotion over self-reliance and industrial policy. A summary of the conflicts between globalization and consociationalism is given in Table 8.1.

In addition, the new global order has endorsed a new morality and a culture of prudence to supplement the ideology of a minimally regulated market system. Individual liberty and responsibility, which Hayek regarded as the high morals of a civilized society, are promoted

Table 8.1 Areas of conflict between globalization and consociationalism

Globalization	*Consociational arrangement*
Requires state disengagement	Requires an engaged state
Leads to loss of policy autonomy	Requires autonomy in policy-making
Narrows the scope of democracy	Broadens the scope of democracy
Economic process is autonomous of political authority process	Economic process takes place within the political process
Growth-first strategy of development	Growth-with-redistribution strategy of development
Emphasizes international competitiveness	Addresses social injustices
Trade is viewed as an engine of growth	Subordinates trade to broader development goals

at the expense of the instincts of solidarity and altruism. Again the moral foundations of society are taken out of public debate and public decision. The more the balance of power shifts from labour to capital and from the state to the market and international organizations, the more citizens are locked out from major decisions. To conclude this section of the discussion, the mounting dictatorship of capital in the unfolding global order has created an environment that is highly hostile for the survival of consociationalism with a social democratic face.

SOUTH AFRICA'S RESPONSE TO THE DILEMMA

Given the identified conflicts between globalization and consociationalism, it becomes imperative to examine how the South African state is dealing with the dilemma. A conclusive answer to this question is not yet possible since the post-apartheid regime has been in power for only three years at the time of writing. Nevertheless, an analysis of the trends can provide some tentative answers.

The responses of the South African government are essentially limited to the following three options. One option is for the South African state to abandon consociationalism and adopt globalization. This option, of course, implies that the state would largely disengage from the economy and abandon redistributive policies to address the legacies of apartheid. This option would not be possible without the defeat of the working class and the rest of the victims of apartheid in their struggle to shape the nature of post-apartheid South Africa. These social classes, whose interests conflict with globalization, have not yet been fully conquered by domestic and global capital. The labour unions and the left in the country are still reasonably potent. As a result, the South African state has not yet openly repudiated consociationalism in favour of globalization.

A second option is to subordinate globalization and the market system to the consociational arrangement and to pursue a strategy of a mixed economy and self-reliance with a growth-through-distribution policy. On the eve of its coming to power, the ANC notably modified the radical socioeconomic programmes it had espoused as a liberation movement. Nevertheless, its RDP programme promised a self-reliant mixed economic strategy in which the state would be actively involved in the reconstruction of the economy and in correcting the problems of maldistribution left behind by the apartheid system. However, it is increasingly becoming clear that the ANC has not been able to pursue a self-reliant and redistributive strategy as outlined in its RDP programme. As Stephen Gelb notes, the fear of 'strike of capital' (its ability to exit) has prevented the adoption of this strategy.[29] In other words, the South African leaders are fully aware that they live in a new era of fast-moving capital that punishes countries that fail to liberalize their economic policies to make them capital-friendly. As a result, the government has notably modified its RDP programme.

A third option available to South Africa's leaders is to attempt to follow some middle-of-the-road strategy (a compromise of the compromise). This implies that the state would attempt to follow a middle road between globalization and the consociational arrangement at least until such time that the balance of social classes pushes it to one side. Indications are that the South African state has opted for this option.

There are a number of measures that the South African government has already undertaken that show it has embraced economic liberalization in line with globalization. One such measure is its agreement with the WTO to liberalize its trade. The country concluded an agreement with the WTO in 1994 committing itself to the reduction and restructuring of import tariffs, the removal of import surcharges and phasing out of the country's General Export Incentive Scheme. The import surcharges were abolished as early as October 1995 and the General Export Incentive Schemes were repealed in July 1997. Tariff rates have been slashed from 15 per cent in 1994 to 10 per cent in 1996, and are expected to come down to 8 per cent in 1999. The government also agreed to deregulate financial markets and to gradually relax exchange controls.[30] The rand depreciated by about 21.9 per cent between the end of 1995 and the end of 1996, although from December 1996 to the end of July 1997 it appreciated by 4.9 per cent. These measures were aimed at strengthening the competitiveness of the country's economy and facilitating the integration of the South African economy into the global economy.

The ANC's agreement to privatize state-owned assets is another indicator. By the end of 1995, the ANC, under pressure from international finance capital, released a document ('The State and Social Transformation') in which it proposed a dramatic reversal of the state's role in the public sector through partial privatization and a range of deregulatory measures. At the beginning of 1996, government and labour accepted the National Framework Agreement (NFA) which laid down guidelines for restructuring state assets. The NFA clearly represented the abandonment of transformation as originally formulated in the RDP. According to the RDP, the basic needs of the majority of South Africans were to be achieved through an efficient and vibrant public sector under state ownership and control. With the NFA, public ownership of assets was dropped. Government's role has been reduced to the task of managing the gradual privatization of the public sector.[31]

Other indicators include the adoption in June 1996 of a new macroeconomic strategy, the Growth, Employment and Redistribution (GEAR) programme which essentially conforms to the logic of globalization with its rather tight fiscal policy. Supply-side measures to support industrial restructuring have also been adopted by the National Economic Development and Labour Council (NEDLAC) as a result of South Africa's entry into the global market.

Lack of notable progress in reducing poverty among the victims of apartheid is another critical indicator that the government has not been able to aggressively pursue its original redistributive policies. The most important mechanism for reducing absolute poverty is employment creation and in this regard the performance of the South African government has been disappointing. There has been some progress in expanding the participation of black South Africans in the public sector. By the end of 1996, the proportion of black South Africans in the public service has risen to about 65 per cent.[32] However, there has not been a corresponding progress in the private sector. From the end of 1996 to the end of the second quarter of 1997, for example, total employment declined by 62 000 jobs falling to roughly the 1981 level. Globalization and technological advance are believed to be the most important factors for the decline.

Progress in the areas of land reform and housing also show that the ANC has not aggressively pursued the RDP programme. A 1997 Idasa survey, for example, showed that 72 per cent of South Africans felt that their group was not getting what it deserved in terms of housing.[33] In regards to land reform, the Department of Land Affairs has attempted to bring about land restitution, land redistribution and tenure reform through a market mechanism. Land Reform Pilot Programme, which is a kick-start measure, is under implementation in all provinces. Yet, as Richard Levin notes, this limited measure is not likely to satisfy the land needs of the majority for a long time.[34] Delivering substantial land through the market to apartheid's rural victims in an era of growing state disengagement is not very promising.

The South African government has not abandoned the consociational arrangement completely. It continues to pay some attention to the demands of labour and the disadvantaged segments of society. Increases in public expenditures on social services in the annual budgets reflect continued concern for social justice. There have been important deliveries in state-sponsored programmes in health and in the provision of water and electricity.[35] The publication of the Green Paper in March 1997 and the Employment Standards Act (ESA), which replaces the Basic Conditions of Employment and Wage Acts, also reflect some level of concern for the interests of workers, although workers have not found these arrangements to be satisfactory. The Congress of South African Trade Unions (COSATU) also continues to have influence over government due to its alliance with the ANC. Yet the ANC's initial compromise of refraining from nationalization has not been sufficient and it has been forced to make further concessions. The ANC has largely conceded control over macroeconomic policy to the investment community severely weakening the consociational arrangement.[36]

In conclusion, the country's consociational arrangement has already been undermined by globalization. Labour in the country was relatively well-organized in the 1980s. However, unions in the country have already lost many of their leaders to the government and to private business. Changing industrial structures are also undermining the traditional membership of unions. The weakening of unions in conjunction with the absence of an effective political organization to the left of the ANC has allowed the ANC to gravitate to the right. The emergence of a rising black bourgeoisie in post-apartheid South Africa is also changing the nature of struggle in the country. This new vibrant social class is likely to abandon its former allies in the struggle against apartheid and join the ranks of the country's old ruling bloc in promoting globalization. Given this changing balance of social classes in favour of capital, genuine social democratic consociationalism is unlikely to survive the onslaught from globalization.

This creeping victory of globalization over consociationalism is, however, a serious threat to the country's peaceful transition and state building. As Mattes and Thiel note, the South Africa of the 'First World' and the South Africa of the 'Third World' are not likely to coexist peacefully without redistributionist consociational arrangement.[37] *There is thus the danger that the 'miracle' achieved by consociationalism may be undone by liberalization.*

Notes and References

1. Arend Lijphart, 'Prospects for Power Sharing in the New South Africa', in A. Reynolds (ed.), *Election '94: South Africa* (New York: St Martin's Press, 1994), pp. 221–31.
2. Arthur W. Lewis, *Politics in West Africa* (London: Allen & Unwin, 1965); and Arend Lijphart, *Power Sharing in South Africa* (Berkeley: University of California Press, 1985).
3. Donald L. Horowitz, *A Democratic South Africa? Constitutional Engineering in a Divided Society* (Berkeley: University of California Press, 1991).
4. Walker Connor, *Ethnonationalism: The Quest for Understanding* (Princeton: Princeton University Press, 1994).
5. Courtney Jung and Ian Shapiro, 'South Africa's Negotiated Transition: Democracy, Opposition and the New Constitutional Order', *Politics and Society*, vol. 23, no. 3 (September 1995), pp. 269–308.
6. Jacques–Mariel Nzouankeu, 'The African Attitude to Democracy', *International Social Science Journal*, vol. 128 (May 1991), pp. 373–85.
7. Maxwell Owusu, 'Democracy and Africa – A View from the Village', *The Journal of Modern African Studies*, vol. 30, no. 3 (1992), pp. 369–96.
8. World Bank, *World Development Report 1996* (Oxford and New York: Oxford University Press, 1996).
9. *Ibid.*
10. James Rinehart, 'The Ideology of Competitiveness', *Monthly Review*, vol. 47, no. 5 (October 1995), pp. 14–23.
11. Bryan T. Johnson and Thomas P. Sheehy, *1996 Index of Economic Freedom* (Washington, DC: Heritage Foundation, 1996).
12. M. Horseman and A. Marshall, *After the Nation State* (London: Harper-Collins, 1994).
13. Leo Panitch, 'Rethinking the Role of the State', in J. H. Mittelman (ed.), *Globalization: Critical Reflections* (Boulder: Lynne Rienner, 1997), pp. 83–113.
14. Daniel Drache. 'New Work and Employment Relations: Lean Production in Japanese Auto Transplants in Canada', in R. Boyes and D. Drache (eds), *States Against Markets: The Limits of Globalization* (London: Routledge, 1996), pp. 227–49.
15. Winfried Ruigrok and Bob van Tulder, *The Logic of International Restructuring* (London and New York: Routledge, 1995).
16. International Labour Office (ILO), *World Employment 1996/97: National Policies in a Global Context* (Geneva: ILO, 1996), p. 49.
17. *Ibid*, p. 52.
18. *Ibid.*, pp. 69–77; and Roberto Patricio Korzeniewicz, 'World-Economic Trends in the Distribution of Income, 1965–92', *American Journal of Sociology*, vol. 102, no. 4 (January 1997), pp. 1000–39.
19. Samuel Brittan, 'Can Democracy Manage an Economy?' in R. Skidelsky (ed.), *The End of the Keynesian Era: Essays on the Disintegration of the Keynesian Political Economy* (New York: Holmes & Meier, 1977), p. 49.

20. W.H. Hutt, *The Keynesian Episode: A Reassessment* (Indianapolis: Liberty Press, 1979), p. 128.
21. F.A. Hayek, 'The Miscarriage of the Democratic Ideal', *Encounter*, vol. 50 (1978), pp. 14–17.
22. F.A. Hayek, *Law, Legislation and Liberty: A New Statement of the Liberal Principles of Justice and Political Economy*, vol. 1 (London: Routledge, 1982), pp. 32–33.
23. Benjamin R. Barber, *Jihad vs. McWorld: How Globalism and Tribalism Are Reshaping the World* (New York: Ballantine Books, 1995), p. 243.
24. Giovanni Sartori, 'Rethinking Democracy: Bad Polity and Bad Politics', *International Social Science Journal*, vol. 129 (August 1991).
25. Philippe C. Schmitter, 'Democracy's Future: More Liberal, Preliberal, or Postliberal?' *Journal of Democracy*, vol. 6, no. 1 (1995), pp. 15–22.
26. Bruce Western, 'A Comparative Study of Working-Class Disorganization: Union Decline in Eighteen Advanced Capitalist Countries', *American Sociological Review*, vol. 60 (April 1995), pp. 179–201; and G. Esping–Andersen and K. van Kersbergen, 'Contemporary Research on Social Democracy', *Annual Review of Sociology*, vol. 18 (1992), pp. 187–208.
27. ILO, *World Employment 1996/97*; and B. Western, 'A Comparative Study of Working-Class Disorganization', *op.cit.*
28. Vivian A. Schmidt, 'The New World Order, Incorporated: The Rise of Business and Decline of the Nation State', *Daedalus*, vol. 124, no. 2 (Spring 1995), pp. 75–106; and Vincent Cable, 'The Diminished Nation State: A Study in the Loss of Economic Power', *Daedalus*, vol. 124, no. 2 (Spring 1995), pp. 23–53.
29. Stephen Gelb, 'South Africa's Post-Apartheid Political Economy', in L. A. Swatuk and D. R. Black (eds), *Bridging the Rift: The New South Africa in Africa* (Boulder: Westview, 1997), p. 50.
30. Republic of South Africa Budget Speech by the Minister of Finance, Mr Trevor A. Manuel, 12 March 1997, p. 6.
31. *South Africa Labour Bulletin*, vol. 21, no. 3 (June 1997), p. 11.
32. Public Service Commission, *Public Service Commission Annual Report 1996* (Cape Town: Cape and Transvaal Printers, 1996), p. 18.
33. Robert Mattes and Hermann Thiel, 'Consolidation and Public Opinion in South Africa', *Journal of Democracy*, vol. 9, no. 1 (1998), p. 103.
34. Richard Levin, 'Land Reform: Politics, Policies and Prospects', in E. Maganya and R. Houghton (eds), *Transformation in South Africa? Policy Debates in the 1990s* (Johannesburg: Institute for African Alternatives, 1996), p. 115.
35. Kenneth Good, 'Accountable to Themselves: Predominance in Southern Africa', *The Journal of Modern African Studies,* vol. 35, no. 4 (1997), p. 548.
36. Gelb, 'South Africa's Post-Apartheid Political Economy', *op.cit.*, p. 51.
37. Mattes and Thiel, 'Consolidation and Public Opinion in South Africa', *op.cit.*, p. 102.

9 Avoiding Globalization: The State and Depoliticization in Nigeria

Julius O. Ihonvbere

INTRODUCTION

The recent crisis in Asia has drawn attention to the need for a *holistic* and *dynamic* understanding and appreciation of what globalization represents for nations in the periphery.[1] On the one hand, the crisis showed that economic growth *per se* was not enough, especially when it is constructed on largely bad debts, over-extension of responsibilities, excessive political control and manipulation of the economy and unrealistic expansion of economic activity at the expense of genuine development. On the other hand, the crisis demonstrated that for economies that held out promise and showed the capacity to deliver if adequate supports were provided, the major economies of the world and the multilateral organizations would respond to their needs. This explains, at least in part, the massive bailout organized for the so-called Asian Tigers and the keen interest of the IMF, the World Bank and the United States in the crisis and process of recovery. More critically, the process of recovery has furthered the rapid incorporation of the Asian economies into global capitalism.

The imposition of painful IMF conditionalities will open up these economies to global forces. This scenario fits perfectly into the IMF's definition of globalization as 'the growing economic integration of goods, services and capital markets'.[2] Of course, globalization is much more than an economic affair. Its impact on cultural, political, environmental and social dynamics within and between nations is equally critical. Yet, it is agreed in the literature that for underdeveloped, mismanaged, crisis-ridden and politically unpredictable and uncertain economies, globalization would mean more crisis than benefits. To be sure, the current euphoria about globalization (which has been temporarily minimized with the deepening economic crisis in Asia) often ignores the existential conditions of oppressed, marginalized and depoliticized people all over the world: the unemployed, women, rural people, minorities and so on. The benefits to the big investor, the transnational corporation, the privileged, public officials, the speculator and banker are often presented above the needs and crises of the disadvantaged majority. Yet, it is how the pains, crises and hopes of these majorities are articulated and addressed that will ultimately dictate the content and context of globalization in most regions of the world.

This is an opportune time to examine the place of Nigeria in the emerging global divisions of labour and power. For a country with all that it takes to emerge as a regional 'power-house' – economic resources, a large urban class, an aggressive bourgeois class, a large population and a prominent location in regional and global politics (at least, relative to other African states) – the recent turn of events in Nigeria has shown very clearly how poor management of national resources and opportunities can create conditions which subvert possibilities for growth and development.[3] In the current global dispensation, these conditions translate directly to a limited or very much mediated capacity to take advantage of the opportunities provided by globalization, not to mention the ability to resist the negative consequences of global integration.

AFRICA IN THE NEW GLOBALIZATION

The end of the cold war and the increasing integration of the global economy, with the triumph of the market and the demise of communism, have posed severe challenges and opportunities for the African continent. On the one hand, there is the opportunity to fully integrate into the emerging global capitalist order to exploit the developments in science and technology, the new information revolution and the expansion of the global market. Such an integration, it is argued, will create new and extensive opportunities for trade, investment, foreign aid and support for other developmental objectives.[4] On the other hand, the changes in the global market hold risks of further marginalization and the further redirection of investments and aid to other parts of the world. The complaints about aid and compassion-fatigue by the donors is evidence of increasing frustration with the intractable and complex problems of the continent. It is contended by those who see the deepening crisis of the region as an inhibition to full and effective participation in the new global order that the legacies of colonial and neo-colonial exploitation and mismanagement, the crisis of the state and society and conditions of poverty, foreign domination, instability, and institutional and infrastructural decay and dislocation make participation in the global order impossible:

> The 'marginalization of Africa' is not just speculation. Not only are foreign governments closing embassies and cutting back aid flows, but Africa's role in the world economy is also shrinking... Sub-Saharan Africa is seen less and less as a credible or useful economic and diplomatic partner and increasingly as a humanitarian problem for the world.[5]

The World Bank has concluded that 'The plight of the African continent remains the most serious challenge for the emerging world order'.[6] This sort of projection raises several questions not just about the future of Africa, but also about its post-cold war relations with other regions of the world. What sort of internal restructurings are needed to empower the region to take advantage of current and future changes in the global order? Is the global system structured in such a way as to make it possible for a debt-ridden, crisis-ridden and poverty-stricken region to effectively and profitably participate in the emerging global dispensation? How will ongoing implementation of orthodox structural adjustment packages as well as difficult political liberalization programmes in the context of deepening crisis and global marginalization facilitate or mediate Africa's participation in the new globalization?

THE STATE AND DEPOLITICIZATION IN AFRICA

It is essential to articulate briefly the place of depoliticization in the entire agenda of the post-colonial state in order to fully demonstrate why it has become an obstacle to growth and development on the one hand and why it is working strenuously to avoid globalization on the other. A product of imperialism, the African state inherited a distorted, disarticulated, foreign-dominated and badly fractured social formation. This is reflected in Kidane Mengisteab's analysis of South Africa and W. Ofuatey-Kodjoe's analysis of Ghana elsewhere in this volume. Lacking legitimacy or a constituency, the state relied immediately on inherited relations of power, politics, production and exchange to maintain its hegemony and reproduce the larger society. This included the adoption of legal frameworks, tax collection systems, revenue allocation to benefit the elite and urban centres, maintenance of the neo-colonial educational system, the consolidation of unequal exchange arrangements with the metropole and a steady process of domesticating and containing platforms of opposition and democracy. Its institutions lacked legitimacy, its custodians were weak and badly fractionalized and had only a tenuous relationship to productive activities. This necessitated the heavy reliance by the dominant elites on the state for accumulation. This situation in itself promoted the steady privatization of the state, its resources and means of coercion. For an elite that was so weak and fragmented in its political and economic purposes, the state became an instrument for reproducing narrow interests and curtailing dialogue, disagreements and constitutionally guaranteed liberties.

The momentum of the independence struggle, though in many instances a struggle of limited objectives and confined to urban locations, was contained and redirected to more mundane and opportunistic ventures. Within the first decade of political independence, ethnic differences had been further manipulated and politicized as were religions, regional and other primordial identities just as the colonial state had done. The military was politicized and opposition parties, newspapers and organizations were either banned, chased into exile or forced underground. One-party states emerged all over the continent rationalized on spurious grounds such as the need for unity for development. Civil society was steadily suffocated as trade unions were banned or converted into party units, academics were terrorized for expressing their views, private media outlets were banned or harassed while pro-government media received huge subsidies, employment came to be based on non-meritorious considerations and foreign aid was squandered on prestige projects.

Within a decade and a half, African leaders had *squandered* opportunities for mobilization, growth and self-reliance, and had mortgaged their economies. They had generated deep and often violent conflicts many of which precipitated military coups, counter coups, ethnic massacres, the massive displacement of people (especially women and children) and the emigration of professionals and scholars abroad. Violent opposition movements emerged further compelling desperate regimes to divert scarce resources to defense and security. The environment of depressed wages, economic mismanagement, political violence and policy unpredictability forced investors to hold back on new investments, engage in internal sourcing and to rely on the manipulation of corrupt local structures rather than engage in massive research and development. In these conditions, it was easy for the majority to disengage from politics, redirect their loyalties and energies elsewhere and to question every national policy from what was regarded as a violent, desperate, inefficient, corrupt and unsteady neo-colonial state.

The impact was severe on national institutions: the judiciary became a laughing stock, the police and army as well as security agencies were privatized, the various government departments became inefficient and largely irrelevant to the needs of the people and the government was now regarded as enemy: a wicked, elite- dominated, exploitative, violent and unreliable institution and force. As its tenuous legitimacy melted, its custodians became even more desperate. They invented ideological diversions, constructed expensive personality cults, looked for scapegoats, diverted resources to strengthen their own security and further alienated the people by increasing taxes or not being able to meet their basic human needs. Political monolithism was strengthened in the effort to flush out all forms of opposition, and the disconnection of the state from the larger society proceeded unmediated. What emerged was a situation of war between the state and an intimidated civil society. To the state, civil society was a dangerous terrain accommodating terrorists, saboteurs, tax dodgers, radical students, intellectuals and lawyers and the bastion of unpredictable political action. To the people and their communities, the state was a ruthless, useless and 'irrelevant' institution to be avoided, cheated, subverted and dismantled if and when opportunities permitted. The closure of democratic openings and the near total abolition of pluralism at all fronts generated crises, suspicions, contradictions and conflicts within and between communities culminating in national political and social instability, even economic decay. Herein lies the problem. How can such a state encourage and mobilize the citizenry to reach the highest points of their creative endeavors? How can such a state lay the foundation for industrialization, growth and rapid accumulation in an increasingly competitive and complex global system? Let us use the example of Nigeria as a brief case-study.

NIGERIA AND THE 'NEW' GLOBALIZATION

If there was one country in Africa that had the opportunity to build a viable economic base in the 1970s, it was Nigeria. Without doubt the country, with its huge market, robust urban centres, oil revenues, attraction to transnationals, vibrant capitalist culture and influence in the global system had the chance to exploit opportunities in the global order. Unfortunately this did not happen. The opportunities were squandered and negated by a combination of structural factors and forces: an unstable and non-hegemonic state; an irresponsible, divided, quarrelsome and dependent bourgeoisie; inefficient and ineffective bureaucracy; weak industrial and economic structures; a predatory economic culture addicted to corruption, waste, mismanagement and the 'quick buck' mentality; and foreign domination, manipulation and exploitation. The chances for using oil rents to reverse the trend and constraints of underdevelopment were frittered away. State power was used to rationalize and legitimize not just corrupt attitudes, but also a subservient and unequal relationship with profit and hegemony-seeking transnational corporations. As Adonis Hoffman recently concluded: 'Once expected to become black Africa's economic showpiece and continental powerhouse, Nigeria now faces a political and economic crisis of historic proportions. Its relations with the West are at an all-time low'.[7] This is certainly a sombre conclusion given the centrality of Western connections and relations in the new global dispensation. For Nigeria, this 'all-time low' relationship holds rather negative implications.

Nigeria's economic woes and squandered opportunities have been adequately covered in the literature.[8] Regime after regime have engaged in unbridled waste and plunder of national resources. Agriculture has been neglected and infrastructure has decayed. The rural majority remain the 'wretched of Nigeria', while urban workers frequently cannot provide for their families. The country has become a classical example of a kleptocracy where nothing is done on the basis of merit. Institutions have lost credibility and national symbols have been overtaken by particularistic interests. In spite of flamboyant foreign policies and the use of oil rents to blur the edges of contradictions and conflicts, Nigeria has moved from being a middle- to a low-income nation with the vast majority of the people thoroughly alienated from the state. Aside from the hundreds of thousands of Nigerians who have thronged to other African, Middle Eastern, Asian, European and American cities in search of jobs and better pay, locally, violence and deteriorating socioeconomic conditions have become part of daily life. This situation has not been helped by idiosyncratic leadership and the militarization of national life.

Today, there is really no 'economy' to write about in Nigeria in spite of vitriolic and often dubious claims by government officials, the Federal Office of Statistics (FOS) and the Central Bank of Nigeria (CBN). For instance, in General Sani Abacha's address to the nation on 1 October 1996, he claimed that the 1996 'Budget of Consolidation' had been designed to consolidate the gains of the 1995 budget. He then announced that official and independent assessments had 'shown greater success over the previous year. We have now achieved considerable economic stability in various sectors and are in a position to plan ahead for the future'.

This sort of *self-deception* is not what is required to move into the twenty-first century or to perform maximally in the new globalization. Nations are undertaking very serious socioeconomic and political re-evaluations of existing policies and postures and making hard and painful choices. Ignorant, illiterate, repressive, corrupt and unenlightened leaders are being displaced as authoritarian and generally undemocratic patterns of governance are being challenged and reconstituted. The emerging competitive global order is not based on rhetoric, defensive radicalism, data manipulation, propaganda and doctored truths. In the very same broadcast, for instance, General Abacha declared:

> Our nation in the past three decades, missed the opportunities to harness its resources properly, control areas of wastage and utilize such resources for development-orientated projects and programmes. We have also realized that in all that we did, the mobilization of our population in the rural areas towards meaningful development has not been effectively achieved. This state of affairs has led to a continuous rural–urban drift, creating serious socio-economic problems for our people... The problem of unemployment, crime and poverty, which affected our society for a time now, must be addressed on both short and long-term bases.[9]

This certainly does not portray an economy that had met all its targets and one that was poised to take advantage of the new opportunities and challenges provided by the new globalization. Under the Abacha dispensation, the Nigerian economy has moved from crisis to crisis, negating all indicators of progress, stifling creativity and investment, suffocating civil society and subverting opportunities for strengthening the expanding structures of growth and development.[10] There is widespread agreement that the rapid deterioration of the Nigerian economy and society will make it impossible for the nation to retain the status it had previously attained within the continent of Africa, much less globally. While it is true that investment still flows into the enclave oil industry, the same cannot be said for the rest of the economy. A summary of the nature of the Nigerian economy is provided by Sunday Adewusi, a former inspector-general of police and now Chairman of the United Bank for Africa (UBA):

> The domestic economy was characterized by very low performance in the productive sectors in 1993, with gross domestic product recording a decline of 2.9 per cent. This was due largely to the constraints in the procurement of raw materials and equipment for the manufacturing sector, the very high interest rates in the financial market, depreciation in the value of the naira and the political impasse occasioned by the unsuccessful attempt at the enthronement of a democratic government in the country. Company closures, staff lay-offs, price increases and perennial shortage of foreign exchange continued unabated. The progressive slump in oil price in the international market, from $17.30 per barrel in January 1993 to $13.55 per barrel by March 1994, further worsened the prospects of increased foreign exchange earnings for the country.
>
> The external payments position worsened, with total external reserves plummeting from $1349.6m in 1992 to $972.3m by the end of October 1993. At the same time, the external debts increased from $27.5bn in 1992 to $28.72bn by October 1993 with very high arrears of due but unserviceable obligations to the tune of $4.54bn . . . the financial sector . . . witnessed intense liquidity crunch due to political tension.[11]

If Adewusi's assessment was made in 1993, let us see what one of Nigeria's biggest banks, the UBA had to say in mid-1997. In its bi-monthly report, the UBA noted that the Nigerian economy was in a 'parlous state or slumber' and that the

> possibility of meeting the set target growth of 5.5 per cent GDP remains ambitious. The viability of the real sector remains in doubt because the sector has continued to be characterized by perennial fuel shortage, power outage, inventory build ups and pessimistic investment climate or low marginal efficiency of capital or poor profit expectation.[12]

Identifying what the state of the economy was, the UBA noted that

> The main weak spot remains investment. Investment trends remain stagnant with falling building investment and flat machinery and equipment spending. Low levels of capacity utilization . . . have held back investment spending through 1996 into 1997 . . . business

> leaders' opinions on the state of the economy remain gloomy with the continued fragility of domestic demand.[13]

Clearly, therefore, the Nigerian economy is not making the robust strides which public officials often throw around. In reality, the deteriorating economic condition has been complicated by a series of internal and external political miscalculations.

While it is true that the Sani Abacha junta inherited a badly pillaged, terribly managed and decadent economy, it has not deviated in any way from the policies of the past which mortgaged the future of the economy and society. In fact, in several areas, especially on the political front, the Abacha junta has worsened the economic situation with far-reaching implications for investor confidence, foreign investment and growth. According to Joseph Ode,

> For Nigeria, all indices of economic health in the past few years have been reading negative. A near-triple-digit inflation, high unemployment rate, low industrial and agricultural output, a depreciating national currency, balance of payments deficits and burgeoning external debt. All these tell the story of a prostrate economy.[14]

While the Abacha government has shown a pathological fixation on the exchange rate of the local currency without an equal interest in production and productive activities, the foreign exchange market and frequently changing regulations have only provided an opportunity for government officials, speculators and military officers to engage in rapid primitive accumulation. As the UBA noted in mid-1997, following an official devaluation of the naira as a solution to high interest rates, 'the enhanced foreign exchange demand was found to be mainly used for speculative purposes as the rent-seekers and arbitrageurs capitalized on the glaring loopholes in the provision of the budget which allowed unlimited purchase of Business Traveling Allowance (BTA) and Personal Traveling Allowance (PTA) to engage in capital flight'.[15] With the current currency crisis in East Asia, it seems that the Nigerian state and its custodians are not drawing critical lessons from the experiences of other nations and regions. This hardly sounds like a verdict on an economy that is aware of and prepared to gain from, the openings in the new global order.

Nigeria has always had poor governance. Yet, the current military regime is certainly the most corrupt and repressive in terms of its politics and policies. The present government seems to believe that it can mobilize the people and lay the foundation for growth, stability and development while at the same time terrorizing them and their organizations. If anything, the changes in the global system goes against such an archaic strategy of primitive accumulation through unmediated violence.[16]

A simple look at the state of the economy and society in early 1998 reveals a frightening and sorry state of affairs: children are engaged in prostitution; workers are not paid regularly for work performed; the cities have become centres of crime and drug trafficking and the United States has decertified Nigeria for its uncoordinated and unserious approach to the drug issue; assassinations have become a national trademark with several opposition leaders assassinated or nearly assassinated; the roads are in total disrepair; schools are either closed, without teachers, laboratories are empty and libraries are at least seven to ten years behind in the relevant literature.[17] Rural areas remain neglected and marginalized, receiving little attention in official policy and in budgetary allocation, though over 85 per cent of the populace continue to live in these areas. Corruption has become not just a way of life, but life itself.[18] Military officers live above the law; the judiciary has been totally intimidated, corrupted, compromised and rendered useless; traditional institutions have been domesticated and bastardized; trade unions, student associations, prodemocracy movements and other popular coalitions have been suppressed and their leaders jailed or forced into exile; unemployment and underemployment have reached unprecedented levels.[19] It is not surprising, therefore, that local and foreign investors have become 'risk averters' in the Nigerian economy, not only because returns are low, but because the political climate continues to generate dangerous tensions which are not conducive for business.

In 1991 the CBN announced that 67 per cent of urban residents were unemployed.[20] Graduates of the country's 97 polytechnics and universities simply disappeared into the informal sector, engaging in desperate efforts to keep body and soul together.[21] The health-care delivery system 'is still in the doldrums', with deteriorating facilities, lack of funds and equipment and with qualified staff abandoning the hospitals and clinics for greener pastures.[22] It has been estimated that about 10 million Nigerians live outside the country, with many engaged in occupations that have nothing to do with their qualifications and experience. In 1996, 1.3 million Nigerians applied for the 4000 immigrant visas allotted by the United States. Personal and collective liberties have been openly abridged.[23] Transportation and communications are still archaic with most banks, hospitals, universities and businesses unaware of the utility of computers. The military junta, in fact, declared that the internet was a security risk because it allowed opposition movements to communicate with the outside world and foreign governments! In an age where computers are helping to extend the frontiers of information and knowledge and helping to speed up transactions, Nigeria is falling behind. The supply of electricity is still as erratic as ever with serious implications for all sectors especially industry. Power outages can last for several weeks or months with no official explanation. It is difficult to recount the tales of pain and frustration which local and foreign businesses have experienced as a result of erratic power supply in Nigeria. This is often accompanied, ironically, with fuel and especially diesel shortages in a country which is the largest oil producer in Africa and a member of the Organization of Petroleum Exporting Countries (OPEC).

Finally, in spite of the proliferation of states, local governments, ministers, parastatals and banks, the Nigerian economy is still largely a 'pirate economy'. The economy is not governed by any rules and is therefore dependent on informal regulations. To make matters worse, in this era of democracy, democratization, good governance and globalization, the Nigerian state remains distant, aloof, violent and insensitive to the plight of the majority, while the elites and the custodians of the state remain corrupt, irresponsible, largely unproductive and highly factionalized and fractionalized on regional, ethnic and religious lines. Thus, given the degree of decay and deterioration, the alienation of productive communities, the marginalization of the people, rural neglect, corruption and institutional fragility, along with declining interest from foreign investors, an economic recovery agenda can only succeed if it mobilizes the entire populace through democratic means.

So far, a democratic agenda has not been designed or presented by the military junta, which seems to be preoccupied with manufacturing and chasing political opponents all over the country and abroad.[24] The situation in contemporary Nigeria is so futile that many Nigerians now compare the present to the days of the civil war (1967–70) – most Nigerians have reached the conclusion that things were better at that time. Others openly complain that the colonial days were much better and that political independence has made little difference in the quality of their life. In fact, many now feel that independence has been more of a curse than a blessing, as the gains from the so-called freedom from colonialism cannot be seen. In a world where people of all ages are discovering new boundaries of knowledge and articulating powerful ideas that are bound to shape the future, such defeatist, fatalistic and submissive attitudes hardly support an agenda for a productive and rewarding participation in the new world order.

CONCLUSION: TOWARDS THE TWENTY-FIRST CENTURY

Without a doubt, the deepening socioeconomic and political crisis in Nigeria works directly against the ability of the political economy to benefit from globalization or to generate a capacity to resist the negative pressures of globalization. For a country that cannot construct viable and fairly predictable political platforms and relations in the twenty-first century, it is doubtful that the forces of globalization, positive and negative, will take it seriously. With dilapidated infrastructures, a patently corrupt elite (Nigeria is ranked by Transparency International as the most corrupt of 56 nations in its 1996 and 1997 survey) and a state which seems totally disconnected from civil society, Nigeria, in spite of its vast potentials, is clearly not poised to participate in the emerging global order in an assertive way. True, investments continue to flow into the enclave oil industry. Even then, communal clashes, protests by workers and increasing acts of sabotage are beginning to affect the flow of production activities. Also, the increasing calls for sanctions against Nigeria's military junta, which continues to test the will of the international community, do not hold out a positive future for the oil sector.

The spate of investment, interest and attention which South Africa seems to be receiving is evidence of the underlying strength of its economy. It is expanding steadily and investing in the southern Africa region. African Americans and several international corporations are going to South Africa and Ghana rather than to Nigeria. Tourists are visiting Senegal, Côte d'Ivoire, South Africa, Zimbabwe and Ghana rather than Nigeria. Nigeria, on the other hand, is contracting and losing credibility in the West African sub-region, losing ground to Ghana in international organizations and being challenged by Cameroon over the Bakassi Peninsular.

In spite of very generous incentives to foreign investors, responses have been 'lukewarm'.[25] In November 1990, the Confederation of British Industry (CBI) hosted a conference in London on 'Investment Promotion in Nigeria'. The Nigerian delegation announced that the government had implemented an 'open door policy' and done away with all previous regulations on trade, investment and foreign exchange.

Ironically, in spite of this liberalization, the Nigerian delegation was spurned by British investors who pointed at the near total breakdown of law and order, widespread corruption, bureaucratic bottlenecks and inefficiency, frequent coups and violent riots and general economic mismanagement. Today, the situation is much worse. Hangings, judicial murders, assassinations, arranged fires, strikes, rumoured coups and the growing influence of speculators who have taken charge of the *agbero* (tout) economy have become the mainstay. The apparently officially-sponsored attacks against the Ogoni people, the less-than-fair trial of the leaders of the Movement for the Survival of Ogoni People (MOSOP), the detention of hundreds of pro-democracy and trade union leaders like Beko-Ransome Kuti and Frank Kokori and the harassment of popular groups under the Abacha junta, have only increased the doubts of investors and Western nations about the future of the Nigerian economy. The recent spate of country-wide bombings which forced Western embassies to issue security alerts to their citizens in and outside Nigeria, can only fuel further disinterest in the economy.[26]

As indicated earlier, foreign investors also point to the massive decline in the purchasing power of the majority of Nigerians, the inefficient supply of electricity, poor communications facilities and the unstable and weak currency, the naira. These drawbacks can only further Nigeria's marginalization in the new global order. It is clear that propaganda, repression, defensive radicalism and diversions cannot alter the country's new irrelevance in global geostrategic and economic calculations. A new internal order is certainly a prerequisite for an effective participation in the global system. There is an urgent need to open up Nigeria's political landscape and to mobilize the people beyond gender, regional, ethnic and religious lines for the critical task of reconstruction, growth and development. As Adebayo Adedeji has noted, 'full democratization of all aspects of economic and social activities and in all stages from decision-making to implementation' must occur before recovery can take place and that 'it is only through the motivation and empowerment of the people as well as the ensuring of the equitable distribution of income that development can take place on a sustainable basis'.[27]

A clear social policy to improve the demand side of the economy is required if Nigeria is to be taken seriously in the new globalization.

Inflation has wiped out the savings of millions of Nigerians and proletarianized the middle classes. In early 1998, the Nigerian government liquidated over 27 banks with many more on the verge of insolvency. Companies and other investors are unlikely to come to Nigeria if people cannot purchase their products, unless Nigeria is to be converted into just a cheap labour market. If the people cannot buy what is being imported or produced, there is no way the economy can grow. In the first place, productivity cannot be expected to improve when producers are virtually dying of hunger with no access to basic facilities. This social policy will include a determined agenda to curb rural poverty and alienation, control inflation, generate employment, provide limited but effective welfare programmes, redirect migration to the rural areas, resuscitate agriculture which continues to provide employment for over 70 per cent of the Nigerian people, check crime and insecurity. This is the sort of agenda that new investors seek.

Economic recovery and growth requires a developmental state, not a state which is unsteady, unstable and insecure. A state led by educated, democratic, mobile and visionary persons who do not measure the well-being of the nation in terms of their personal bank accounts, the number of cars they own, how many 'enemies' they have executed or jailed and how much they have looted and stored in foreign banks. The nature, composition, efficiency and openness of the state means a lot and makes a great difference to the economy. The challenge for the immediate future is therefore the restructuring of the state to be accountable, efficient, effective, transparent, predictable and capable of supporting the necessary projects to encourage private and collective initiatives.

Only such a state can create the environment for strengthening local investors. Also, only such a state can appreciate the salience of science and technology in the current global environment of laser technology and the information superhighway. Local entrepreneurs cannot expand, generate employment, use local raw materials and strengthen themselves when they cannot borrow, import spare parts, sell their goods and compete effectively with cheaper imports as a result of trade liberalization. This means that a blanket trade liberalization is a disastrous policy for any dependent and underdeveloped nation to follow in the current global order of trade blocs and high protectionism. Until these and other reforms and transformations take place, Nigeria will not and cannot be a serious actor in the new globalization. It might remain somewhat influential in the West African (even African) region, but such influence will not be sufficient to attract the sort of global support and generate local creativity so much needed to survive in the current capital-driven global order.

Notes and References

1. Seth Mydans, 'An Asian "Miracle" Now Seems Like a Mirage', *New York Times*, 22 October 1997; David E. Dsanger, 'Shaky Asia, New Shivers', *New York Times*, 24 November 1997; 'Asia's Economic Crisis: How Far is Down?' *The Economist* (15 November 1997); and Seth Mydans, 'Thailand Economic Crash Crushes Working Poor', *New York Times*, 15 December 1997.
2. IMF Builds on Initiatives to Meet Challenges of Globalization', *IMF Survey*, 26 September 1997, p. 1.
3. Adebayo Olukoshi and Osita Agbu, 'The Deepening Crisis of Nigeria Federalism', in A. Olukoshi and L. Laakso (eds), *Challenges to the Nation-State in Africa* (Uppsala: Nordiska Afrikainstitutet, 1996), p. 77.
4. See 'Sub-Saharan Africa: Route to Success Lies in Sound Economic Policies', *IMF Survey*, 20 February 1995.
5. Carol Lancaster, *United States and Africa: Into the Twenty-First Century* (Washington, DC: Overseas Development Council, policy essay no. 7, 1993), p. 19.
6. World Bank, *World Development Report 1995: Workers in an Integrating World* (Washington, DC: World Bank, 1995), p. 122.
7. Adonis Hoffman, 'Nigeria: The Policy Conundrum', *Foreign Policy*, vol. 101 (Winter 1995–96), p. 146.
8. See Julius O. Ihonvbere, *Nigeria: The Politics of Adjustment and Democracy* (New Brunswick, N.J.: Transaction Publishers, 1984); Toyin Falola and Julius O. Ihonvbere, *The Rise and Fall of Nigeria's Second Republic, 1979–84* (London: Zed Books, 1985); and Julius O. Ihonvbere and Timothy M. Shaw, *The Illusions of Power: Nigeria in Transition* (Lawrenceville, NJ: Africa World Press, 1998).
9. Sani Abacha, address delivered to the nation, 1 October 1996.
10. See Julius O. Ihonvbere, 'Dead End to Democracy in Nigeria?: Explaining the 1993 General Abacha Coup', in M. Jones (ed.), *1994 Association of Third World Studies Proceedings* (Statesboro, Ga.: Georgia Southern University, 1995); Hoffman, 'Nigeria: The Policy Conundrum'; Oyeleye Oyediran (ed.) *Governance and Development in Nigeria: Essays in Honor of Billy J. Dudley* (Ibadan: Oyediran Consult, 1996); and Peter Lewis, 'Endgame in Nigeria? The Politics of a Failed Democratic Transition', *African Affairs*, vol. 93 (1994), p. 372 .
11. Sunday Adewusi, Chairman's Statement to the Shareholders of the United Bank for Africa PLC at the 33rd Annual General Meeting, 8 September 1994, at the Nicon Noga Hilton Hotel, Abuja, Nigeria.
12. 'Problems and Issues in the Nigerian Economy on the Rise in Domestic Lending Rates and Fall in Saving Rates', *UBA Bi-Monthly Business and Economic Digest*, vol. 20, no. 2 (May–June 1997), p. 2.
13. *Ibid.*, 3.
14. Joseph Ode, 'Rich But Poor', *Newswatch*, 10 October 1994, p. 28.

15. 'The Travails of the Depreciating Value of the Naira', *UBA Bi-Monthly Business and Economic Digest*, vol. 20, no. 2 (May–June 1997), p. 3.
16. See Julius O. Ihonvbere, *Africa and the New World Order* (New York: Peter Lang Publishing, 1998); Boutros Boutros-Ghali, 'Democracy: A Newly Recognized Imperative', *Global Governance*, vol. 1, no. 1 (Winter 1995); and Mark T. Bereger, 'Post-Cold War Capitalism: Modernization and Modes of Resistance After the Fall', *Third World Quarterly*, vol. 16, no. 4 (December 1995).
17. For a critique of the educational system see Collins Edomaruse, 'Reversing the Gear at 36', *Thisday*, 1 October 1996.
18. See Mercy Atte, 'Corruption: The Worm Lives', *Newswatch*, 10 October 1994; Ihonvbere, *Nigeria*, *op.cit.* Peter O. Agbese and Julius O. Ihonvbere, *The State and Structural Adjustment in Nigeria* (Washington, DC: Howard University Press, 1988); and Nigerian newspapers and magazines which publish incredible stories of corruption and mismanagement on a daily basis.
19. See the annual reports of the Committee for the Defence of Human Rights (CDHR), the Civil Liberties Organization (CLO), the Constitutional Rights Project (CRP) and the Campaign for Democracy (CD), for factual accounts of these and other developments.
20. Wale Akin-Aina, 'Social Services – Crumbling Like Cookies', *Newswatch*, 10 October 1994.
21. See Julius O. Ihonvbere, *Nigeria*, *op.cit.*
22. *Ibid.*
23. For a very detailed account see US Department of State, *Nigeria: Country Report on Human Rights Practices for 1996* (Washington, DC: US Department of State, 1977); Michael Birnbaum, *Nigeria, Fundamental Rights Denied: Report of the Trial of Ken Saro-Wiwa and Others* (London: Article 19, 1995); and Wole Soyinka, *The Open Sore of a Continent: A Personal Narrative of the Nigeria Crisis* (London: Oxford, 1996).
24. The Nigerian economy has been in crisis for a long time. The current junta has simply deepened the contradictions and crisis. See 'Manufacturers Association of Nigeria in Business Concord', 12 December 1987, for an earlier verdict on the state of the economy.
25. See 'Investment in Nigeria: Open Door Policy', *West Africa*, 3–9 December 1990.
26. See Deborah Robinson, *Ogoni – The Struggle Continues* (Geneva and Nairobi: World Council of Churches and All-Africa Conference of Churches, December 1996).
27. Adebayo Adedeji, 'Foreword' to *The African Alternative Framework to Structural Adjustment Programmes for Socio-Economic Recovery and Transformation* (Addis Ababa: ECA, 1989), p. iii.

10 Ideology, Politics and Public Policy in Ghana: 1982–96

W. Ofuatey-Kodjoe

INTRODUCTION

Some writers on the subject of relations between the Third World state and globalization have suggested that the states in the South have lost their hegemony over their economies, and have become merely vehicles for the implementation of policies established by international financial institutions (IFIs).[1] Others take the view that in addition to their role as transmission belts for the policies of international financial institutions, these states also try to buffer their economies from the more harmful effects of externally derived policies.[2] Still others argue that while these states are carrying out the 'liberalization' policies mandated by IFIs, they try to do so 'without putting at risk the social and political power of the ruling class'.[3] As Ould-Mey has noted, in order to implement the unpopular economic policies called for by IFIs, these states try to sharpen their legitimacy, and contain the internal social and political ramifications of these 'reforms'.[4]

On 31 January 1981, a military coup toppled the Third Republic of Ghana and brought into power a group of people headed by Jerry John Rawlings.[5] The radical populist rhetoric of the new regime led many observers to expect that the government would adopt anti-IMF (International Monetary Fund), 'self-reliant' policies to deal with the economic crisis facing the country at that time. Therefore it came as a complete surprise when in April 1983 the Ghana government adopted a structural adjustment programme, under the auspices of the World Bank and the International Monetary Fund, which was so comprehensive that Ghana became the 'poster boy' of structural adjustment.

The case of Ghana is instructive in part because it represents one of the most intensive applications of IFI conditionalities, and it has been touted as the most successful of these ventures. Indeed, some commentators have suggested that the Ghanaian experience should be used as a model for other countries facing economic difficulty.[6] It has also been known to face the most systematic and pervasive internal opposition from virtually all sections of the Ghanaian population.[7] What is remarkable is that the Rawlings regime has been successful at weathering this internal opposition. In fact, after 15 years of existence the regime is the longest lasting government in Ghana since independence. Furthermore, it has been able to transform itself from a military dictatorship into an elected civilian regime, thereby acquiring some internal legitimacy to complement the massive external support that it has received from the international community.

The purpose of this chapter is to investigate the political strategies that the Rawlings regime has used to overcome the internal opposition to the reforms that it has been carrying out in Ghana as part of the World Bank and IMF-mandated Economic Recovery Programme (ERP). Following the preceding studies of South Africa and Nigeria, this chapter is divided into three parts: an analysis of the nature and impact of the ERP on the Ghanaian public, the patterns of opposition that the government faced while trying to implement this programme, and the strategies that the government has used to impose its policies on a population which at times has been very hostile.

THE NATURE OF THE REGIME

In the immediate aftermath of the coup, a small group of people emerged to determine and articulate the objectives of the coup, and to develop the institutions which would be needed to accomplish those objectives. This group was a heterogeneous collection of men surrounding Rawlings. Among them were people like Zaya Yeebo and Kwesi Botchwey, who had been his colleagues in the radical organizations with which he had been associated after he had been retired from the air force.[8] Some of them were soldiers, like Sergeant Alolga Akata-Pore who had assisted him in making the coup. Still others were personal friends and associates like his confidant and ideological mentor, Capt. Kojo Tsikata (rtd), and his cousin Tsatsu Tsikata. Among the most conspicuous and influential at this time were the leftists and the members of the various progressive organizations. Although the coup had caught many of them by surprise, they felt a certain sense of ownership of the 'revolution' because of their previous relationship with Rawlings and some of the other coup-makers.

Ideologically, this group included students, intellectuals and labour leaders 'who share[d], at various levels of clarity, socialist notions about a just society'.[9] Other ideologies were also represented at Gondar Barracks. There were many liberals and conservatives and plain opportunists, some of them affiliated with the proscribed political parties, who made private overtures to Rawlings and some of the other coup-makers hoping for jobs and special favours. Some of them wanted to get involved in the 'revolution' because they saw an opportunity to influence 'the process' or hijack it. The lobbying at Gondar Barracks was intense. As a result, the original group that coalesced around Rawlings was quite ideologically diffuse. To be sure there was a strong leftist and radical tendency. However, there were other tendencies as well. Thus, in the fluid and confusing situation following the coup, these people saw themselves not as colleagues, but as ideological adversaries in serious contestation for power. In their view, they were engaged in a zero-sum game the object of which was to eliminate the 'enemy' factions and seize control of the government.

The first problem that the 'revolution' had to deal with was to acquire some sort of *legitimacy* for the regime. This was considered important because unlike the 1979 Rawlings coup, this was not intended to be a house-cleaning operation, or just another coup. The 'revolutionaries' wanted it clearly understood that the objective of the insurrection was, in the words of Rawlings, 'to create a revolution . . . - something that would transform the social and economic order of this country'.[10] They intended a fundamental transformation of Ghanaian society; the kind of transformation that would 'afford everyone the opportunity to participate in the decision- making process of this country'.[11] In addition, they wished to establish a society in which there would be no more exploitation of the 'ordinary people', a society in which they would be able to enjoy the resources of the country more equitably. The source of the legitimacy of the regime was placed squarely on 'the will of the people'. As Rawlings remarked, 'it is the people only who have the right and power to determine, through the defence committees, the type of government under which they would like to live'. He added later that 'the 31 December Revolution has launched People Power in this country'.[12] Armed with this populist legitimacy, they set about creating the institutions they would need to move the 'revolution' along.

Before achieving the objectives of the revolution, the insurrectionists recognized that there were several short-term, instrumental objectives that had to be attained. First among these was the creation of the institutional basis for defending the revolution and carrying the country through a transitional period, until the establishment of the true people's democracy.[13] There were other objectives, as well, such as the restoration of the economy and the reconstitution of the state machinery. In addition, it would be necessary to eliminate corruption, remove some of the most glaring inequities in the society, retrieve some of the ill-gotten gains of the privileged and punish those who had engaged in the most extreme, illegal and corrupt ways of amassing wealth at the expense of the people.[14]

Beyond these declarations, the 'revolutionary' leadership did not seem to have any specific ideas about how to accomplish these objectives, or what institutions were going to be devised for that purpose. There was a great deal of animated talk about mobilizing workers, students and other 'progressive forces', but there was little or no clarity about the specific nature of these efforts. As it turned out, these methods were worked out 'on an *ad hoc*, haphazard manner by informal caucus around Rawlings',[15] frequently under circumstances of passionate and vitriolic disagreement between the different tendencies within the 'revolutionary' leadership. Policy-making within the leadership reflected the varying orientations of the core group and so what emerged as an ideology was a kind of radical populism and nationalism, without a coherent programme and no machinery to implement a programme if one existed.[16] It was into this cauldron of intense struggle among themselves for control of the state apparatus that the issue of the formulation and implementation of economic policy was thrown.

When the Rawlings government took over the administration of the country, the most pressing policy problem was the state of the economy, As Capt. Tsikata noted in an interview, 'We felt we had to do something, because in a few months the whole country would have ground to a halt'.[17] The Provisional National Defence Council (PNDC) did not have a clear idea of how to arrest the almost daily precipitous deterioration of the economy. It was clear, however, that government revenues had to be increased, government expenditures had to be curtailed, the inflation rate had to be checked and the currency had to be stabilized.[18] The initial policies of the government attempted to attack these problems through partial demonetization of the economy, aggressive revenue collection and the rescue of tons of cocoa beans from the interior for export.[19]

In the early part of 1982, Rawlings appointed an inner core of advisors to serve on the National Economic Recovery Committee.

This group was charged with the responsibility of developing economic policy. In August 1982, the group decided that the *ad hoc* policies that were being implemented would not solve the problem of the economy in any fundamental or long-lasting way. They also decided that the best way to go would be to negotiate with the international financial institutions for financial assistance and if necessary accept some of their well-known conditions.[20] Pursuant to this decision, they produced what came to be known as 'the Abbey Report' named after its author, Dr Joseph Abbey. The main features of this plan were:

1. a massive devaluation of the Ghanaian currency (cedi) in order to provide incentives to export producers;
2. increase in cocoa producer prices;
3. strict control over government budget deficits;
4. increased effectiveness in revenue collection;
5. reduction of subsidies on some goods and services;
6. the introduction of user fees on basic government services (education, hospital costs); and
7. introduction of price decontrols.[21]

The radicals in the PNDC bitterly opposed this proposal. They rejected devaluation, price decontrols and the elimination of subsidies as selling out to imperialism and devastating the living conditions of Ghanaians.[22] The outline of the document which they presented, the *Graham Report*, produced by Yao Graham of the New Democratic Movement (NDM), contained counter-proposals, including the nationalization of some foreign industries and the mobilization of workers and farmers to increase production.[23] There ensued an intense debate within the PNDC as to the economic direction to be taken by the 'revolution'. The debate turned out to be inconsequential, because Rawlings and his faction had already decided to go ahead with the World Bank and IMF negotiations. In fact, while the debate was being held, Kwesi Botchwey was already in Washington negotiating with the representatives of the IFIs.[24]

What emerged out of this process was the Economic Recovery Programme, which was introduced in the April 1983 budget and whose objectives were as follows:

- To eliminate, through planned institutional changes, local and foreign exploitation which manifests itself in rampant malpractice in internal and external trade and in tax evasion and avoidance:

- To increase production to modest but realistic targets in a selected number of agricultural products and select manufacturing industries in the first year:
- To increase production of food and industrial raw materials and export commodities to planned levels in the context of the Three-Year Medium-Term plan:
- To lower the rate of inflation through prudent fiscal, monetary and trade policies:
- To improve the distribution of goods, services and incomes.[25]

Programmatically, the ERP had three basic aspects: exchange policies, export promotion policies and import reduction policies. The exchange policies involved the massive devaluation of the currency and the progressive elimination of import subsidies (with the exception of 23 essential commodities).[26] The export promotion policies were geared towards the expansion of the productive base of export commodities especially cocoa and gold and the encouragement of export-oriented industries through foreign investment and privatization.[27] The import reduction policies involved a programme for the stabilization of wages and prices and a reduction of government spending.[28] The adjustment programme that was presented to the Ghanaian people was presented as the ERP.

There is near unanimous agreement that the ERP has been successful in stopping the downward trend of the Ghanaian economy. The inflation rate, which peaked at 121 per cent after the initial devaluation in 1983, dropped to 25 per cent in 1994. Meanwhile, gross domestic product (GDP) rose from 0.7 per cent in 1983 to 5.5 per cent in 1984 and has been hovering around that rate ever since. The modest growth was accomplished in the face of a great many difficulties; the expulsion of about one million Ghanaians from Nigeria, reductions in agricultural earnings, the falling prices of gold and cocoa and problems associated with delays in the disbursement of aid.

However, the programme has been extremely hard on the Ghanaian people. The devaluation of the currency from 2.75 cedis = US$1 in 1983, to 1725.7 – US$1 in 1996 has caused extreme pain among the people, especially the poorest people. In addition, unemployment has increased and although goods are plentiful in the shops they are beyond the means of most Ghanaians.[29] The Programme of Action to Mitigate the Social Costs of Adjustment (PAMSCAD), which was instituted with so much fanfare, has not lived up to its promise.[30]

PATTERNS OF OPPOSITION TO THE REGIME

At the beginning of the 'revolution' the internal support for the PNDC came from five groups. First, there were the left-wing intellectuals who were organized in the groups making up the progressive 'movement'. The second leg of support was composed of organized labour and the leadership of the Ghana Trade Union Congress (GTUC). The third support base of the regime were the other ranks and junior officers of the army who had been radicalized by their association with the progressive forces during the 'first coming' of Rawlings. The fourth base of the regime was the leadership of the National Union of Students (NUGS), based at the three universities where there was always a ready source of radical thinking. The fifth support base was organized by the PNDC itself out of the spontaneous outbreak of populist sentiment into the People's Defence Committees (PDCs) and Worker's Defence Committees (WDCs). The initial radical populist tinge of the 'revolution' was due to the combination of these groups, identified generally as youthful, populist, leftist and socialist.

This support base did not last long, however, and as early as the summer of 1982 serious disagreements developed between the 'movement' and the PNDC over a range of issues, especially the ERP. By mid-1984, the PDCs and WDCs which had been created by the Rawlings group had been disbanded and the rest of the support system: organized labour, the students, the left intellectuals and the soldiers had become completely alienated from the government.[31] In December 1983, A.K. Yankey was elected president of the GTUC in spite of the opposition of the PNDC. One year later, commenting on the rift between the GTUC and the PNDC on the question of the ERP, he noted that 'the government that said that the coup of 31 December was a revolution for the workers and masses is now running the country like a business'.[32] According to the unions, the government's policies – devaluation, privatization, massive retrenchments of workers, intervention in collective bargaining – have worked consistently against the people. In addition, the workers were adamantly opposed to the reluctance of the government to consult with them on national issues, especially ERP policies. Third, the workers have expressed their frustration with the government's abuse of human rights, especially the practice of arresting and detaining union leaders without due process.

The radical intellectuals were similarly antagonistic to the PNDC. As mentioned before, many of the members of these groups felt some ownership of the revolution at the outset. They fought in and out of the decision-making core to acquire control over the economic policies of the government. There were some individuals, like Kwesi Botchwey and others in the NDM who were able to stay on in the government and even had some influence in it. However, since 1983 when the radical 'alternative' lost the struggle for the control of the government and most of them resigned or were purged, the radicals have maintained a consistent position of confrontation with the PNDC, especially on the issue of the ERP. As they see it, this confrontation is due to profound ideological differences between the PNDC and themselves.[33]

By mid-1983, the students were also at odds with the government. The extreme dissatisfaction of the students with the April 1983 budget was based on their view that the switch by the Rawlings government from a radical populist orientation towards what they perceived as collaboration with imperialism was a shameless sell-out of the Ghanaian people. Later on, they added to their grievances those government policies associated with the ERP which had directly affected them, such as the withdrawal of government subsidies on school fees, books and allowances, and the two-year national service requirement. In addition to these grievances, the students also protested against governmental abuses, corruption and especially the numerous violations of human rights.

The main opposition to the regime came originally from the professionals, the majority of the academics, the Churches and the upper and middle classes in general. Alarmed by the 1982 policies, these groups organized their antagonism to the government around the issues of constitutionalism and civil liberties.[34] However, the real issue seems to have been their apprehension that they might lose economic and political power to the lower classes. After the failure of some elements within this group to topple the government in April 1982, many of them have taken refuge in a general 'withdrawal' from participation in public life. In spite of the fact that the policies of the government began to be viewed by the commercial bourgeoisie as advancing their own economic interests, they have not been fully supportive of the PNDC. They complained about a number of issues, including the fact that high interest rates, severe liquidity problems and trade liberalization have put them in a non-competitive situation.[35]

Since 1986, local business owners have started to give the government some guarded support. In June 1988, the president of the

Association of Ghana Employers, J.V.L. Phillips, said at its annual meeting 'We, the employers feel that the government has embarked on the right policy, that is, privatization'.[36] On 13 June 1988, while calling for the 'promotion of genuine democratic politics', the University Teachers Association of Ghana issued a statement acknowledging the positive effects of the ERP and PAMSCAD.[37] The majority of the middle class and the intelligentsia have supported the businesspeople, especially on the issues of human rights and due process and they have bitterly opposed the government's attack on civil liberties.[38]

REGIME STRATEGIES

As soon as Rawlings and his core group decided to go into negotiations with the IFIs, they decided that they would need to develop some strategies not only to implement the structural adjustment programmes (SAPs), but to keep control of the revolution and eventually stay in power. Thus the struggle for the control of the state and the struggle for control of economic policy were carried out simultaneously. They felt that what they needed was a coordinated strategy for controlling the minds of the people, mobilizing and maintaining a support system and overcoming opposition. Consistent with the populist orientation of the 'revolution' and the insistence that the source of its legitimacy was 'the people', the logical strategy for developing a coalition to support the government would have to be the mobilization of the people. Before that could happen, however, they first had to seize control of the government from the other factions involved in 'the revolution', and keep all decision-making firmly within their grasp.

The problem of making sure that decisions concerning the implementation of their economic policy would remain in their hands was considered crucial by both Tsikata and Rawlings. This was a crucial problem because of the extreme factionalism within the group, their ideological diffuseness and the possibility that someone or some people might highjack the 'revolution'. The solution was to develop the capacity to make decisions within a small cabal, without interference from the PNDC. This turned out to be a struggle, and the members of the PNDC on the left did not give in easily. The strategy that Rawlings used was to isolate the left, divide it and finally eliminate it from the important decision-making centres in the government.[39]

Between 1982 and 1983, several disputes occurred within the PNDC. The issue of the economy led to confrontations (including armed skirmishes between Rawlings and his allies and some of the radicals). These confrontations gave Rawlings the opportunity to engage in a systematic purge of the left and their allies in the army. As a result some of the them resigned, some were executed and some fled the country.

Another technique used by Rawlings and his inner core of decision-makers was to use the PNDC as a showpiece while locating the actual decision-making process within unidentified bodies which they dominated. At first, Rawlings engaged the radical left in the PNDC. However, due to their resistance to the policies mandated by the IFIs, he decided to shift decision-making authority from the PNDC to other bodies. As a group, the PNDC had met only infrequently even at the outset. After the coup attempts in 1982 it never met at all, even though directives continued to be issued in its name. By 1985, Rawlings had shifted a significant amount of power from the emaciated PNDC to a new cabinet dominated by seven ministers from the Limann era.

One strategy that the government employed was to try to mobilize a coalition for support of the ERP. The first effort at mobilization gave birth to the organization of the PDCs, the WDCs and the Interim National Coordinating Committee (INCC). In early 1982 Rawlings called for the formation of Peoples Defence Committees and Workers Defence Committees. These bodies were envisaged as the 'power base of this country',[40] the duties of which were to

> defend the rights of the ordinary people, to expose and stop corruption and other counter revolutionary activities ... maintain collective national discipline and supervision of national resources ... and afford everyone the opportunity to participate in the decision- making process in the country.[41]

These bodies soon became a serious point of disagreement between the radicals and the right-wing members of the PNDC. One of the points at issue was the role to be played by the INCC, which was formed on 1 February 1982 to oversee these bodies. The leadership of the June Fourth Movement (JFM) and Peoples Revolutionary League of Ghana (PRLG) saw the INCC as a body of limited membership, serving as the 'nucleus for the eventual development of a political movement'.[42] Tsikata and Rawlings wanted a body which would be open to all and have only minor administrative functions. At first it seemed as if the left had won. The INCC became very active in coordinating the activities of all the defence committees in the country; it helped to establish some of them, it established a cadre training school at the Afienya Youth Training Centre, developed Defence Committees in the army and police force and published a newspaper, the *Nsamankow*, for its members. However, this assessment was premature. After the initial unsuccessful attempt by Rawlings to curb the organization, he changed its name to the National Defence Committee (NDC) and assumed its chairmanship in July 1982.[43] In 1984, Rawlings further consolidated his power over these organizations by transforming them into Committees for the Defence of the Revolution (CDRs) and placed them under the control of Regional Secretaries of the PNDC, who changed their tasks from that of controlling the workplace to one of mobilization.[44] In December 1984, Rawlings announced the termination of the WDCs and PDCs.

Other PNDC techniques are evident in the way the regime handled the trade unions, in relation to the problems of wages, prices and public employment reform. Right at the outsets the government realized that these aspects of the ERP would devastate the living standards of the workers and that the trade unions would be expected to mount a strong protest. The government singled out the trade unions for special concern not only because they were capable of causing widespread political unrest, but also because they were strategically located to undermine the ERP, given their pivotal role in the production process. Therefore, since early 1982, the government has been deliberately attempting to bring the unions under its control. The first strategy of the government was to take over the unions and use them to mobilize the people and the workers in an 'army of the employed' as an organized popular base to support the government in the policies that it wanted to implement.

Capitalizing on the reputation for corruption among union leaders, the PNDC used its populist image to wean many workers away from the traditional leadership. In 1982 the PNDC supported many actions of workers against their unions, up to the point of finally deposing some of the union leadership, appointing new union leaders and putting the affairs of the workers under an Interim Management Committee appointed by the PNDC.[45] In addition, the government attempted to marginalize the traditional unions by using the WDCs as counterfoils on the shop-floors, in the hope that they would then be able to gain control over the unions.[46] This strategy had only limited success, and therefore the government decided to use unambiguous frontal attacks.

These attacks involved the use of populist rhetoric, repression by state security organs, disruption of union organization and the use of other organizations such as the CDRs and NUGS to oppose union protest. The rhetorical attacks on the unions were virulent, depicting workers as selfish and threatening that the government would not tolerate the behaviour of a few union leaders acting irresponsibly. Consistent with this rhetoric, the government showed no hesitation in crushing union workers' disputes

Another group that the PNDC attempted to control was the organization of students. Due to their support of the populist rhetoric of Rawlings and the PNDC right after the coup, students were the first to rally to the revolution as a group. On 11 January 1982 they formed the Youth and Students Task Force (YSTF) and engaged in a variety of activities such as carting cocoa from the interior for export, organizing literary classes for peasants and workers and helping to organize PDCs. On 16 April 1982 the PNDC decorated the NUGS as a reward for their dedication and help. Thereafter, the PNDC made several attempts to coopt the NUGS leadership as informers with promises of jobs in the government. However, after the 1983 budget the relationship between the PNDC and NUGS went steadily downhill. By 1987 the situation was so explosive that the PNDC was sending police to the campuses to crush student demonstrations. Since then, the universities have been closed from time to time as a government response to student unrest.[47]

The government's attempt to mobilize a coalition to support its policies has not succeeded. The PDCs and WDCs had great difficulty due to some confusion in their objectives, functions and guidelines; conflicts with existing political and administrative institutions; and corruption and other abuses by ubiquitous opportunists.[48] The CDRs have not fared much better. In his speech on 31 December 1986, Rawlings admitted that these institutions had failed due to lack of resources and other organizational weaknesses.[49] The attempt by the government to reach some kind of accommodation with the radical organizations was not successful, and therefore the idea of a coalition of workers, students, defence committees soldiers and intellectuals has not materialized. On the other hand, the farmers and rural folk who stand to gain from the ERP have not been organized. The difficulties of mobilizing the population has been particularly acute in the rural areas and the relationship between the Rawlings group and the rural constituencies has continued to be cool.[50] The launching of the Mobilization Squads (Mobisquads) represented a campaign to increase the participation of rural folk in the 'revolution'. The results have been indifferent.

Other people that the Rawlings group has been trying to woo are the middle-class folk; the professionals, business and commercial elites. Since the very inception of the 'evolution', the PNDC made overtures to eminent persons to join the government and give their services to the nation. However, the suspicion with which these middle-class people view the 'revolution' and the unpredictable and threatening behaviour of the cadres, has caused them to be slow to respond. The National Commission for Democracy (NCD) has also had difficulty in mobilizing the population. For a short time, the District Assembly Elections seemed to have breathed new life into the NCD; however, the fact that a third of the membership are appointed by the PNDC has sapped some of the enthusiasm out of the population. Six years after the beginning of the revolution there were still no organizations for the mass of the people and a 'culture of silence' seems to have descended on the population.[51]

Due to the inability of the NDC government to create and maintain the coalition that can provide support for the implementation of the ERP, as well as provide general support for the government, it has had to resort to the strategies of *neutralizing* opposition through diversion, containment or elimination. One technique that the regime has used is populist rhetoric. Rawlings came into power with a certain amount of political capital with the common people, especially the urban working poor and lower classes, due to the reputation he gained in his 'first coming' as an honest, patriotic man of the people. He has continued to get some mileage from this capital in attempts to isolate some of the opposition to the policies of the PNDC. The use of this technique by members of the PNDC has been particularly noticeable in their dealings with organized labour.

One of the most potent techniques for neutralizing opposition is the pattern of violence that seems to have characterized the rule of the PNDC. Since 1982 the regime has been engaged in numerous violations of human rights, including summary executions, beatings and torture, disappearances and detention without trial. It is generally acknowledged that between 1982 and 1984, these incidents were more sporadic and unregulated. However, since the mid-1980s they seem to have been more systematic, more orchestrated and more policy-related. This pattern of activity led to the politics of intimidation, which is described by NUGS in a letter to the government: 'we are now existing under a rule of terror, an era where any view opposed to the government is crushed with weapons of destruction, where even public opinion is suppressed, press freedom is biased and the rule of law and natural justice is denied to Ghanaians'.[52] During the days of the Armed Forces Revolutionary Council (AFRC), Rawlings developed a reputation for being ruthless and tough. This reputation and the extreme violence of the first few years of the PNDC makes the direct and implied threats credible enough to intimidate the population. To support the intimidation technique, the government frequently engages in massive show of force, with armoured vehicles, anti-riot squads and fighter aircraft. This, coupled with the well-publicized activities of the Special Reserve Battalion (Commandos), the Bureau of National Investigations (BNI) and special tribunals has driven people into the notorious 'culture of silence'.

With the introduction of electoral politics the government has developed the usual methods of patronage politics, so that the offering of rewards and punishment has become an important feature of the way in which structural adjustment projects are sold to the public. For instance, prior to the election campaign in 1992 the government decided to win over the urban/worker electorate by endorsing an 80 per cent increase in a wage settlement. The blatant nature of this sort of electoral 'investment' became obvious in the following year when the government introduced a levy on fuel, followed by a further retrenchment in public employment and divestiture of several state enterprises, in order to counter the 70 per cent inflation and budget deficits. It is well-established that the success of the regime is due, at least in part, to the large sums of money spent in the rural areas in order to acquire and maintain the support of the rural constituencies.

One difficulty that faces the regime as it attempts to create a support base is the repressive nature of the government. To be sure, the government has made attempts to eradicate the harassment and brutalizing of people that characterized the initial phases of the 'revolution'. However, the harshness of the economic recovery programme and the security threats the regime has had to face from the left and the right has encouraged the government to indulge in authoritarianism and civil rights violations. Aspects of this pattern include the use of the Preventive Custody Law (1985) to detain people without due process and the arbitrary practices of some of the Public Tribunals. There is a widespread perception in Ghana that one criticizes the government at the risk of one's life or liberty. It is due, in part, to this perception that many people have sought refuge in the 'culture of silence'.

CONCLUSION

The Rawlings regime, *in both its military and elected incarnations*, has imposed on the Ghanaian public the economic liberalization policies mandated by the World Bank and the IMF in the face of intense and sustained opposition by virtually all sectors of the society. How was it able to do this? The answer seems to be found in the willingness and the ability of the regime to do a number of things. In Ghana, the first thing the regime did was to seize control of the decision-making power and then proceed to make the decisions about the economy in secrecy. Once the decision had been made to adopt the package and to implement it, the government then decided to deal with opposition within its own ranks; it isolated different groups from their potential allies, used inducements when it could and, above all, used a variety of repressive measures when they thought it was necessary against the opposition forces.[53] This is similar to the pattern of state repression in Nigeria which Julius Ihonvbere outlined in the preceding chapter.

The main opposition forces against the regime were urban low-income consumers: bureaucrats and workers. These were the people who suffered most from the adverse effects of the ERP. As a result, the most vocal protests have come from workers and their representatives. However, the workers have been joined by white-collar workers, students and leftist intellectuals. For them, the usual form of protest has been demonstrations and street action. The middle class has also suffered, but not as much as the lower classes. Ghanaian businessmen are disgruntled by the unwillingness of the government to shield them against devastating competition from foreign companies. Furthermore, the SAP has left them facing extremely high interest rates, causing them to endure lack of capital and serious liquidity problems. Thus the government seems to be facing a paradoxical situation in which it seems to be having more and more disagreements with its 'natural constituency' while receiving increasing support from the upper and middle classes who have been considered the class enemies of the 'revolution'. In addition, the rural population has been particularly difficult to organize. Consequently, the regime has found it very difficult to put together any sustained coalition to support the ERP policies. Its only alternative has been to neutralize or suppress any opposition and coerce the Ghanaian people into accepting the reforms.

Rawlings has dealt with opposition in a variety of ways:

- first, he has relied upon his residual appeal as a populist and the appeal of his rhetoric;
- second, his regime has adopted the structural reforms in a manner that effectively deflects the ill effects of the reforms away from his government;
- third, his alliance with elements in the military has allowed him to physically crush and psychologically demoralize any emerging opposition;
- fourth, he has been able to revert to lavishing patronage on his supporters and bribing sectors of the population (in the 1992 elections); and
- finally, he has effectively used the usual techniques of electoral politics to keep himself in power and to establish some legitimacy and continuity for his government.

All of this has come at some cost to the viability of both the ERP and the government. The Ghana case supports the experience of other countries in Africa, Latin America and Asia, that it is easier for an authoritarian government to suppress opposition to SAPs than it is for democratic governments. Some would argue that the programme could not even have been started if Rawlings had not captured the government through the use of force and been willing to use coercion to implement the SAP.[54] Another advantage that authoritarian regimes have in this regard is the absence of organized opposition parties. In such situations the only way for people to protest against the policies of the government are through sporadic and anomic demonstrations, or through underground activities. Of course this plays into the hands of the government, because it brings the issue into an arena in which the government can use repressive measures in the name of national security. The elimination of subversives and coup-plotters is a legitimate function of the state and Rawlings and his group have proved to be especially successful at it.[55]

However, it seems that as the government has become a little more open in the aftermath of the 1992 elections, the ability of the government to continue in this vein may have been compromised. On the other hand, the regime seems to be learning how to use other methods which may be less coercive, but more effective in their persuasiveness. As we have seen, in order to win the election in 1992, Rawlings had to revert to bribing labour by endorsing wage hikes which could not have been justified in terms of the ERP. Furthermore, he was willing to withdraw the value-added tax which led to the devastating *kumi preko* demonstrations in 1995, leading to the resignation of finance minister Kwesi Botchwey. Rawlings also agreed that the government would provide 7.4 billion cedis in redundancy pay to workers who lost their jobs.[56]

Ghana's experience demonstrates that in order to implement a structural adjustment programme, a country needs an authoritarian regime. At the very least we may have to concur with Lal's observation that the imposition of these unpopular IFI-mandated programmes requires 'courageous, ruthless and perhaps undemocratic government'.[57] Moreover, the success of the programme may depend on the ability of the government to isolate the decision-makers from all sectors of the society and a regime needs to be able to manage effectively its relations with key groups within the society in order to establish a reform coalition. Failing that, the government would have to be prepared to neutralize opposition to its policies through a mixture of incentives and coercion. Given the extreme unpopularity of these programmes, the probability is that the regime would have to be ready to use repression.

In Ghana, the Rawlings regime introduced the SAP into the country as a result of secret negotiations with the IFIs. It followed through with a concentration of power in the hands of a few top decision-makers. It attempted to ease the process of implementation by coopting all the various opposition groups, which turned out to be almost the entire country. This effort was predictably unsuccessful. Thereafter the government decided that the opposition would simply have to be neutralized, or eliminated. In this exercise, the politically weak and the powerless and the poorest sections of the society for whom the 'revolution' was supposedly launched, became the major victims of the programme. As usual the politically powerful of the society have been protected.[58] Thus the case of Ghana confirms the experience of other countries in Africa and elsewhere in Latin America and Asia, that in acting as *transmission belts* for IFI policies, the states in the South do so in ways that have maintained the position of the ruling classes.

Notes and References

1. Paul Hirst and Grahame Thompson, 'Globalization and the Future of the Nation State', *Economy and Society*, vol. 24, no. 3 (August 1995).

2. Mohameden Ould-Mey, 'Global Adjustment: Implications for Peripheral States', *Third World Quarterly*, vol. 15, no. 2 (1994).
3. Clive Thomas, *Restructuring the World Economy and its Political Implications in the Caribbean* (London: Mancel, 1989).
4. M. Ould-Mey, 'Global Adjustment', *op.cit.*, pp. 33–4.
5. For general analyses of the 31 December coup, see Donald Rothchild (ed.), *Ghana: The Political Economy of Recovery* (Boulder: Lynne Rienner, 1991); Kwame Ninsin, 'Ghanaian Politics after 1981: Revolution or Evolution', *Canadian Journal of African Studies*, vol. 21, no. 1 (1987), pp. 17–37; and Donald Ray, *Ghana: Politics, Economics and Society* (Boulder: Lynne Rienner, 1986).
6. Ho-Won Jeong, 'Ghana: Lurching Toward Economic Rationality', *World Affairs* (Washington, DC), vol. 159 (1996), pp. 64–71.
7. Jon Kraus, 'The Political Economy of Stabilization and Structural Adjustment in Ghana', in D. Rothchild (ed.), *Ghana: The Political Economy of Recovery* (Boulder: Lynne Rienner, 1991), p. 125.
8. Among these were the June Fourth Movement (JFM), the Kwame Nkrumah Revolutionary League, the Movement on National Affairs, the New Democratic Movement, the Pan-African Youth Movement and the Peoples Revolutionary League of Ghana. These radical organizations had a history of working together on many protest activities. In 1980 Rawlings had joined the JFM and became its president in the following year.
9. Kwame Ninsin, 'State, Capital and Labour Relations, 1969–87', in I. Hansen and K. A. Ninsin (eds), *The State, Development and Politics in Ghana* (London: Codesria, 1985), p. 19.
10. Jon Kraus, 'Ghana's Radical Populist Regime', *Current History* (April 1985), p. 164.
11. *People's Daily Graphic*, 12 January 1982.
12. K. Ninsin, 'Ghanian Politics After 1981', *op.cit.*, p. 24.
13. Zaya Yeebo, 'Ghana: Defence Committees and the Class Struggle', *Review of African Political Economy*, vol. 32 (1985), p. 66.
14. Eboe Hutchful, 'From "Revolution" to Monetarism: The Economics and Politics of the Structural Adjustment Programme in Ghana', in B. K. Campbell and John Loxley (eds), *Structural Adjustment in Africa* (London: Macmillan, 1989), p. 101.
15. Z. Yeebo, 'Ghana', *op.cit.*, p. 67.
16. E. Hutchful, 'From "Revolution" to Monetarism', *op.cit.*, p. 93.
17. Interview, August 1988.
18. Baffour Agyeman-Duah, 'Ghana, 1982–88: The Politics of the PNDC', *Journal of Modern African Studies*, vol. 25, no. 4 (December 1987), p. 630.
19. Donald Rothchild and E. Gyimah-Boadi, 'Ghana's Economic Decline and Development Strategies', in J. Ravenhill (ed.), *Africa in Economic Crisis* (New York: Columbia University Press, 1986), *op.cit.*,pp. 630–31.
20. J. Kraus, 'The Political Economy of Stabilization', p. 124.
21. *Ibid.*, p. 125.
22. Zaya Yeebo, *Ghana: The Struggle for Popular Power* (London: New Beacon Books, 1991), pp. 114–30.
23. J. Kraus, 'The Political Economy of Stabilization', *op.cit.*, p. 125.

24. Z. Yeebo, *Ghana*, *op.cit.*, p. 117.
25. J. Kraus, 'The Political Economy of Stabilization', *op.cit.*, pp. 186– 7.
26. J. Kraus, 'Ghana's Radical Populist Regime', *op.cit.*, p. 186.
27. D. Rothchild and E. Gyimah–Boadi, 'Ghana's Economic Decline', *op.cit.*, p. 268; and D. Ray, *Ghana*, *op.cit.*, p. 132.
28. D. Ray, *Ghana*, *op.cit.*, p. 132.
29. *West Africa*, 26 March 1984, pp. 654–5.
30. Jeffrey Herbst, *The Politics of Reform in Ghana, 1982– 91* (Berkeley: University of California Press, 1993), p. 121. The focus of the Programme of Action to Mitigate the Social Costs of Adjustment (PAMSCAD) was to find jobs for the unemployed and redeployed in small businesses and on farms; and it was designed to concentrate on projects that emphasize community initiative and the delivery of basic services to the rural and urban poor. Adotey Bing 'Ghana: Adjusting the Social Conscience', *Africa Recovery*, 26 August 1988. This programme failed because it was severely underfunded. For analyses of the economic and social effects of the ERP see Kwesi Jonah, 'The Social Impact of Ghana's Adjustment Programme, 1983–86', in B. Onimode (ed.), *The IMF, the World Bank and the African Debt* (London: Institute for African Alternatives, 1989); and J. Kraus, 'The Political Economy of Stabilization', *op.cit.*
31. K. Ninsin, 'Ghanian Politics After 1981', *op.cit.*, p. 33.
32. A.K. Yankey, 'How Ghana's Labour Movement Sees the IMF', *Lagos Guardian* (Nigeria), (December 1985), p. 10.
33. Z. Yeebo, *Ghana*, *op.cit.*, p. 276.
34. E. Gyimah-Boadi and Donald Rothchild, 'Rawlings, Populism and the Civil Liberties Tradition in Ghana', *Issues*, vol. 12, no. 3/4 (Fall/Winter 1982), p. 68.
35. Roger Tangri, 'The Politics of African Government- Business Relations in Ghana', *Journal of Modern African Studies*, vol. 30, no. 1 (1992), p. 101.
36. *West Africa*, 13 June 1988, p. 1012.
37. *Ibid.*, p. 1092.
38. Thomas M. Callaghy, 'Lost Between State and Market: The Politics of Economic Adjustment in Ghana, Zambia and Nigeria', in J. M. Nelson *Economic Crisis and Policy Choice: The Politics of Adjustment in the Third World* (Princeton, NJ: Princeton University Press, 1990), pp. 281–2.
39. Interview with Kojo Tsikata, 1988.
40. Z. Yeebo, *Ghana*, *op.cit.*, p. 92.
41. *People's Daily Graphic*, 12 January 1982.
42. Z. Yeebo, *Ghana*, *op.cit.*, p. 71.
43. *Ibid.*, p. 72.
44. See Ho-Won Jeong, 'The Structural Adjustment Programme in Ghana', *Journal of Law and Political Science*, vol. 3 (January 1995), p. 7.
45. J. Herbst, *The Politics of Reform in Ghana 1982–91*, *op.cit.*, p. 66.
46. Immanuel Hansen and Paul Collins, 'The Army, the State and the "Rawlings Revolution" in Ghana', *African Affairs*, vol. 79, no. 314 (January 1980), p. 179.
47. Z. Yeebo, *Ghana*, *op.cit.*, p. 237.

48. B. Agyeman-Duah, 'Ghana, 1982–88', *op.cit.*, p. 624.
49. *Ibid.*
50. Z. Yeebo, *Ghana, op.cit.*, p. 70.
51. *People's Daily Graphic*, 6 April 1987.
52. NUGS statement, 1983.
53. See H.-W. Jeong, 'The Structural Adjustment Programme in Ghana', *op.cit.*
54. J. Herbst, *The Politics of Reform in Ghana, 1982–91, op.cit.*, p. 46.
55. During the first ten years of the regime there were upwards of 15 documented unsuccessful attempts to topple the government. This is evidence of the ineptitude of the coup-plotters, luck and the extraordinary effectiveness of the regime's security system.
56. H.-W. Jeong, 'Ghana', *op.cit.*, p. 4.
57. Deepak Lal, *The Poverty of 'Development' Economics* (London: IEA, 1983), p. 33.
58. Z. Yeebo, *Ghana, op.cit.*, p. 205.

11 Liberalization and Retrenchment in the Middle East and North Africa

Manochehr Dorraj

INTRODUCTION

The two predominant forces of social change in the Third World in the late twentieth century are religious revivalism and democratization. The emergence of this new apparently contradictory phenomenon is itself a byproduct of globalization and the two divergent forces of economic integration and cultural particularism that it puts in motion. The magnitude and vibrance of these two phenomena in the Middle East and North Africa have been quite divergent. While Islamic revivalism has been the predominant social force in the region in the last two decades, the forces of democratization and their achievements have been relatively meagre and negligible. Another peculiarity of democratization in the region is its convergence with Islamic. Due to global and regional religious revival, and the political weaknesses of secular forces, Islamists have been in the best position in many parts of the Muslim World to take advantage of political openings and mobilize themselves for contestation of political power. This reality has put the issue of compatibility of Islam and democracy to the forefront of political debate among Muslim theologians, intellectuals and western academicians. Reconciling a sacred faith with democracy, whose historical roots are attributed to western cultural and institutional traditions, has posed a host of challenges for theoreticians as well as political practitioners.

It is instructive, for didactic purposes, to make a distinction between *democratization* and *liberalization* and to define our terminologies. *Political liberalization* is defined as a process that involves 'the expansion of public space through the recognition and protection of civil and political liberties, particularly those bearing upon the ability of citizens to engage in free political discourse and to freely organize in pursuit of common interest'. *Political democratization* 'entails an expansion of political participation in such a way as to provide citizens with a degree of real and meaningful collective control over public policy'.[1] Given the fact that elite-initiated political compacts in the Middle East and North Africa remain highly manipulated, and free contestation of political power is not yet a part of the rules of the game, it is more appropriate to speak of possibilities of liberalization and not democratization in the region. In fact, while the desire on the part of the masses for freedom and political participation is genuine, what has transpired in many parts of the Middle East and North Africa in the last decade can be described as a facade liberalization in which the elite tolerates freedom of speech, press and assembly, only insofar as its power is not seriously threatened. When the opposition becomes menacing, those in power quickly employ the old tactics of intimidation and repression to remind the opposition who are the real wielders of power and the enormity of the price that the opponents would have to pay to challenge the regime. Therefore, it is more appropriate to describe the Middle Eastern experiment with liberalization as one where the political power would be less authoritarian and arbitrary rather than democratic in the western sense of the word.

This chapter consists of three central parts. The first focuses on the problematics of liberalization and retrenchment, the causes and the preconditions of liberalization, and the obstacles to it. The second part delineates the tensions between Islam and democracy, and in the final part I analyse studies of liberalization in Algeria, Egypt and Jordan, with a particular focus on the role of Islamist groups and the state response to them in the last decade. The chapter concludes by offering observations on the limitations of the Middle Eastern liberalization experiment and charts a dialectic of liberalization and retrenchment that moulds the dynamic of the present struggle between the forces of change and the forces of the status quo.

THE GLOBAL AND REGIONAL CAUSES OF LIBERALIZATION

The causes of liberalization in the last decade are both international and domestic. Because the internal political life in many parts of the region is stifled, the intellectuals eagerly follow what happens abroad and draw inferences for the domestic scene. The impact of the global democratization which began in the 1970s in Spain, Greece and

Portugal, and continued in Latin America, the former Soviet Union and Eastern Europe in the 1980s, ushered in a new era of political awakening among the masses and dictated a new course of action to the authoritarian regimes of the Middle East and North Africa. The shift in global and regional political realities increasingly rendered liberalization not only a desirable, but also a necessary option for maintaining long-term stability. Closely related to this was the demonstration effect of the global movement toward democratization in the Third World. Middle Eastern leaders had to either face the realities of the new global environment in which they were functioning, or run the risk of becoming increasingly irrelevant. Hence, the fate of such dictators as Romania's Ceausescu, who seemed invincible only a few months prior to his execution, did not go unnoticed among the Middle Eastern autocrats. The message was loud and clear: reform or face the possibility of violent revolution and death.

Because of the global communications revolution and the sprawling of satellite television, videos, faxes, e-mails and so on, authoritarian leaders can no longer insulate their people and keep them ignorant of political realities outside as well as inside the country. The fall of the Soviet Union and the collapse of Communism in East and Central Europe were also significant. Since some of the Middle Eastern countries such as Algeria, Libya and Syria had partially opted for command economies as the Soviets abandoned socialism, and in pursuit of new trade partners and economic investment had abandoned their former allies, these countries had to opt for privatization and economic reform as well. The change in policies of the IMF and the World Bank made the reception of their loans contingent upon implementation of 'structural reforms'. This policy encouraged privatization of state-owned enterprises, put an end to state monopoly of foreign trade, removed barriers to free trade, and abandoned state subsidies in order to trim the bloated state expenditure. To be sure, in many parts of the Middle East and North Africa, privatization and economic liberalization has been accompanied by the persistence of repression and authoritarianism.

Insofar as the dismantling of a command economy reduces state control of the economy, it also reduces the resources available to the state to maintain total control over the society. Though uneven in some cases, for the most part the diffusion of economic power may also enhance the diffusion of political power.[2] But this is only one side of the story. While many Middle Eastern regimes have opted for economic liberalization and marketization, they have resisted political liberalization. Syria, Libya and Iran provide clear examples. Moreover, insofar as privatization and the disappearance of state subsidies removes a social safety network for the poor, and expands the gap between the rich and the poor, economic liberalization can actually pauperize the poor and render political liberalization a meaningless exercise for a large sector of the population. Privatization and expansion of free trade, designed to further integrate the Middle East into the global economy, also makes the region more susceptible to the boom and bust cycles prevalent in a capitalist system. While the vast resources of many western nations would enable them to withstand such crises, the meagre resources of many Middle Eastern nations would make it arduous to bear the social and economic cost of such upheavals. Therefore, the contradictory consequences of economic liberalization may function as a catalyst for, as well as an obstacle to, democratic consolidation insofar as it requires eliciting the support of the lower classes.[3]

Among the important domestic factors responsible for political liberalization are the decline of oil prices since 1986. The plummeting of oil prices and the inability of the government to buy off the opposition has forced the elite to grant concessions. As the political costs of repression, demonstrated by the fate of the Shah of Iran, proved to be too high, and the state's ability to buy off political acquiescence diminished, many regimes opted for token power-sharing and social compacts. Algeria provides a good example. Another major factor was the debt crisis: prior to 1992, the burden of the debt crisis in countries such as Egypt, Yemen, Morocco and Algeria further exacerbated the financial crisis of the state and compelled it to allow electoral participation in order to stave off genuine democratization in which the contestation of power is permitted.

By the 1980s, the Middle Eastern middle class had come into its own. Its ranks were swelling, and it was becoming more conscious, mature and politically seasoned. Hence, the incipient civil society, the associational life and non-governmental organizations were sprouting throughout Middle Eastern cities. The middle class had the aspiration as well as the instruments for a more substantial voice in the process of decision-making. Finally, with the Iranian revolution of 1979 having run its course, and the Shi'ite political extremism of the 1980s highlighted by car bombing and hostage-taking having reached a dead end, the majority of the Muslim activists of the 1990s were increasingly disposed to opt for the ballot box and electoral politics as a tactic to achieve their goals. These factors pressured the elites to enter into social compacts and open up the political process, albeit with limited and manipulated scope.

LIBERALIZATION AND CIVIL SOCIETY

Civil society is defined as a 'melange of associations, guilds, syndicates, federations, unions, parties, and groups come together to provide a buffer between state and citizen'.[4] Civil society is that area of social life that is neither familial and intimate, nor state-controlled and directed. It includes non-governmental and voluntary organizations, guilds, associations, interest groups and political parties. The more powerful are such non-governmental instruments of interest-articulation and political participation, the more likely the prospects for liberalization. Others also add the issues of civility, denoting tolerance, respect for intellectual pluralism and democratic ethos as essential components of a civil society.[5] The emergence of non-governmental organizations without a tradition of civility may not culminate in the creation of a vibrant civil society.

Civil society aggregates, mitigates and mediates between the people and the state in an attempt to influence policy. It is also a temporal and cultural phenomenon in the sense that it assumes different forms in different polities and cultures. Moreover, civil society is not a cause of democracy; it is a prerequisite for it. Civil society does not flourish under the following three conditions: a state of revolution, foreign intervention and absolute dictatorships. Revolution polarizes the society and is based on mass mobilization. Often, organizations deemed as 'counter-revolutionary' are suppressed, and mass mobilization from above may replace genuine participation from below. Foreign intervention, based on subjugation and domination of native population leaves no room for interest-articulation of such forces. Dictatorships also stifle any semblance of independent political organization that may become an alternative to the state power. A vibrant civil society may emerge as a result of steady economic growth, the increasing strength of the middle class, the emergence of non-governmental organizations and popular demand for participation. But a civil society may also emerge when the political order collapses due to war, conflict or corruption. In such cases the emergence of a civil society may be linked to weak national integration and the rise of ideological and communal groups. Amidst the political vacuum induced by the collapse of the central government, in search of empowerment, such groups can play an instrumental role in creating a political space between the state and society at large.[6]

The state's strategy in regard to civil society is varied. In some places it has used either political pressure or reward, or a combination of the two, to coopt the opposition. An example of this strategy can be found in Jordan, Turkey, Yemen and Kuwait. Another strategy has been the penetration of non-governmental organizations by the ruling party, as has occurred in Syria. The third policy option is the complete suppression of the civil society, as is the case in Iraq, Sudan and Libya. Despite its immense poverty and social problems, Egypt, which has one of the more vibrant civil societies in the Arab World, is considered to have a better prospect for liberalization than the rest of the region. The prospects for civil society in Tunisia also seem promising. With no powerful military competing with the ruling party for power, no ethnic conflict, a large and well-educated middle class and a decentralized economy, Tunisia is in a better position than most Arab nations to develop a viable civil society.

In countries where a centralized dictatorship has decimated the civil society, such as Iraq, Sudan and Libya, the prospects for liberalization are slim as long as the present authoritarian regimes stay in power. In Yemen, where the state bureaucracy and coercive apparatus are not powerful institutions, some gains have been made to liberalize the political system, despite the country's poverty. Whereas the petrodollar has bestowed enormous wealth upon the Saudi monarchy to centralize its power and buy off or suppress the opposition, the Jordanian monarchy, lacking such resources and facing a politicized populace, has been forced to opt for liberalization and token power-sharing as the survival strategy in an age when monarchs are endangered species. In the past, the absence of democracy in the Middle East was attributed to the existence of authoritarian regimes and the weaknesses of associational life. Now, with the emergence of Islamist movements, 'the explanation shifts to one emphasizing that Middle East societies are so strong that they are in danger of overpowering the state'.[7]

The failure of democracy in the Middle East has been attributed to numerous factors. Some scholars consider the patrimonial and paternal political culture of the region – in which kinship, tribal, sectarian, and ethnic loyalties take precedence over national goals and civic values – as an impediment to the growth of autonomous and democratic institutions.[8] The social grip of neo-patrimonialism over the society has proven to be resilient indeed. This is why one observer concludes that 'the most interesting Western democratic models for this part of the world are not so much those founded on national/individual/democracy as those where a certain degree of community organization is seen to be legitimate'.[9] The primacy of collectivity and corporate organization over the individual has deep roots in Islamic history. Therefore, the challenge is to dissect how the modern state, while providing an alternative source of loyalty to the religious, tribal and ethnic attachments, in a dialectical twist and through its authoritarian nature simultaneously reinforces the bonds of the primordial. One may take refuge in the primordial in the face of the omnipresent repressive hand of the state. In such circumstances the individual has a precarious existence, and the passage available for democratic political life remains fraught with obstacles and constraints.

Hence, individual liberty is the result of a delicate balancing act between state power and the grip of primordial loyalties (the *asabiyya*). As Salame notes,

> individual liberty therefore, means to use the new state to relax the hold of *asabiyya* so as to emerge from its system of values, to rebel against its established powers, while still parading the original *asabiyya* in an attempt to limit the growing ascendency, authoritarian if not arbitrary, of the state apparatus in the process of being established.[10]

This dialectical relationship between state power and primordial loyalties also has a global dimension in which the integrative and homogenizing forces of globalization instigate the rise of cultural particularism, ethnic, national and religious identities. It is in this unfolding dialectic that the rise of the primordial loyalties in the postmodern world (including the Middle East) must be understood. Only by building viable institutions capable of rising above such loyalties can the traditional patron–client relationships, pervasive in the region, be surpassed, and the ruler and the ruled be bound on the basis of a new social contract.

Others see the weaknesses of civil society as the major impediment to democratization.[11] Due to long years of political repression and authoritarian rule, non-governmental organizations and associational life have not yet established themselves. Thus, the weaknesses of civil society render the power of the state unchallenged. Insofar as the state remains the only source of information and dispensation, and the independent vehicles of interest-articulation continue to be feeble, the public has very few resources to defend its rights. This predominant role of the state has led some scholars to conclude that 'the key element on the road that may lead to democracy is the state, rather than individual, the community, the nation, the class, or the market; and moreover it preceded these other elements too'.[12] Although the primacy of the state, given its enormous resources and the monopoly of power, cannot be understated, it is also the case that the Middle Eastern state remains vulnerable to mass and community action, not to mention the subverting forces of the market and globalization.[13]

Yet, others consider Islam incompatible with democracy, and perceive Islamic culture as a major obstacle to democratization.[14] Given the predominant role of Islamic culture in political and social life, and the recent rise of Islamic revivalism, it is imperative to further discuss the tension between Islam and democracy and to briefly sketch the role of Islamists and the state's response in the process of liberalization in the last decade.

ISLAM, DEMOCRACY AND LIBERALIZATION

The theoretical issues surrounding the compatibility of Islam and democracy are numerous and complex and they constitute a separate area of study that the limitations of space would not permit us to explore here. In this chapter we are concerned with how attempts at liberalization which have been submerged by Islamic revivalism, and the emergence of Islamic movements as the main opposition forces, have manifested themselves in the political arena. In other words, we are more interested in exploring Islamists' political agenda and the state's policy response as it pertains to liberalization and retrenchment. This is the same task which Behzad Yaghmaian undertakes in the following chapter on Iran.

There are two views on the compatibility of Islam and democracy. First, there is a liberal view which holds that because democratic states are based on the separation of religion and politics, Islam and democracy cannot be reconciled. Since Islamists present themselves as the sole representatives of a revealed religious truth, they cannot respect the principle of intellectual pluralism and democratic governance in the western sense of the word. The second view is the Islamist interpretation, as enunciated by Muslim traditionalists, which is essentially communitarian rather than democratic. It places priority on the religious foundation of the state rather than on its democratic content. In other words, its primary objective is to enforce the rule of Shari'a

(Islamic law), safeguard the sanctity of Islamic moral ideals, and create an Islamic order. It is less concerned with whether such a social order would be democratic or authoritarian. Hence, while some Islamic societies may conduct 'free and fair elections', they often lack the supporting structures, the high level of development, the democratic ethos of tolerance and intellectual pluralism, and the viable civil society that are necessary for a successful democracy. Nonetheless, the impact of the Iranian revolution on the one hand, and the political illegitimacy of the state and its inability to provide the basic goods and services on the other, have contributed to the increasing appeal of political Islam since 1979.

As the economic crisis mounts throughout the Muslim world, and the state has proved incapable of providing for basic needs, many Islamic groups have emerged as agents of social welfare and providers of goods and services. Muslim charitable non-governmental organizations are active in providing free health care, education, low interest loans and community services and renovations. This not only has enhanced their popularity, but it has also positioned them to act as an alternative source of power. Indeed, in many parts of the region Islamist organizations have been transformed into movements of grassroots participation and empowerment, especially among the lower echelons of society. By embracing their religious faith, those who are materially underprivileged and poor compensate for their low economic status by feelings of moral superiority that religious conviction bestows upon the individual.

Because of the suppression of secular and socialist forces throughout the Middle East and North Africa, with the political openings made possible by liberalization of the last decade, Islamists have found themselves in the best possible position to harvest the fruits of this new political atmosphere. In order to cope with the new global and regional realities discussed above, the Islamists began to reassess the former politics of fury and wrath prevalent in the early 1980s, and for the most part they have opted for a more moderate course of parliamentary and electoral politics in the last decade. Political liberalization and the participation of the incipient civil society in decision-making, albeit distorted and manipulated, became, in Binder's words, increasingly 'self-evident and meaningful to the mass and the elite alike' in many parts of the region.[15]

In recent years, parts of the Muslim world have witnessed certain attempts to expand political participation, which have included allowing the opposition to run candidates and participate in electoral politics, relaxing the tight censorship of the press and tolerating greater freedom of speech, albeit limited and controlled. These developments have been most vivid and prominent in Algeria, Egypt and Jordan. The study of Islamists in these countries and the state's response sheds light on their increasingly significant role in the process of liberalization. It also reveals some of the complexities and nuances in the dialectics of liberalization and retrenchment in the region.

Algeria

The plummeting of oil prices in 1986 and the Algerian government's imposition of austerity programmes instigated several days of rioting in 1988 in which young Muslims figured prominently. Starting in 1987, several major developments indicated that the new Islamic awakening had developed deep roots in Algerian society. In July, 187 Muslim militants were put on trial for 'plotting' against the state. Although the violence of the extremists received the widest attention from the media, this event signified the depth of discontent in Algerian society. Islamic organizations originating around small groups of intellectuals, clergymen or cells on the margin of politics had entered into the mainstream by establishing their movements on local and municipal levels. This trend was reflected in the burgeoning number of private Islamic institutions and the growing public accommodation of Muslim tenets in Algeria. In 1987, an estimated 6000 schools and 3000 clinics had been established by Islamic groups or individuals.[16] By February 1989, the socialist government of Benjedid was clearly losing ground to the Islamists when the majority of Algerian people approved a new constitution, intended to end the ruling National Liberation Front's monopoly on power.[17]

In some of the other North African countries, opposition political parties are banned. In Libya, for example, politics is intended to have popular participation, but the creation of political parties and organizations independent of the state is banned. As a result, the people enjoy no free elections and have little voice in retaining their current leadership. What opposition there is remains trapped in the popular committees, which are not subject to general election. In Algeria, however, during Benjedid's second-term presidency after the constitutional revisions of 1989 were approved, opposition parties permeated the political landscape. After the constitutional revision of 1989, voting became mandatory under Algerian law. This legitimized the existence of independent political parties alongside the National Liberation Front (FLN), thus opening the door for multi-party elections.[18]

The new constitution came into effect later in 1990 when the FLN, Algeria's leading party, legalized 20 political parties, a free press and the liberalization of the economy. Though considered the 'boldest democratic experiment in the Arab world', Algeria's ruling party was not rewarded for its initiatives.[19] In fact, it was later defeated by Islamists in municipal elections. The Islamic Salvation Front (FIS) captured 54 per cent of the vote whereas the FLN captured only 34 per cent. Therefore, faced with a combination of violent public demonstrations against the government austerity programme since 1986, ushering in the constitutional reform of 1989, the government of President Benjedid was compelled to concede to political liberalization. The June 1990 local elections demonstrated government commitment to liberalization. The government not only allowed for political contestation, but at least temporarily it seemed to have accepted its defeat at the hands of its political rival, the Islamic Salvation Front. The victory of the FIS, however, alarmed foreign investors. Equating Islamic revivalism with the political and economic risks associated with the possible action of extremists, many investors withdrew much needed capital for economic reconstruction.

There was also a widely-shared fear among the secular forces that the ascendance of Islamists might represent the ushering in of 'a reign of virtue and terror'. However, these reactions were more accurately 'a referendum on the postcolonial state and its entire baggage: one-party rule, the command economy and the repressive state'.[20] The so-called defeat of secularism indicated the widespread malaise and dissatisfaction in Algerian society. For the young urban poor and the half-educated masses who make up to 60 per cent of Algeria's 24 million people, the saga of the ruling party and its 'combatants' mobilizing the Algerian nation in its struggle against France is ancient history. They have no memory of the 1956 revolution. Thus, the FLN leadership cannot appeal to them on the basis of their revolutionary credentials or nationalist legitimacy. In their lifetime the state has devoured independent institutions, labour unions, professional associations, political parties and the bazaar.[21] Islam was the only social and cultural force that the state could neither devour nor ignore and the only force capable of maintaining any ideological rigour to mobilize the opposition. Therefore, in the elections of 1989 and 1990 Algerians were voting as much against a corrupt and repressive system as for Islam.

The leaders of the 1956 revolution had used Islam effectively to rally the people against French dominance. After the revolution they continued to use Islam to legitimize a one- party socialist rule. Whereas 'secular Islam' seemed successful until the late 1970s, by then, partially inspired by the example of Iranian revolution, a populist Islam was emerging to fill a desire for a more personal and politicized faith. Amidst increased centralization and bureaucratization of power and a declining economy, the ideological appeal of political Islam grew.[22] For the young generation with no memory of the Algerian revolution, Islam was also the source of identity and cultural authenticity. While the state had integrated all of Islam's 'official' institutions into the government, unofficial mosques began to spring up all over the country funded by private sources.[23] The Islamists not only wanted the state to enforce the Shari'a, but they also aspired to create an Islamic government and build a new Islamic society. This explains why they called for a boycott of the constitutional referendum of February 1989. So far as the FIS were concerned, the new constitution would not have enhanced the Islamization of the Algerian society. Hence, as the government proved incapable of providing the basic goods and services for the populace – a reality accentuated by plummeting oil revenues since the oil price crash in 1986 and the ensuing earthquake of 1989 – the mosques and the FIS stepped in to provide such services. The mosques also provided Qur'anic lessons for an increasing number of believers, thus proselytizing and politicizing them in the process.[24]

As the FIS ranks grew, so did the divisions within it. Sheikh Abbas Madani, for example, approved of a multi-party democratic system; his firebrand deputy Imam Ali Belhadj considered anything short of establishment of an Islamic government and society unacceptable. The violence and intolerance of the extremist wing of the FIS alienated more moderate Islamic groups, such as HAMAS, and eroded its base of support among the people. HAMAS, one of the main rivals of the FIS, denounced a one-party Islamic system and called for the creation of an Islamic society through a gradual, nonviolent course of action.[25] In April 1991, Benjedid moved to change the electoral laws, including banning political campaigns in the mosques, forbidding proxy voting and dividing Algeria into 500 constituencies to be elected through unified lists. This was a clear attempt to curb the influence of the FIS and culminated in clashes between government and FIS forces. By June 1991, these violent confrontations escalated leading to the arrest of FIS leaders Belhadj and Madani and the postponement of the scheduled legislative and presidential elections. The FIS scored an impressive victory in the first round of legislative elections held on 26 December 1991, winning 189 of the 430 seats, compared to 20 for the secular socialist forces (FFS) and 16 for the FLN. After the overwhelming FIS victory, Benjedid reportedly had worked out a power-sharing agreement with the FIS leaders.

Benjedid had his own reasons for accommodating the Islamists. Facing their growing strength, he realized that the old method of repression and intimidation would no longer be a long-term deterrent against the growth of their movement. Instead, by inviting them into the government where they would be subjected to the same degree of day-to-day scrutiny and criticism placed on his government, he hoped that he would be able to weaken if not coopt them. But under pressure from the army, Benjedid resigned. Then, the second round of runoff national elections, set for 16 January 1992, which would have given the FIS a strong parliamentary majority, was canceled. Subsequently, the FIS, which had enjoyed a legal status since 1989, was banned. The elections were postponed hoping the government would be able to improve the deteriorating economic conditions, which included 22 per cent unemployment and spiraling inflation. Clearly the Algerian secular elite sees the roots of FIS appeal in deplorable economic conditions and hopes that improving the economy will weaken the base of support for the FIS.

After the resignation of Benjedid and the appointment of an emergency council of national salvation, made up mainly of the FLN leaders, the army and the security apparatus carried out a 'soft-gloved coup'; the government announced a state of emergency and clamped down on the opposition. The government-appointed court declared the FIS unconstitutional on the grounds that no party can claim to represent Islam. Islam is the religion of all Algerians, the government argued; therefore, no group could monopolize the mantle of Islam for political purposes. A five- member committee led by Mohammad Boudiaf, one of the former leaders of the FLN in exile in Morocco since 1963, replaced Benjedid. The two FIS leaders, Abbas Madani and Ali Belhadj, were sentenced to 12 years imprisonment each, and many lesser known members and supporters of FIS were executed or imprisoned. Many who had won local and regional elections on the FIS ticket were also arrested and the councils and assemblies in which the FIS had done well were dissolved. These policies were followed by street demonstrations and violent clashes between the army and FIS supporters in which many died and thousands were arrested and persecuted by the security forces. These events abruptly halted the liberalization process in Algeria. The return of repression is also indicative of the tenuousness and fragility of liberalization in the Third World, especially when political liberalization is not accompanied by the expansion of economic rights – that is, adequate food, clothing, shelter, medical care, employment and the ability to make a decent living.

The assassination of Benjedid's successor, President Boudiaf, by an alleged FIS supporter in June 1992 further damaged the possibility of reconciliation between the government and the FIS in the near future. As the government campaign of crackdown against FIS supporters intensified in the ensuing months and years, Algeria's short-lived romance with liberalization, which had opened up a glimmer of hope in many parts of the region, came to a tragic end. The government of Zeroul that replaced Boudiaf had to face the hardening position of the Islamic opposition and come to terms with terrorist activities of the armed Islamic group (GIA), a splinter from FIS. The activities of this group since 1994 have included the assassination of French and Italian citizens, as well as Algerians who are associated with the military regime. The kidnapping of Yemeni and Omani ambassadors, and the launching of attacks against the French embassy have been among other major activities of the group.

In 1994, President Zeroul, known as a conciliator, met with the imprisoned leaders of FIS and called for a dialogue with all political forces. But FIS and GIA were not among the groups that responded to his call. In September 1994, the two leaders of FIS, Madani and Belhadj, were released from prison. Since his release from prison, facing the suspicions that he intended to create an Islamic totalitarian state, Madani has asserted his respect for constitutional and democratic rule and a peaceful transition of power. These developments, however, did not help to alter the course of violence chosen by the GIA extremists or some of the ranks of FIS armed attachment (AIS). As the cycle of violence, which has cost many innocent civilian lives, continues, a sector of the Algerian military establishment sees the non-negotiation and the military defeat of GIA as the only solution to the present impasse of violence and bloodshed. It is not clear how much authority Zeroul exercises over this faction of the army. These developments clearly indicate that in light of a sagging economy and declining legitimacy, the political space in which the Algerian elite can maneuver is shrinking considerably.

Egypt

Some of the first tentative steps to opening up Egyptian society were taken under the rule of President Anwar Sadat. Sadat's economic *infitah* (liberalization), however, was accompanied by increased bureaucratization of power and rampant corruption. Sadat was preoccupied with his image abroad and at home. To forge a democratic image, and to create a loyal opposition, he founded the Socialist Labour Party in 1978 and put it under the leadership of his brother-in-law while banning the real opposition parties, such as the New Wafd and the National Unionist Progressive parties. In 1981, he also banned the Socialist Labour Party after it escaped his control. Therefore, Sadat's claim of pluralism was a sham from the outset.[26] He also made the mistake of attacking all of his Muslim opponents. Instead of distinguishing between extremist underground groups and mainstream religious organizations, he attacked the Islamic movement as a whole. This policy engendered the radicalization and fostered the unity of the Islamic opposition. In addition, his attempt at indiscriminate adaptation of western culture and his political accommodation of Israel further alienated the Islamic majority of Egyptian citizens.

Sadat's economic policies also polarized Egyptian society by widening the gap between the rich and poor. His policies brought 'materialism but not prosperity' and further undermined the Egyptians' faith in their government to create real economic reform.[27] Thus Sadat, though claiming political and economic reform, was not taking any real strides towards democracy, but only tiptoeing around the same authoritarian structures which had for centuries served despotic rulers. As dissent began to mount and legal political parties were banned, the opposition resorted to violence.[28] On 6 October 1981, Sadat fell victim to his own policies and was assassinated by Muslim extremists.

Having observed the fate of his predecessor and the Shah of Iran, Sadat's successor, Hosni Mubarak, took steps to open up Egyptian society and improve the lagging economy. Mubarak chose to accommodate the opposition by allowing them to participate in the political system, and he permitted the certification of a variety of diverse opposition parties. Laws passed in 1986 allowed the independents one representative per district. In 1987, opposition parties won 108 of 448 seats, the largest ever since the formation of the Egyptian parliamentary system in 1924.[29] Mubarak has also tolerated opposition by allowing a 'lively' opposition press to emerge and operate. This policy is an important step away from traditional oppressive measures and authoritarian policies and has enhanced the growth of associational life and non-governmental organizations.

Another major consequence of Mubarak's accommodationist policies of the 1980s was the deradicalization of a considerable sector of the Islamic opposition. Mubarak allowed moderate Islamic groups to compete more openly in the political system, a policy that has led to the isolation of the extremist wing and tempered the moderate opposition. Many Muslim leaders advocated 'incremental social change through peaceful dialogue, patient politicking, and personal example'.[30] Thus, through toleration, Mubarak managed to temporarily tame the core of the radical Islamic opposition Sadat had indirectly created through repression.

The change in political orientation of the Muslim Brotherhood also played a significant role in ushering in a new era of compromise and accommodation between the Islamists and the secular state in Egyptian politics. Realizing that the politics of confrontation had produced meagre results in the past, the Muslim Brotherhood seized the opportunity provided by Mubarak's conciliatory overtures to Islamicize society gradually through legislation and eliciting governmental support to enact Islamic laws.

As the economic crisis of Egyptian society intensified in the 1980s, rendering the government incapable of providing some of the basic public services, the Muslim Brotherhood and its umbrella organizations stepped in to fill the void. Islamists have established alternative schools, day-care centres, health-care clinics and many other guilds and associations. These organizations work under the rubric of *jamiyyat khayriyya* (Muslim charitable associations). As these Islamic charitable organizations expand throughout Egypt, they have become more than mere public service outlets. They have been transformed into organs of self-control, local autonomy, mass mobilization, and grassroots participation. Realizing the extent of their popularity, the government has provided these organizations with funds in an attempt to prevent their conversion into organs of dual power. In so doing, Mubarak's regime hopes to take some credit for the success of these organizations. Meanwhile the government, aspiring to associate itself with these popular movements, often totally manipulates and dominates these organizations for its own ends. Although some associations and non-governmental organizations have succumbed to the pervasive corruption of the Egyptian society, others have developed a life and dynamism of their own, often filling the vacuum created by the decline of state and its inability to provide basic goods and services.

Faced with the increasing popularity of Islam and its cultural and institutional symbols, Mubarak's regime opted to patronize 'the moderate' Islamic trend, the Muslim Brotherhood. Through such state-supported Islamic institutions as al-Azhar, the Ministry of Awqaf (religious endowments), and the Supreme Council of Islamic Affairs, the regime took the initiative to carry out the policy of Islamization from above as a safeguard against any radical initiative from below. Consequently, Egyptian society has gradually become Islamicized through the sanctions and blessings of a secular state. The Shari'a has become the official source of legislation, all publications must abide by an Islamic code of censorship, the discussion of Islamic subject matters in mass media is overwhelming and the president officially inaugurates the main religious events. The government has also taken an active role in building mosques and establishing Muslim associations and Qur'an schools. While accommodating the moderate wing of the Islamic movement, the government has not hesitated to crack down on its more militant wing. During 1989–90, for example, thousands of activists who demanded the full implementation of Islamic law were arrested. Members of 'Salvation from Hell' were imprisoned for creating a paramilitary organization which had 'declared Egypt's rulers and society "infidel" and attempted to kill two cabinet ministers and a journalist who had denounced the activists as religious extremists'.[31]

More positive attitudes towards the democratic rules of the political game and the Muslim Brotherhood's willingness to participate in the political process have evoked an accommodating response from Mubarak's regime. Mubarak's overture toward the Muslim Brotherhood has further legitimized them, breaking the barrier of fear prevalent in authoritarian states. Consequently, mass support for the Brotherhood has increased in the past decade. Their base of support cuts across class lines, but they are particularly strong among educated middle-class professionals and their organizations. The 1987 election results were indicative of the Muslim Brotherhood's growing strength. Whereas in the 1984 parliamentary elections, in alliance with the New Wafd party, they gained 15 seats in parliament, in 1987, in alliance with the Socialist Labour Party, they gained 23 seats. Due to new electoral laws which abolished the old-party list in favour of individual candidates and thus put the large parties at a disadvantage, the Muslim Brotherhood decided to boycott the election of 1990.

Because of its access to state resources and the concomitant power of dispensing patronage, the ruling National Democratic Party (NDP) has a privileged position in any electoral competition. The NDP won 73 per cent of the votes in the 1984 parliamentary election, 70 per cent in 1987, and 80 per cent in 1990. Since the 1992 crackdown on

Islamists in Algeria, the Egyptian government also escalated its crackdown of the two extremist Islamic groups, Gamaat Islamiya and El Jihad. Gamaat Islamiya, in turn, has intensified its attack on government officials, intellectuals they perceive to be critical of Islam, and tourists. Attacks on tourists are designed to financially paralyze the Egyptian government which heavily relies on income from tourism. In 1994, the government stepped up its anti- terrorist campaign and arrested as many as 10 000 members and supporters of the two Islamic organizations. Using the ruling national democratic party's 80 per cent majority in parliament, Mubarak's government has passed legislation to curb the influence of the Muslim Brotherhood in trade unions, bar associations and other non-governmental organizations. The Muslim Brotherhood has not as yet been formally recognized as a legal political party and cannot run candidates directly.

These events clearly demonstrate the limitations of elite- initiated democratization. Once unleashed, however, the democratic process has a life and dynamics of its own. Government patronage of moderate Islam and its support for Islamic programmes and institutions has further legitimized the Islamization of Egyptian society. Among the inadvertent outcomes of this process are that an Islamic society may find a secular state increasingly irrelevant and unsuitable for the conduct of its affairs, or that the secular elite may have to go through an Islamic metamorphosis and 'rediscover' its Islamic roots in order to survive. The Mubarak government has opted for the latter strategy.

Jordan

In contrast to Egypt, which is deeply steeped in the history and traditions of its illustrious past civilization, Jordan is one of the most artificial countries of the Fertile Crescent States, one whose very existence is challenged by the commitment of the large segment of its population to Palestinian nationalism. Jordan came into existence after the disintegration of the Ottoman Empire at the end of World War I. The British partitioned Transjordan, thus defining the territory of Jordan. The creation of the State of Israel in 1948 and the loss of the West Bank and Jerusalem to Israel in the 1967 war further accentuated the insecurity of Jordan's borders. These factors have made Jordanian nationalism comparatively weak and diffused. Thus, the binding ideological force in the country's political life has been Islam and the monarchy. This fact partially explains the recent success of the Muslim Brotherhood in Jordanian politics.

The Muslim Brotherhood was founded in Jordan in 1934. From the outset, the relationship between the monarchy (King Abdullah) and the Islamists was one of mutual accommodation. Both sides had found such relations expedient as well as beneficial. Even when King Hussein banned all political parties in 1957, the Muslim Brotherhood was allowed to continue its political activities, which included participating in electoral and parliamentary elections. Therefore, in contrast to Egypt where the history of the Muslim Brotherhood until very recently was marked with violent and bloody clashes with the state, in Jordan the opposite is largely true. This, however, does not suggest that the relationship has been free of conflicts. For example, faced with deteriorating relations between Syria and Jordan, King Hussein used the Muslim Brotherhood to organize paramilitary camps on the Syrian border in 1980, but as the relations between the two countries improved, the king publicly attacked the Brotherhood and ordered the arrest of some of their leaders in 1985.

Several important factors prompted King Hussein's decision to open up the political system in Jordan. First, the major component of the Jordanian economy, the remittances of its guest workers in the Gulf states, began unravelling with the plummeting of oil prices from $38/barrel in 1981 to $9/barrel in 1986. The depleting oil income of the Gulf states forced them to replace their educated Palestinian labour force from Jordan with less expensive Pakistani and Indian workers. Tens of thousands of Palestinian guest workers left the Gulf states for Jordan by 1988. This homeward migration compounded the unemployment problem in Jordan. According to one estimate, between 1990 and 1995, 35 per cent of professionals (teachers, engineers and scientists) were unemployed and 50 per cent of all university graduates could not find jobs. The unemployment became particularly acute in the period leading up to the Gulf war. The Gulf war also exacerbated the economic problems of Jordan by disrupting the link to Jordan's all-important trade partner, Iraq. The Jordanian support for Iraq during the war also eliminated the grants that Jordan received from the oil-rich Gulf states.[32]

The major catalyst, however, came in 1989 when the International Monetary Fund's economic rescue package for Jordan imposed an austerity programme that cut back government subsidies with dire economic consequences. Prime Minister Zaid al-Rifai raised the price of fuel and basic commodities to respond to the International Monetary Fund's economic programme which was to reschedule Jordan's $6.5 million debt. This policy triggered massive price riots in the southern part of the country, a region in which both the king and the Brotherhood enjoy considerable support. As Jordan's economic crisis became more acute, the king was in need of a new social compact. Unable to deliver financial rewards, he now had to grant concessions and relinquish some of his power as an absolute monarch.

Partially influenced by the success of Mubarak's liberalization in the 1980s and the global trend toward democratization, the king began to ease the pressure on the opposition in general and the Islamists in particular. As a gesture of good will, King Hussein dismissed Rifai. The king also opened up the political process and expanded participation. In an attempt to create a new 'political compact' with his people, he declared an amnesty for political prisoners, and on 8 November 1989 the king gave his blessings for the first democratic parliamentary election in 22 years. Since political parties were banned, the Muslim Brotherhood was in an excellent position to take advantage of the new more open political atmosphere. It is not surprising that the Brotherhood and its Muslim allies won 34 of the 80 seats in Parliament.[33] The new prime minister, Mudar Badram, represented the Brotherhood's position in the cabinet. His request to administer the nation's education and social development ministries, however, was turned down by the king.

Among the first steps of the new administration was the lifting of the martial law which had been in effect since the Arab–Israeli war of 1967, and declaring a political amnesty. What followed was a number of impressive electoral victories for the Muslim Brotherhood. On 1 January 1991, in response to the Gulf crisis and mounting domestic pressure, the king reversed his initial position of exclusion of Islamists from his government and included five members of the organization in his cabinet. This initiative brought recognition to the Brotherhood and legitimized them even further. The Muslim Brotherhood joined forces with nationalist, liberal and leftist parties during the Gulf war to denounce the anti-Iraqi coalition. Given the large Palestinian population of Jordan and the close Jordanian economic ties with Iraq, Saddam Hussein's attempt to wrap himself in the Palestinian flag during the war evoked a positive response in Jordanian society, a response that the Muslim Brotherhood could not afford to ignore. This policy, however, has cost the Brotherhood the patronage of the Saudi and Kuwaiti governments, the two historical allies of the Brotherhood in Jordan.

To institutionalize the democratic process further, King Hussein approved a national charter on 9 June 1991 which allowed a multiparty system, codified the rule of law, enhanced the freedom of the press, and guaranteed greater rights for women. Liberalization in Jordan has involved certain mutual-trust-building steps on the part of King Hussein and the ruling Hashemi'ite family and the opposition. In return for allowing a multiparty system and the participation of the opposition in parliamentary politics, King Hussein asked for their pledge of allegiance to the monarchy and a pluralistic system. In 1991, Jordan ratified a national charter which codified the opposition's pledge to respect the institution of monarchy led by the Hashemi'ite clan.

The limitations of elite-initiated liberalization, however, were exposed on 17 June 1991, when the king dismissed the cabinet he had appointed in January and appointed his cousin, Sherif Said Ben Shaker, a loyalist, to replace Taher al-Masri, a liberal, as Prime Minister. The removal of the Muslim Brotherhood from the cabinet was designed to facilitate Jordan's participation in the American-initiated Middle East peace conference in Madrid during the months of October and November 1991. The leader of Muslim Brotherhood al-Khalifa explained: 'We will not participate in any government that will negotiate with Israel or with its American partner'.[34]

Alarmed by violent confrontations between the Islamists and the army in Algeria, the king hoped that slowing down the pace of liberalization would avert a showdown between the government and the opposition. By putting his cousin in power, the king also hoped to insulate the government from a frontal assault by the opposition. The opposition would know that an attack on the government would be regarded as an attack on the king, something the opposition could not afford at this stage.

While courting the moderate Muslim Brotherhood, the king did not hesitate to suppress the more militant members of 'Mohammad's Army'. Perhaps as a direct signal to the Islamists, and in reaction to bloody events in Algeria, the king ordered the execution of eight members of this antimonarchial Islamic group in 1992. The message sent to the Muslim Brotherhood and other opposition forces was quite clear: they would only be tolerated as long as they remained a loyal opposition and supported the institution of the monarchy. Hence, while parliamentary politics is accepted as part of the rules of the game, much of the legislation before parliament comes from the government, and the king holds the power to dismiss leaders and even to dissolve parliament as he pleases. This is why some scholars have aptly described the Jordanian liberalization as an experiment in 'facade democracy'. A facade democracy is defined as 'a system where liberal-democratic institutions, processes and safeguards are established by law but are in practice so manipulated or violated by a historic oligarchy as to stay in office'.[35]

In 1992, the parliament passed a law allowing political parties to participate in the parliamentary election of 1993. The result of the election of 1993, in which the Muslim Action Front actually lost seats in parliament, was indeed pleasing news to the king. Unlike Algeria, where future elections were cancelled when it became clear that FIS has substantial support among the populace, the Jordanian government managed to diffuse the support of Islamists before they could take control of government. By opening up the political system, the king managed to foster competing opposition groups and effectively end the monopoly of Islamists in the political arena. Therefore, he did not have to resort to violence to crush the Islamic opposition as the Algerian government did.[36]

With the signing of the peace treaty with Israel in 1994, many Jordanians expected economic dividends, which have not yet materialized. Kabariti, the new prime minister, hopes that Jordan's support of the Palestinian cause will continue to keep the Islamist and the leftist forces at bay. In addition, in 1996, criticism of the government for abuse of human rights increased. Criticism of the king is punishable by imprisonment, as Leith Shbeliat, the president of Jordan's Engineers' Association, found out. The course of the Jordanian democratic experiment is indicative of the very fragile nature of liberalization under an authoritarian regime with a weak democratic institutional infrastructure and a highly insecure political elite perched atop the system.

CONCLUSION

While influenced by such factors as the global impact of democratization, the maturing of the middle class, the growth of the incipient civil society, and the increasing mass pressure for political participation, political liberalization in the Middle East and North Africa is, for the most part, a manipulated phenomenon to bolster regime legitimacy. Another attribute of Middle Eastern liberalization is that economic liberalization runs ahead of political liberalization. While many regimes have displayed a willingness to bow to the exigencies of the global market in this age of economic interdependence, only a few have opted for a token power-sharing and none has permitted a genuine contestation of power and fully-fledged democratization. While many countries have readily opted for marketization and the IMF- instigated programme of 'structural reforms' and neoliberal economic policies, they have been hesitant to plunge into the uncharted waters of democratic governance. Egypt, Jordan and Algeria provide a few examples.

Liberalization in the Middle East is circumscribed and limited by several factors. The first is the economic and political weaknesses of the elite. Such chronic crises as unemployment, inflation and inadequate goods and services were rampant in Algeria, Egypt and Jordan throughout the 1980s. Hence, the base of support of the secular regimes in these countries remained narrow and tenuous. In the face of austerity programmes and economic hardships on the one hand, and state monopolies of political life on the other, the appeal of the official nationalist and 'socialist' ideologies of the postcolonial states began to wane. The old nationalist coalitions which defined and gave impetus to the ideology of Arab nationalism, socialism and pan-Arabism was now being replaced by potent populist Islamic trends. By the 1980s it was abundantly clear that without the traditional basis of legitimacy, religion – in this case the blessing of the increasingly popular Islamic groups – the modern state would be incapable of sustaining and exercising its authority effectively. Facing a more educated and politically awakened urban population whose passivity could no longer be bought easily, the ruling elites decided to tap new sources of legitimacy and broadened the basis of consensus.

The second factor is the lack of institutionalization of liberalization itself. Insofar as liberalization remains dependent on 'the good will' of the 'benevolent leader', it will remain tenuous and unstable. This especially holds true in the Middle East and North Africa where authoritarian political culture has deep roots and charismatic arbitrary rule abounds.[37] To transform liberalization from a temporary cosmetic into a permanent and meaningful feature of the system, democratic institutions and processes must be built that will endure longer than individual leaders.

Due to a long history of political repression in the three case studies, with the exception of the Egyptian Muslim Brotherhood, no enduring tradition of institutional pluralism and genuine political participation from below existed. Often charismatic leaders used elite-initiated mass mobilization to replace genuine political participation. The lack of such a tradition also explains the underdevelopment of democratic Islamic theory to legitimize the Muslim parties' participation in the democratic process. In other words, in this realm, theory lags behind the spontaneous action and initiative of the Muslim masses. But as participation becomes more self-conscious and mature, more sophisticated corroborating Islamic theories of democratic participation are bound to appear to justify calls for the institutionalization of pluralism and democracy.

As our case studies indicate, the success of liberalization has been very uneven so far. *Political extremism has also enabled the governments of the region to reach out to smaller, insignificant Islamic or secular opposition parties while discrediting and cracking down on the more powerful Islamic organizations.* Hence, while Islamic groups have proven quite capable of harnessing and mobilizing the manifold public discontent against the secular state, so far they have very little to offer in terms of concrete programmes that would remedy the social and economic malaise. They have also done little to allay the fear among secular groups that, once in power, the Islamists would not monopolize all power and suppress their opponents. The challenge before Muslim democrats is to bridge the gap between Islamic ideals and a programme of action which safeguards democratic institutions and procedures.

Notes and References

1. R. Brynen, B. Korany and P. Noble (eds), *Political Liberalization and Democratization in the Arab World*, vol. 1 (Boulder: Lynne Rienner, 1995), p. 3.
2. M. Dorraj, 'Privatization, Democratization, and Development in the Third World: Lessons of a Turbulent Decade', *Journal of Developing Societies*, vol. 10, no. 2 (Spring 1994), pp. 173–82.
3. M. Moonshipouri and M. Dorraj, 'Democracy and Human Rights in the Third World: A Comparative Assessment', *Journal of the Third World Spectrum*, vol. 4, no. 1 (Spring 1997), pp. 85–111.
4. A.R. Norton (ed.), *Civil Society in the Middle East*, vol. 1 (Leiden: E.J. Brill, 1995), p. 7.
5. R. Brynen, B. Korany and P. Noble, *Political Liberalization*, *op. cit.*, p. 3.
6. *Ibid.*, p. 12.
7. A.R. Norton, *Civil Society in the Middle East*, *op. cit.*, p. 25.
8. H. Sharabi, *Neopatriarchy: A Theory of Distorted Change in the Arab Society* (New York: Oxford University Press, 1988). See also H. Sharabi (ed.), *The Next Arab Decade* (Boulder: Westview, 1988), pp. 2–3.
9. G. Salame (ed.), *Democracy Without Democrats?: The Renewal of Politics in the Muslim World* (London: I.B. Tauris, 1994), p. 10.

10. *Ibid.*, pp. 10–11.
11. A.R. Norton, *Civil Society in the Middle East*, vol. 1, *op. cit.*
12. G. Salame, *Democracy Without Democrats? op. cit.*, p. 13.
13. M. Dorraj, 'State, Petroleum, and Democratization in the Middle East and North Africa', in M. Dorraj (ed.), *The Changing Political Economy of the Third World* (Boulder: Lynne Rienner, 1995), pp. 119–27.
14. S. Huntington, *The Third Wave: Democratization in the Late Twentieth Century* (Norman: University of Oklahoma Press, 1991). See also L. Diamond, M. Lipset and J. Linz, *Democracy in Developing Countries* (Boulder: Lynne Rienner, 1988), p. xix.
15. L. Binder, *Islamic Liberalism: A Critique of Development Ideologies* (Chicago: University of Chicago Press, 1990).
16. R. Wright, 'The Islamic Resurgence: A New Phase?', *Current History*, vol. 87, no. 526 (February 1988), pp. 53–4.
17. 'Chadli Bids Farewell to Socialism', *Africa Report*, vol. 34, no. 1 (May–June 1989), p. 10.
18. *Ibid.*
19. 'Can Islam, Democracy, and Modernization Co-exist?', *Africa Report*, vol. 35, no. 4 (September–October 1990), p. 9.
20. F. Ajami, 'The Battle of Algiers: A Referendum on the Post Colonial State', *The New Republic*, 9 July 1990, p. 12.
21. *Ibid.*
22. For an analysis of Algerian Islam and its relation to civil society and the state, see M. Arkoun, 'Algeria', in S.T. Hunter (ed.), *The Politics of Islamic Revivalism: Diversity and Unity* (Bloomington: Indiana University Press, 1988), pp. 171–86. See also F. Burghat and W. Dowell (ed.), *The Islamic Movement in North Africa* (Austin: University of Texas Press, 1997).
23. R. Tlescani, *State and Revolution in Algeria* (Boulder: Westview, 1986).
24. 'Islam's Gains', *The Economist* (16 June 1990), p. 45.
25. D. Brumberg, 'Islamic Fundamentalism, Democracy, and the Gulf War', in J. Piscatori (ed.), *Islamic Fundamentalism and the Gulf Crisis* (Chicago: American Academy of Arts and Sciences, 1991), p. 202.
26. J. Waterbury, *The Egypt of Nasser and Sadat* (Princeton: Princeton University Press, 1983). See also R.A. Hinnebusch, Jr., *Egyptian Politics Under Sadat: The Post- Populist Development of an Authoritarian-Modernizing State* (Boulder: Lynne Rienner, 1985, 1988).
27. T.W. Lippman, *Egypt After Nasser: Sadat, Peace, and the Mirage of Prosperity* (New York: Paragon House, 1989), p. 247.
28. *Ibid.*, p. 215.
29. M. Makram-Ebeid, 'Political Opposition in Egypt: Democratic Myth or Reality?' *Middle East Journal*, vol. 43, no. 3 (Summer 1989), pp. 423–37.
30. R. Bianchi, 'Islam and Democracy in Egypt', *Current History*, vol. 88, no. 535 (February 1989), p. 94.
31. J. Esposito and J. Piscatori, 'Democratization and Islam', *Middle East Journal*, vol. 45, no. 3 (Summer 1991), p. 430.
32. R. Delwin and W. Irelan, 'Education Policy and Human Resource Development in Jordan', *Middle Eastern Studies*, vol. 28, no. 1 (January 1992), pp. 178–215.

33. B. Milton-Edwards, 'A Temporary Alliance with the Crown: The Islamic Response in Jordan', in J. Piscatori (ed.), *Islamic Fundamentalism and the Gulf Crisis* (Chicago: University of Chicago Press, 1991), pp. 90–92.
34. J. Esposito and J. Piscatori, 'Democratization and Islam', *op. cit.*, pp. 430–31.
35. B. Milton-Edwards, 'Facade Democracy and Jordan', *British Journal of Middle Eastern Studies*, vol. 20, no. 2 (1993), p. 192.
36. S. Ibrahim, 'Crisis, Elites, and Democratization in the Arab World', *Middle East Journal*, vol. 47, no. 2 (Spring 1993), pp. 292–305. See also Y.M. Ibrahim, 'Jordanian Voting Strongly Endorses Peace Efforts', *New York Times*, 10 November 1993, A8.
37. For a study of social roots of authoritarianism in the Arab world, see K. Hasan al-Naqeeb, 'Social Origins of the Authoritarian State in the Arab East', in E. Davis and N. Gavrielides (ed.), *Statecraft in the Middle East: Oil, Historical Memory, and Popular Culture* (Miami: Florida International University Press, 1991), pp. 36–70.

12 Global Accumulation and Structural Adjustments in Iran

Behzad Yaghmaian

INTRODUCTION

During the past two decades, developing nations have been pursuing the now universal policy of neoliberalism in regulating conditions of accumulation. In developing countries, neoliberalism has been framed and enforced in the context of structural adjustment policy (SAP) by the World Bank and the International Monetary Fund (IMF). The implementation of SAP, in most cases, has resulted in the erosion of wage-earners' purchasing power and the deterioration of their standard of living. Being guided by the regulatory conditions of global accumulation, states face new contradictions in their attempts to reconcile the 'national' and 'global' imperatives while resolving domestic tensions created by SAP.

The following chapter is an inquiry into the state's response to people's reactions to structural adjustment policy in Iran. Despite the rhetorical anti-West, anti-capital stands of the state, Iran implemented a comprehensive structural adjustment policy after 1989. Iran's welfare state and interventionist policies were replaced with market and price liberalization. State subsidies were slashed or reduced, and some public enterprises were privatized.

The objectives of this chapter are to analyse Iran's transformation of policy and to study the responses to social and economic consequences of SAP on the part of the wage-earners and the state. In the following section, I present a theoretical discussion of the dynamics of state/wage-earners' relationship within the context of SAP and larger mandates of global accumulation. This includes an analysis of SAP and the specificity of the state's response to the imperative of global accumulation. The section theorizes the dynamics of the state/people relationship where a civil society is lacking or weak and fragile. The second section considers the contradictions and dilemmas of the state in Iran, and using the analysis presented in that section I move on to discuss the radical transformation of the state's economic policy and the implementation of SAP in the aftermath of the war between Iran and Iraq. I then address the economic impacts of SAP on the standard of living of wage-earners, and the complexity of people's reactions to SAP in the absence of civil society and institutions of collective action. Finally I explore state responses to people's reactions and the imperatives of global accumulation.

GLOBALIZATION, STATE, WAGE-EARNERS AND STRUCTURAL ADJUSTMENT POLICY

This section locates structural adjustment in the regulatory configuration of global accumulation, and demonstrates its role in securing the conditions of global profitability of transnational capital. The continuing internationalization of accumulation and the gradual dominance of global production[1] have led to the ascendance of neoliberalism – the regulatory mechanism for global accumulation. In developing countries in the past two decades, the regulatory requirements of international accumulation have been primarily enforced by the IMF and the World Bank through structural adjustment policy. Structural adjustment policy helps shape national wage regulation and the national institutional restructuring conducive to international accumulation. It facilitates the integration of the world market by enforcing unilateral nation-state actions for the restructuring of national sites. Structural adjustment is an integral part of the internationalization of neoliberalism through the enforcement of neoliberal trade and macroeconomic policies in loan-seeking countries. Though different in its national specificity, structural adjustment policy typically includes liberalization of prices, imports, the financial sector, foreign exchange and labour markets, and creates the institutional configuration and the regulatory arrangements necessary for international accumulation.

Market liberalization is driven by the mobility/flexibility requirements of transnational capital and complements the broader global liberalization of investment and production. Trade liberalization, the creation of a friendly environment towards national investment (inward direct foreign investment) by deregulating local markets and offering low wages, the privatization of state-owned enterprises, and the reduction of government expenditures are all policies that aim at reproducing the regulatory conditions of global accumulation.

Two essential components of the mobility/flexibility phenomena are the restructuring of the labour market and the creation of flexible labour regimes. Labour-market liberalization is the path to the increased control of capital over labour through the 'flexibility' of task assignments, hiring and firing of workers, and so on. The liberalization of the labour market is, in essence, a 'euphemism for the disempowerment of labour'.[2] Flexible labour regimes allow the existence of diverse labour processes, and forms and layers of exploitation of labour by capital. It is this flexibility that has helped attract transnational capital to various industries of developing countries (including textiles, clothing, electronics, and so on) under the policy of export-led growth and structural adjustment.

In addition to the institutional restructuring of the labour market, structural adjustment leads to a decline in real wages through both nominal wage reductions (in some cases) and foreign exchange market liberalization and the depreciation of the local currency. Real exchange rate depreciation is used to increase the international competitiveness of the national site by lowering the real cost of labour. Capital-shortage and loan- seeking nation states compete to increase the attractiveness of their national economy as a site of investment and production through real wage reduction and flexible labour regimes. Structural adjustment is the institutionalization of these policies across nation states – an attempt to change capital–labour relations by reducing labour's bargaining power against capital. Structural adjustment also enforces the free international mobility of commodity and productive capital by mandating trade liberalization and removing state control of foreign direct investment. Loan-seeking nation states are required to accept the structural and regulatory conditions of global capital by removing national obstacles to international accumulation.

The international regulation of accumulation is a tenuous enterprise that is embedded in various intraclass and interclass contradictions and conflicts. The contradiction between labour and capital, and the resulting competition of capitals and the conflict between nation states, are inherent destabilizing factors that function as counter-tendencies within the emerging global regulatory trend. The implementation of SAP is constrained by class and non-class processes and conflicts, and the ability of the nation state to resolve the contradictions of capital and create the necessary national social harmony. The demands of global accumulation on the one hand, and the negative social and economic impacts of SAP and other regulatory measures of accumulation on the other, make the fulfillment of the state's functions both tenuous and contradictory. The specificity of state reactions in resolving its contradictions depends, to a large extent, on the existence of civil society and the organic institutions of popular democracy, and on wage-earners' abilities to organize effective institutions of collective dissent and opposition to the state's regulation of accumulation. In the final analysis, the state's ability to forestall wage-earners' articulation of a collective voice is fundamental to the successful and uninterrupted implementation of SAP and regulatory conditions of global accumulation.

The distribution effects of SAP and its impact on the standard of living of the poor lead to diverse reactions on the part of the affected population. I argue here that the *specificity* of the forms and context of people's response to SAP is, among other factors, determined by the extent to which civil society and the institution of collective action exist. In countries where civil society is institutionalized and entrenched, reactions to the economic consequences of SAP often occur in the form of collective action and public response. Where unions and labour associations, grassroots non-class organizations representing the group interest of an affected population, and, in general, social movements (old and new) are institutionalized and collective action (even partially) is a part of everyday culture, public opposition becomes a dominant form of reaction to SAP. Such reactions, by and large, remain within the confines of legally-defined citizens' rights. Resistance and collective action at the point of production, strikes, class and non-class struggles beyond the labour process, collective lobbying for favourable state regulation and so on have been the common forms of collective response to such policies.[3]

Contrary to this public manifestation of dissent and discontent, where civil society and institutions of collective action are weak or nonexistent, a process of internalization of economic and social catastrophe occurs leading to individual and personal reactions on the part of the affected population. The individual sphere replaces the collective, and personal response takes the place of public reaction and protest. A state's regulation of the personal sphere and its control of the life channels of the society, and the absence of citizens' rights and freedom of assembly, make the formation of a public voice impossible within the confines of legally sanctioned action.

In the absence of the sites of collective action and public voice, a process of retreat to personal struggles for survival occurs, leading to diverse manifestations of individually crafted coping mechanisms. The internalization of discontent produces a complex set of responses and/or mental and physical reactions. Corruption, bribery, manic anxiety, fear and repression, suicide, heart attack and crime become social epidemics, leading to alienation and social hostility among victims of economic policy. The fear of tomorrow and the anxiety about one's inability to survive the battle of everyday life further deepen the retreat to the sphere of personal struggles. The generalized internalization of discontent leads to intensified competition for survival and an acute sense of alienation.

The internalization of discontent thus shields the state from collective opposition to its policies. At the same time, the state's ban on collectivity and public manifestations of dissent lead to sporadic, unorganized and spontaneous ruptures and collective actions that take place outside the parameters of a legally sanctioned public voice. Collective action in such cases takes the form of riots, looting, burning of the property of 'others', and direct confrontation with the state and its organs of repression. Here, economic protest is inherently political. The fusion of the 'political' and the 'economical' occurs in practice from the inception of public action. The state often responds with the use of force, brutalizing those who dared to step outside the sphere of personal and internalized reaction. In such cases, collective opposition to state policy (SAP) is by nature a challenge to the integrity of the state and its power. It is that fundamental challenge that leads to immediate repression and brutalizing of the public voice.

Thus, collective resistance to the regulatory imperatives of global accumulation is either nonexistent or challenges the state as an agent of social cohesion and harmony. It is the fear of a breakdown of social peace that, in special circumstances, compels the state to temporarily retreat from the full implementation of SAP and pursue income redistribution policies that can level off the tempo of collective resistance and neutralize the architects of the public voice.

STATE STRUCTURE AND CIVIL SOCIETY: THE CASE OF IRAN

The dominance of the bourgeois mode of production and the weakening of pre-capitalist social formations failed to bring about a civil society and its institutions in Iran. The revolutionary period of 1978–79 that culminated in the overthrow of the Pahlavi regime resulted in the creation of nascent institutions of civil society. But the triumph of the Islamic Republic in February 1979 led to further erosion of the potential for the formation of a civil society in Iran. The state, from its inception, created its institutions of control of economic, political and cultural spheres, and preempted even the weakest institutions and forms of social and cultural life outside what was sanctioned by the government. Newly-created independent workers' councils, women's groups, and other grassroots organizations were replaced by state-controlled political committees in all public enterprises, workplaces, schools and neighbourhoods.

Despite its unity in the forms and extent of social and political repression, the Islamic state has been, from its inception, a divided terrain manifesting the multiplicity of centres of state power in the constitution. In addition to institutionalizing forms of a modern state, the constitution created a separate (state) power with the authority to supervise and supersede the decisions and actions of the 'formal' state. The *fagheeh* (governance of supreme Islamic jurisprudence), or the 'supreme religious leader', was institutionalized in the constitution and granted the power to supervise and rule the three branches of the state. The constitution created an inherent contradiction and duality of power in the state by recognizing free elections and the concept of a republic, while rendering absolute and unlimited power to the supreme spiritual leader.

Besides nominal political differences, the primary factions of the state are identifiable on the basis of broadly-defined economic platforms and representation of social classes. State factions have been fluid, with members constantly changing allegiances and crossing over to competing groups. Pursuing specific economic and political objectives, state factions have also formed coalitions and political blocs within the assembly and in the society at large. Using their power base and their entrenched position within various state institutions, factions that are temporarily pushed outside the executive branch often exert powerful influence (and even control) on executive decisions. In this sense, the state in the Islamic Republic has always been a site of struggle between competing forces. Economic policy has been a contested terrain, and a front from the struggles of equally powerful forces within the state.

From Welfare State to Structural Adjustment: A Transformation of the State Regulation of Accumulation

Broadly defined, three distinct tendencies and power bases have developed within the Islamic Republic, competing for a dominant position in the state and an ultimate determination of policy. The state power has been shared by changing coalitions of the 'Islamic Left', the 'Traditional Right', and a growing tendency of 'Modern Right' known as '*Kargozaran*'.

Advocating a quasi-Soviet-type and Keynesian welfare state, the 'Islamic Left' was the dominant force behind the earlier populist policies of the Islamic Republic. Backed by Khomeini, the tendency successfully fought for state control of foreign trade despite fierce opposition from the 'Traditional Right'. The tendency also instituted an elaborate system of state subsidies, price controls and other economic regulations.

The 'Islamic Left' tendency has been a persistent advocate of a vague notion of Islamic social justice and a staunch opponent of the uncontrolled market economy. The social and economic policies of the tendency were, to a large extent, the realization of the overall populist rhetoric of the Iranian revolution. Immediately after victory, the new state nationalized banking, insurance and most large industrial establishments whose owners had fled the country with large sums of money. State involvement in the economy increased during the war with Iraq through the enactment of macroeconomic planning, a broad programme of income redistribution, and the establishment of consumption subsidies and rationing. By the early 1980s, design and control of production, distribution, trade and pricing were, by and large, in the hands of the state.[4]

The economic and regulatory measures of the 'Islamic Left' were in direct contrast with those of the 'Traditional Right'. Being located in the Bazaar, the power base of Iran's traditional merchant bourgeoisie, the 'Traditional Right' has been an advocate of free trade, privatization, and a reduced state role in the economy. While the 'Traditional Right' primarily focused on the removal of state control from international trade for the enrichment of the merchant class, the 'Modern Right' tendency advocated similar policies with the promise of rationalizing the system of production and distribution. The tendency has been the open advocate of neoliberalism: trade and exchange rate liberalization, removal of state subsidies and price controls, and the reduction of the role of the state in the economy. Led by Iran's last president, Hashemi Rafsanjani, the tendency became an ideological magnet for technocrats and opponents of earlier populist policies of the state. The tendency has been the main force behind the implementation of the World Bank-sponsored SAP in Iran since 1989.

The termination of the eight-year war with Iraq produced the opportunity for the strategic break from the wartime welfare- state policies and the move towards neoliberalism. Contrary to earlier years, the postwar policies were, at least partially, guided by the state's desire to rationalize Iran's position in the world market and normalize its political relations with other states. The need to rebuild the war-torn economy and to revitalize Iran's industrial base were the pragmatic factors behind the policy switch in the postwar years. Given the general scarcity of hard currency and the large reconstruction expenditures after the war, international borrowing became a priority. Like most other developing nations, Iran was drawn to negotiating conditional loan arrangements with the World Bank. The design and implementation of SAP in Iran was therefore, on the one hand, a reflection of the desire of a part of the state to rationalize the country's position in the world economy and to remove the structural obstacles to its further integration in the network of international capital. On the other hand, SAP was a policy requirement of the World Bank and a condition for the Bank's support for Iran in loan negotiations with private lenders.[5]

The attack on the quasi-welfare state that existed during the war was brought about by a coalition between the traditional and modern-right tendencies. The election of Hashemi Rafsanjani as the first president after the war, and the elimination of the position of the prime minister, paved the way for the development of a new policy consensus between the office of the president and the 'Traditional Right' faction within the parliament. Leaving behind their political differences, the tendencies united on liberalizing different primary markets, ending the state monopoly on international trade, launching a comprehensive privatization programme and reducing state subsidies. A political compromise was reached about the nature and forms of state response to people's opposition and reaction to their social, economic and political disempowerment. The state continued to use official and unofficial organs of repression to prevent the formation of collective action in response to its social and economic policies.

The new policy and the transformation of state roles in the regulation and accumulation were formulated in Iran's First Plan (1989–93). The plan was designed by the Office of Budget and Planning (OBP) and approved by the parliament. It called for the privatization of large industries; the partial transfer of state responsibilities to the private sector; the removal of all forms of exports restrictions; the reconsideration of the pricing of domestically produced goods, exports and imports; the reduction of state subsidies for education; gradual pricing of electricity, water, fuel and telephone and postal services according to their cost of production; gradual reduction of the state payroll; and an end to the state monopoly in foreign trade.[6]

A comprehensive structural adjustment policy was unleashed in 1989. During the five years between 1989 and 1993 the state privatized foreign trade and deregulated the domestic market. Subsidies were gradually reduced and eliminated, and the shares of a number of state-owned institutions were floated on the stock market.

Following the general framework of SAP, Iran was advised to pursue the liberalization of the foreign exchange market and the gradual phasing out of multiple pricing of the exchange rate.[7] Due to the centrality of the economic ties between Iran and the United States prior to the 1979 revolution, the dollar played a central role in the Iranian economy. The Iranian state has followed a fixed exchange rate regime of 70 rials per dollar since 1955. Viewing the exchange rate as a tool for economic development and other domestic economic goals, the Islamic state established an elaborate multiple exchange rate system, using differential prices for various categories of imports and national production. While the official rate was used for primary state projects and low-priced necessities, other rates were based on the priority of the specific sector or line of economic activity.[8]

In the years after the revolution, a parallel black market emerged leading to the establishment of rates far above the official exchange rate. The rising demand for foreign exchange during the war, and the limited and fluctuating foreign currency receipts from oil exports (Iran's primary source of foreign currency), led to the creation of an acute foreign exchange shortage, a pervasive speculative frenzy in currency markets, and a steady increase in the exchange rate of the dollar for speculative investment.[9]

Moving towards the gradual liberalization of the foreign exchange market, in mid-1989 the state officially terminated the long-existing multiple exchange rate system and reduced all rates to four categories of official, preferred, competitive and floating.[10] Imported goods were divided into the same four categories and received their respective exchange rates. Basic necessities and investment goods for development projects were entitled to the official exchange rate of 70 rials. Proceeds from exports were exchanged at the preferred rate of 425 rials. House appliances and similar consumer goods imports were granted the competitive exchange rate, and importers of other non-essential imports were allowed to purchase foreign currency at the floating rate from the Central Bank.[11] The floating rate was to be determined by the Central Bank every day based on assessments of market forces. The continuation of the policy eventually led to a further overhaul of the system and the eventual establishment of one single rate determined by supply and demand.[12] All rates were increased over time, and by 1993 most commodities were removed from the official exchange rate category. The floating and competitive rates became dominant in all categories of goods and services.

A single (floating) exchange rate regime was finally established in 1993, the last year of the First Plan.[13] A non-official/free market was allowed to coexist with the official foreign exchange market. The foreign exchange shortage, and the inability of the state to deliver a sufficient supply of foreign currencies at its single floating rate, transformed the unofficial foreign exchanged market into a lucrative site for speculative investment, and led to a continuous long-term decline in the value of the local currency in the free market. The Central Bank's objective was a gradual closing of the gap between the rates in the two markets.

THE SOCIAL AND ECONOMIC CONSEQUENCES OF SAP

It is beyond the scope of this chapter to present an elaborate analysis of the economic consequences of SAP. Such an analysis can be found elsewhere in this volume, particularly the chapters by Richard Harris and Manochehr Dorraj. In what follows I focus on aspects of SAP that most fundamentally affected the everyday struggles for survival. The state's overhaul of the foreign exchange regime and its effect on prices and income distribution, the weakening and removal of subsidies, and the 'rationalization' of prices are policies that most directly affected wage-earners' economic life.

The liberalization of the currency market in Iran resulted in the long-term (though fluctuating) decline in the value of the national currency, and an increasing dollarization of the economy. The free market price of the dollar increased by more than 100 times (or 10 000 per cent) from 70 rials in 1978 (the year before the revolution) to 72 000 rials in May 1995, when the state was forced to retreat from its earlier policies and impose a fixed exchange rate at 30 000 rials per dollar.

The sustained appreciation of the dollar created a lasting frenzy in the foreign exchange market and helped (along with other factors) the transfer of resources from (already weak) productive investment to short-term speculative investment in the dollar. The steady loss in the market value of the rial led to rising prices of most domestically produced and imported consumer goods, and a chronic supply-pushed inflation. The effect of currency liberalization on prices was not coincidental. Being dependent on the import of productive capital (machinery and semi-finished goods), industrial production and capital accumulation are constrained by the availability of cheap imported capital goods. The increase in the foreign exchange rate reduced capital imports and created shortages of necessary parts and materials.[14]

Foreign exchange-generated bottlenecks result in simultaneous declines in output and rising prices. In the case of Iran, the twin problem of inflation and stagnation ('stagflation') was the result of inflation rates of nearly 50 per cent (according to state-generated statistics) and a decline in output growth from more than 10 per cent in 1991 to less than 2.5 per cent in 1994.[15] In addition to affecting domestic production, the depreciation of the national currency also resulted in increased prices of imported basic consumer goods. The simultaneous privatization and liberalization of foreign trade led to the allocation of scarce foreign currency resources to lucrative luxury goods imports, further depriving wage-earners of their potential access to affordable articles of consumption and the meeting of their basic needs.

The unprecedented capital gains from speculative investment in the currency market led to a further accumulation of wealth in the hands of a few, and the reprocessing of this wealth in other speculative ventures including the housing market in a later period. Housing prices and rentals increased in proportions never experienced before, leading to monthly rents that surpassed the incomes of average wage-earners in the capital and other large cities. The psychological impact of the sustained increase in the relative value of the dollar produced further speculative price increases in markets for both tradable and non-tradeable goods. Retailers of even the most basic non-tradeables increased their prices with every increase in the value of the dollar. The result was the vicious cycle of daily price hikes and constant erosion of the purchasing power of fixed-income wage-earners. According to published government statistics, while prices increased on average by almost 50 per cent per year during the 1989–93 period, average wages and salaries only rose by 12 per cent to 17 per cent.

The effect of currency market liberalization on the standard of living of wage-earners was further compounded by SAP's attack on the partial rationing of basic needs and state subsidies, and the rationalization of the price system. Thus, by 1993 a number of staples, including butter, chicken, eggs, soap and laundry detergents were removed from the system of rationing. In addition to removing specific commodities from the system, the state began a new policy of changing the pricing of rationed commodities in 1993. Accordingly, prices of rationed staples were determined on the basis of the conversion of the full cost of imports (import price) at a new exchange rate of 1750 rials per dollar (an increase of 2400 per cent from 70 rials per dollar).[16]

Various studies have attempted to estimate the effects of SAP on the poverty level in Iran. Defining the poverty line as access to a 'normal food intake', research has shown a marked increase in the percentage of the population living below the poverty line after 1989, the first year of the First Plan.[17] In 1989, 45 per cent and 52 per cent of families in urban and rural areas respectively, lived below the poverty line. The share of the population living in poverty had increased by 29.3 per cent and 23.3 per cent in urban and rural areas respectively in 1994. The appreciation of the prices of staples also forced changes in the consumption behaviour of the population, leading to declining nutrition levels. In most cases the daily intake of bread (continuing to enjoy high state subsidization) replaced the consumption of red meat, chicken, rice and other nutritious food. Meat was gradually elevated to a luxury item for many Iranians.[18]

It is important to note that the estimates of poverty outlined above do not include the cost of housing, medical care and other highly inflationary essential goods. Housing expenses alone surpass the monthly income of many employed wage-earners. On average, Iranians spent nearly 57 per cent of their income on rent.

From its inception in February 1979, the state systematically preempted the fragile and newly-born grassroots institutions of people's power and all manifestations of a collective voice. Being denied institutions of civil society and a government of law, people's reactions to the economic and social consequences of structural adjustment have been realized mostly through the internalization of their disempowerment and economic marginalization. In addition to an occasional outburst of open challenges to the state, for the most part wage-earners sought salvation from the painful realities of everyday life through additional sources of income from second and third jobs, bribery and corruption. Trapped in an endless battle of survival and alienated from society, others adhered to violence and criminal activities. Though small in scale, such acts of individual violence have been rising rapidly in the post- liberalization years. Yet, those further alienated from society and defeated by everyday struggles sought salvation in suicide, died of heart attacks, or fell into the abyss of depression, anxiety and manic fear of tomorrow.

A systematic analysis of wage-earners' response presupposes a comprehensive compilation of data on a number of categories, including: the percentage of the labour force occupying more than one job, the increase in financially motivated crime, and suicide and heart attack statistics by age and gender. The collection of this data will allow the construction of an indexes of wage-earners' reactions. Such indices help a deeper analysis of the problem by being studied in relation to customary economic indices such as unemployment, real wages, inflation and poverty line over time.

In general, even if not collected in a systematic way, such data is expected to exist in different forms and to be available from state agencies and libraries. It is also within the domain of normal practice to make this information available for research and scholarly activities. Such has proved not to be the case in Iran where most scholarly investigation is deemed suspicious, and information is the private property of its safekeepers. In Iran, hospital information on suicides and heart attacks are kept like national security records, and curiosity is a crime. This is a country where the state is so sensitive to the most remote possibility of organized opposition that it sensors the most innocent curiosities, punishes those who think and question, and those who dare to create an independent mode of intellectual production.

RETREAT AND REPRESSION: THE STATE'S RESPONSE TO WAGE-EARNERS' REACTIONS TO SAP

The Iranian state has used a variety of methods in curtailing opposition to its policies. The specificity of the state's response at each moment is a reflection of inter- and intraclass struggles, and extraclass processes, in the society. The state, on one hand, must react to the imperatives of global capital (as the dominant social relations of production) and the pressure of regulation within a regime of international accumulation. On the other hand, it must be responsive to competing interests that are rooted in the divisions of capital and various class and non-class alliances that emerge in response to accumulation and regulation. The study of the state's response to people's reactions to SAP must incorporate the tension and competing interests of various tendencies within the ruling classes, and the formation of new alliances between these tendencies and other social forces.

The implementation of SAP in Iran was, from the outset, opposed by the 'Islamic Left' tendency and social forces sympathetic to its social and political agenda. Though out of power, the tendency's critique of SAP was persistently presented to the public through its supporters and influential media including the daily *Salam*, *Mobin*, and the radical Moslem student weekly *Payame Daneshjoo* (*Voice of Students*). *Payame Daneshjoo* focused on researching and reporting the social and economic impacts of SAP and privatization, while exposing the corruption and financial scandals of various state-run enterprises. Though not challenging the legitimacy of the state, 'Islamic Left' and its constituencies have been vocal and open critics of the state's economic policy and its impact on the poor.

The sharp criticism of the state by the student weekly was finally brought to an end when the paper was banned from publication for an alleged defamation of a public official. The headquarters of *Payame Daneshjoo* was attacked by the pressure groups backed by powerful factions within the ruling strata, while equipment was destroyed and the staff threatened. The paper resumed publication after the election of Mohammad Khatami to the presidency of Iran in May 1997. In less than three months, the headquarters of the paper was ambushed, and the editor and other employees were severely beaten and injured.[19]

The poor and the wage-earning class, as discussed earlier, primarily reacted to SAP and its consequences through an alienating process of internalization and the formation of non-collective dissent. The internalization of social discontent and the predominance of isolated and individual sites of struggle for survival shielded the state from potential collective responses to its policies. But on a few occasions, public discontent produced open social ruptures in which the totality of the state was challenged by disenchanted protestors. On these occasions, a form of spontaneous collectivity was generated and channeled against the state as such. The severity of political and cultural repression and economic disenfranchisement led, in some cases, to the formation of collective actions that crossed the usual boundaries of economics and political protest and challenged the legitimacy of the state, while also demanding lower prices, jobs and economic security. In addition to scattered riots and ruptures, there have also occurred short-lived job actions against rising prices and declining standards of living of the workers. In most cases, such actions were settled by the use of force and occasional wage and salary concessions on the part of the state. Despite these sporadic manifestations of public protest, for the most part the state has been able to forestall the formation of collective action through systematic negation of civil society and its institutions.

The state has also been forced to conciliate and retreat from its positions and policies due to opposition from above and the potential for social explosion from below. The most drastic of such retreats occurred in May 1995, when the state abruptly reversed its policy of exchange liberalization and imposed (once again by the use of force and terror) a fixed exchange rate of 300 tomans per dollar. The retreat was brought about by the state's realization of the volatility of the social conditions caused by rising foreign exchange rates and domestic prices. It was a forced retreat caused by an understanding that even terror was no longer adequate for containing wage-earners' rage and the recognition of the limits of their capacity to internalize collective misery. Though unable to curtail rising prices and stabilize currency markets in the long run, the measure temporarily slowed the spreading social tension and created a sense of psychological relief and respite for most fixed-income citizens. Some prices temporarily declined and the state gained people's confidence by its gestures of fighting currency speculators, hoarders and 'foreign enemies of the Islamic Republic'.

As a result of blocking the possibility of fast and short- term gains in currency markets, speculators began an exodus to other lucrative markets for short-term gains. Land and housing markets became targets of attack, leading to an unprecedented rise in rentals and housing prices, and a further erosion of wage-earners' purchasing power. The potential explosiveness of continuous increases in prices and the impoverishment of wage-earners resulted in other compromises on the part of the state. The privatization plan proceeded at a very slow pace and the deterioration of people's standard of living and the escalation of poverty produced a new dialogue (if only rhetorical) around the issue of poverty eradication. The Second Plan (1994–99) included clauses for the enhancement of 'social justice', eradication of poverty, and a reduction in the Gini coefficient.[20] President Hashemi Rafsanjani urged the OPB to develop an anti-poverty programme, proposing the elevation of the standard of living of every citizen of the Islamic Republic to a level above the poverty line.[21] The president of the OPB declared poverty eradication as the precondition for sustainable development, and the 1996 and 1997 state budgets allow for the allocation of funds for alleviation of poverty and the creation of social justice.[22]

Amid compromise, retreat and conciliatory gestures in its economic regulation, the state's negation of rights and the institutions of civil society continued. The result was the further deepening of people's alienation and the emergence of a silent sentiment towards the restructuring of the state and its institutions and practices. The sentiment for change was later galvanized around the presidential candidacy of Mohammad Khatami in May 1997, and was transformed into an unprecedented movement for rights.

The 1997 presidential election polarized and divided the country around the questions of law and civil society. On the one side there was an emergence of an informal grassroots coalition that included millions of intellectuals, journalists, writers, artists, the clergy, technocrats and propertied classes, and the left – a broad spectrum of individuals advocating democracy and social justice. Despite their different economic, political and ideological perspectives, diverse and antagonistic social forces and classes united around Khatami's political platform: the creation of a civil society and the government of law in Iran; freedom of association and political parties; more active involvement of women and youth in society; citizens' right to the privacy of their own space; and protection against widespread lawlessness and the violence of the police and government- supported armed gangs and pressure groups.

On the other side, the 'Traditional Right' rallied behind Nategh Noori, the speaker of the parliament, as the next president of Iran. To most voters, Noori's campaign represented the continuation and further deepening of institutional and systemic violation of rights and liberties. On 23 May, more than twenty million Iranians poured into the voting stations and defeated Nategh Noori as the chosen presidential candidate of the Religious Right. The unprecedented victory of Mohammad Khatami in this latest presidential election was primarily the result of spontaneous and grassroots efforts of ordinary people, who defied all expected behaviour and organized an energetic and vibrant campaign after years of social alienation and hopelessness.

The election created a new sense of activism, hope and trust in one's power to change the existing order. It broke the vicious circle of internalization and alienation, and helped the creation of the people's most vocal and energetic collective voice in the past 18 years. It transformed people's sense of alienation and defeat and channeled their resentment and anger towards the state. The presidential election was a quiet revolution for rights on the part of the ordinary people. On the other hand, the election was also a manifestation of a break within the Islamic Republic. The support for Mohammad Khatami and his platform by politically powerful and influential religious and secular circles and individuals reflects a new response to Iran's social conditions and a call for reform by some factions within the state structure.

Mohammad Khatami's campaign was supported by forces with diametrically opposite views about the economy, including Hashemi Rafsanjani and the 'Modern Right' tendency – the group of technocrats and the clergy that had been behind the implementation of the World Bank-designed structural adjustment policy in the past few years. Khatami's supporters also included the 'Islamic Left' tendency, Abdol Karim Mousavi, Iran's prime minister during the Iran–Iraq war, Behzad Nabavi, an influential figure within and outside the tendency, the Association of Radical Clergy, the Organization of the Mojahedins of the Islamic revolution, and various influential Islamic groups committed to a vague notion of social justice and equity. As discussed earlier, Mousavi and the Association of Radical Clergy have been ardent opponents of privatization and the implementation of structural adjustment policy in Iran.

The question remains as to the future of SAP and the regulatory policies of the new administration in Iran. Mohammad Khatami's coalition benefitted from the selfless participation of millions of unorganized wage-earners who, despite their deteriorating and insecure economic status, energetically supported his presidency on the basis of his political and social platform. The implementation of neoliberal policies in the past eight years has led to a transfer of income and resources from the most vulnerable sections of society to the propertied classes. Despite the persistence of the majority of voters, inflation, unemployment and other economic problems were only marginally addressed by the candidates. The burning issues of privatization, the state's role in the economy, trade policy, and a commitment to full employment and social justice were, by and large, excluded from the presidential campaign. The Iranian economy continues to suffer from severe unemployment, inflation, and a deepening impoverishment of wage-earners.

As of now, no clear economic blueprint has been presented by the new president. During his presidential campaign, Khatami only broadly defined the economic orientation of his administration as 'growth and development with social justice'. He has reaffirmed his commitment to the fulfillment of the Second Plan (drafted and approved by the administration of Hashemi Rafsanjani). In November 1997, the administration announced a new exchange rate policy for holders of foreign currency with no prior obligation to deliver all or part of their holdings to the Central Bank. Accordingly, Iranians obtaining other currencies through sale of assets, employment or other noncommittal sources in foreign countries, can exchange their holdings at rates strictly determined by supply and demands.[23] This is the first indication of at least a partial return to a regime of floating exchange rates.

There are some scattered signs of broad economic orientations of the new administration, indications of a general interventionist approach within the parameters of a constrained and restricted structural adjustment policy. The exact course of economic and social policies of Mohammad Khatami's government will be determined by the intense struggle that is underway within and outside his electoral coalition. At present, all forces are carefully trying to fortify their position. Differences within the supporters of the new president are bound to heighten. Rafsanjani, Iran's last president, is now the chair of the Council for the Discernment of the State's Interest (CDSI), a newly-empowered non-electoral committee with rights and powers that surpass the authority of the president and his cabinet. Unchartered and unapproved by the electorate, the CDSI enjoys the power of practically approving or nullifying the decisions of elected officials. Though no longer the elected president, Rafsanjani has become the second most powerful political figure in Iran in less than a few months.

The new power of Rafsanjani and the CDSI will have significant impact on the future of SAP, the creation and deepening of civil society, and the state's response to wage-earners' collective voice. The empowerment of CDSI has led to yet further multiplication of centres of power within the state, leading to further weakening of the positions of the president and other elected officials. A few days into his presidency, Khatami announced the formation of an economic advisory committee composed of various ministers and public officials to study economic conditions of the country and help formulate economic policy. In less than a week, Rafsanjani's CDSI created a parallel committee with similar tasks and responsibilities.

Clearly, a new potential for positive change has emerged in Iran – a potential whose results will, for the most part, depend on ordinary people's participation and involvement. Given the new political opening (though weak and fragile) and the mobilization of wage-earners during the election, the possibility for the creation of institutions of collective action has emerged. *The creation of a government of law rests on people's ability to sustain their energy and translate their recent experience into existing organizations and institutions of power.* People's frustration with economic problems are on the rise; economic conditions are continuing to deteriorate; unemployment persists; and rising rents and prices of basic necessities continue to erode wage-earners' purchasing power. The future of the relationship between the state, people and the civil society, to a large extent, depends on people's ability to maintain their newly-fostered energy and strengthen their fragile and vulnerable social movements.

Notes and References

1. Peter Dicken, *Global Shift: The Internationalization of Economic Activity* (New York: Guilford Press, 1992); and Dick Bryan, *The Chase Around the Globe: International Accumulation and the Contradictions for Nation States* (Boulder: Westview Press, 1995);
2. Eva Paus, 'Economic Growth Through Neoliberal Restructuring? Insights from the Chilean Experience', *Journal of Developing Areas*, vol. 28 (1994), p. 43.
3. The struggles of labour and students in France since 1995 are prime examples of public response to economic policy in a civil society.
4. Akbar Kamijani and M. Ahmadvand, 'An Analysis of the Theory and Practice of Privatization in Some Countries – A Study of the Iranian Experience', *Eghtesad va Modiriat* (*Economics and Management*), vol. 31 (Winter 1996), pp. 33–73 (in Farsi).
5. The association with the World Bank and the Bank's role in the implementation of SAP has been vehemently denied by state officials in Iran.
6. Office of Budget and Planning (OBP), First Plan, *Socio-Economic and Cultural Development – Islamic Republic of Iran (1989–93)* (Tehran, 1997).
7. Exchange rate is defined here as the domestic currency (rial) price of one unit of foreign currency (say the dollar). Rial is the official name for Iran's currency; but the unit often used by the public, retailers and the media is the toman, an equivalent of ten rials.
8. In 1989, prior to the overhaul of the market, 12 different rates were identified in Iran. Mohammad Rafati and A. Nader Mehregan, *Exchange Rate: From Multiple to a Single Rate* (Tehran: Business Studies and Surveys Institute, 1993), p. 88 (in Farsi).

9. Oil exports have been the source of close to 90 per cent of Iran's foreign currency receipts in recent years.
10. Alireza Shakibai and P. Kamali Dehkerdi, *A Comparative Analysis of Trade Liberalization and its Consequences in Selected Countries* (Tehran: Business Studies and Surveys Institute, 1993), p. 130 (in Farsi).
11. Hossein Adeli, 'The Single Exchange Rate Policy: Results and Prospects', in *The Third Seminar on Monetary and Foreign Exchange Policies* (Central Bank of Iran, 1993), p. 22.
12. M. Rafati and A.N. Mehregan, *Exchange Rate*, *op. cit.*, p. 88, n. 4.
13. Mohsen Noorbakhsh, 'Opening Presentation', in *Report from the Third Seminar on Money and Exchange Rate Policies* (Tehran: Bank Markazi, 1993), p. 13 (in Farsi).
14. See Behzad Yaghmaian, 'Internationalization of Capital and the Crisis of the Iranian Economy', *Review of Radical Political Economics*, vol. 20, no. 4 (1988).
15. Mehdi Taghavi and A. Gharavi Nakhjavani, 'Recessionary Inflation', *Etelaat Siasi va Eghtesadi* (1996), pp. 9–10.
16. Abbas Rahimi, 'Commercial Policy and a Comparative Analysis of Poverty in Basic Goods', in *An Analysis of the Economics of Poverty* (Tehran: Business Studies and Surveys Institute, 1996), p. 84 (in Farsi).
17. A. Rahimi, 'Commercial Policy', *ibid.*; Ali Deani Torkamani, 'An Analysis of Poverty in Iran', in *An Analysis of the Economics of Poverty*, *ibid.*, pp. 53–82 (in Farsi); and Abbas Rahimi, 'The Effect on Poverty Line of Eliminating Subsidies in Iran', *Mahnameh Barresihayeh Bazargani* (*Monthly Commercial Surveys*), vol. 81 (1996), pp. 5–24 (in Farsi).
18. A.D. Torkamani, 'An Analysis of Poverty in Iran'. *ibid.*
19. Among scores of persecuted writers and journalists, the editors of *Adineh* and *Gozaresh Monthly*, two well- respected monthly independent journals with left/liberal tendencies, were arrested and imprisoned. They were accused of 'spying for foreign state', 'insulting the supreme leader *(fagheeh)*', 'using drugs', 'defaming a state-run firm', and other charges. Also arrested was Mohammad Sadegh Javadi Hessar, the editor of *Tous* newspaper. The paper's publication was suspended for its criticism of the state.
20. OBP, Second Plan, *Socio-Economic and Cultural Development – Islamic Republic of Iran (1995–99)* (Tehran, 1996).
21. 'Eradicating Poverty: Perspectives of Officials, Experts and People', *Commercial Surveys*, vol. 105–106 (1996), p. 41 (in Farsi).
22. See Anvar Khamei, 'Poverty Eradication or Poverty Escalation?' *Gozaresh Monthly*, no. 73–74 (1996–97) (in Farsi); Manoochehr Kiani, 'The Impacts of 1997 Budget on the National Economy', *Gozaresh Monthly*, no. 71 (1996) (in Farsi); and Fariborz Raees Dana, 'Under This Antipoverty and Pro-social Justice Budget', *Gozaresh Monthly*, no. 71 (1996) (in Farsi), for a discussion of the limitations and ineffectiveness of this proposal for alleviating poverty in the country.
23. 'Exchange Rates Will be Determined by the Agreement between the Buyers and Sellers According to a Memorandum by the Central Bank', *Hamshari Daily*, 10 November 1997.

13 Liberalization, Globalization and Inequality in South Asia

Mustapha Kamal Pasha

Imbued with Promethean impulse, neoliberal globalization[1] presents to its disciples a brave new world of limitless opportunity: a world of rapid economic growth, technological advancement, a borderless culture of contentment. Sanctified by the collapse of the Second World, the end of the cold war and the consolidation of global hegemony,[2] the new creed has found a receptive worldwide audience. With no feasible alternatives in sight, neoliberal globalization casts an imposing shadow on policy choice and economic practice. Against the backdrop of challenges to statist rent-seeking, bureaucratic insolence in government and governance, and general economic miscarriage, celebrations of neoliberal globalization appear both timely and legitimate.

Acceptance of market fundamentalism is said to furnish the best of all possible worlds. In the new global political climate, antinomies of globalization remain generally repressed, seen mainly as atavistic rumblings of an *ancien regime*, both political and cultural, or as marginal fissures in an otherwise seamless pattern. South Asia offers no exception to the universal tidal wave of neoliberal globalization. In part enamoured by its lure, not discounting the cultural gains of full membership in the new global cultural economy,[3] but mostly driven by structural imperatives, elites and state managers in this part of the global South also seem poised to march to the global market anthem. A closer inspection reveals, however, the patent difficulty of homogenizing the economic prescription inherent in neoliberalism, the avatar of globalization.

Neoliberalism is primarily a *social*, not an economic process, *differentiated* by multiple forms of stratification and antimonies. Furthermore, seeking to depoliticize the political economies of the South, it ends up activating new political passions and interests. The unleashing of new social forces, in turn, conditions the pace and intensity of implementing neoliberal reforms. Domestic opposition in turn redefines liberalization; the legitimacy of liberalization largely rests upon the effective integration of contravening currents into the political process. Thus, what is cast as a *technical* enterprise, is ultimately a socio-political project.

What explains the race to the market in South Asia? Is the currently fashionable wave of economic liberalization in Dhaka, Colombo, Islamabad or New Delhi a byproduct of the end of socialism? Is the spread of neoliberalism to this region an illustration of 'policy bandwagoning', given an emerging 'international policy culture'?[4] As elsewhere, standard interpretations of the march to the market underscore the failures of dirigiste intervention. Advocates of neoliberalism in South Asia cite mounting fiscal deficits, bureaucratic insolence, kleptocracy, unaccountability and economic irrationality of state management among the chief factors for the demise of statism.[5] Alternatively, however, the present sentiment may herald structural alignments and constraints of globalization.[6]

As faith in the new goddess of the market replaces reverence to the state, economies in South Asia are realigning themselves to the imperatives of the global political economy. The 'soft' state[7] experiments with the newest neoliberal doctrines to stay afloat in the global ocean of prices and profits.[8] Notorious for their sluggishness to embrace market rationality on a global scale, South Asian entrepreneurs are now feverishly seeking foreign capital and investment in an effort to consolidate capitalism.[9] For some, South Asia, once a bystander in the global political economy, seems poised for scaling the newly industrializing country (NIC) wall.[10]

This chapter examines the impact of neoliberal globalization in South Asia by highlighting the ambivalence of recent liberalization efforts. While the ostensible aim of neoliberal reforms is to dismantle statist impediments to the market, the actual processes of liberalization have spawned new structures of patronage, incriminating both state and civil society. The graduation of non-governmental organizations (NGOs) in development, for instance, suggests a new division of labour between the state and civil society. In restructuring the state, civil society and the economy, brokers of neoliberalism have been compelled to garner political support from heterogenous constituencies, as in the case of farmers in India, bureaucrats in Pakistan, or the professional middle class in Sri Lanka. Paradoxically, the politicization of liberalization upsets the flow of implementation. Under pressure from domestic opposition to globalization, a new compromise between the state and societal actors often follows. Concessions to specific political elements generally contribute to the rise of new centres of patronage. In this sense, the assumed neutrality of liberalization is compromised.

Casting these concerns aside, an historic bloc of new globalizing elites in the domestic political economy is emerging in each of the South Asian countries. Despite political unrest and instability, in part linked to the effects of neoliberal globalization, agents of this new constellation see their own fortunes wedded to an expanded arena of compromise. State managers tuned into the ascending scale of globalization, vocal political constituencies drawn from the new petty bourgeoisie, propertied groups amenable to adapt to the new social order – are now all willing to embrace neoliberalism.

The growing engagement with, and subordination to, the new global political economy is also producing new forms of inequality. Superimposed on existing structures, globalization accentuates old divisions while generating new ones. With the rise or consolidation of domestic agents in the *globalizing process*, broad changes in polity and culture become attenuated.

This chapter sketches some of the more discernible patterns, with an emphasis especially on the cultural logic associated with globalization. In this respect, my analysis is most similar to the preceding chapter by Behzad Yaghmaian on Islam. The first section illustrates the main contours of liberalization by identifying the common features of neoliberal reforms in different South Asian nations. The discussion here is designed to underscore the difficulty of overcoming the system of state patronage built into an administrative model of development. Ironically, domestic opposition to reform seeks state protection against the uncertainties of the marketplace, invariably reproducing, if in modified form, the system it aims to dethrone. The second section briefly examines the rise of a new convergence on the viability of neoliberal reforms in South Asia. While opposition to reform is quite extensive, the general mood in the region seems one of acquiescence to the *ideological* dominance of neoliberal thinking. The third section expands the discussion on reforms to address the broader *social* impact of globalization on South Asia. Specifically, it examines how the assault on the state is linked to the new inequality and a burgeoning culture of indifference. A new cultural divide can be associated with neoliberal globalization. Following the analysis in the second section on the emerging convergence on neoliberal reforms and the diminished role of the state, the focus here is on the broadening schism between a globalizing 'leisure class' in South Asia and an expanding underclass. The last section draws some tentative conclusions pertaining especially to the new vectors of polarization and politics in the region. It is premature to fully appreciate the impact of neoliberal globalization in South Asia. The analysis in this chapter, therefore, is only suggestive of a general trend in the region, which is most likely to change in the years ahead as neoliberalism deepens or is reformed under domestic political pressures.

LIBERALIZATION AND PATRONAGE

Notwithstanding significant variance in extant institutional and political structures, virtually all South Asian countries (like their counterparts in the Third World) have been characterized by the presence of an interventionist, if inefficient, state. Inheriting the trappings of an 'overdeveloped'[11] administrative and paternalistic state,[12] post-colonial industrialization always rested on extensive state involvement in the economy. In areas as diverse as infrastructure, domestic industrial production, foreign trade, banking and finance, the state was everywhere. Until the recent advent of the neoliberal current, capital outlays in education, construction, and housing, protection via tariffs and quotas, the so-called license-*raj*, privileged access to public funds, and subsidies – in short, all the accouterments of state-supported industrialization – were in place in the early post-colonial phase. In essence, though, a 'mixed' economy imbricating dominant propertied classes and state bureaucrats came to typify the South Asian model of economic growth.[13] Private capital was clearly hegemonic in relation to the state. The state, while quite meddlesome, was generally supportive of private proprietors. The extractive capacity of the state remained fairly limited in areas like strict tax collection.[14] Patronage conditioned the accumulation process in distinctive ways.

Within these broadly defined parameters, the specificity of the state's role in different South Asian countries can be gauged, but only in reference to the density of the social structure (class, caste, ethnic and religious differentiation), the political form (for example, parliamentary democracy in India or authoritarianism in Pakistan), and the nature of class conflict, all contributing to the depth or shallowness of the industrial process.[15] India, with a longer trajectory of industrial growth under colonialism and the relative maturity of its captains of industry, strikes a separate pose. Only the presence of a massive peasant sector in India has provided a countervailing force to the dominance of the industrial sector. The landed elites, often colluding with military and bureaucratic elites, remain entrenched in neighbouring Pakistan.[16] By contrast, the industrial bourgeoisie in Bangladesh is 'the youngest element' in its class structure.[17] Sri Lanka's highly-skilled labour force and professional class may explain its relative facility, notwithstanding ethnic distempers, in implementing neoliberal reforms. In all instances, though, the administrative model of the colonial state has remained deeply etched into the fabric of South Asia's political economy. Compounded by structural rigidities – unequal patterns of wealth distribution, gender, caste and class cleavages – liberalization has been a cumbersome process.[18] To contextualize, despite the euphoria attending neoliberal globalization, the actual trajectory of economic liberalization has encountered complex social forces at all spatial levels in South Asia. Neoliberal reforms have resisted a unilinear or uniform pattern. In most instances, the *political* fallout of the reforms have engendered adjustments to structural adjustment.

In its restricted sense, liberalization in South Asia (as in other parts of the global South) is intertwined with structural adjustment sponsored by international multilateral agencies, with an emphasis on denationalization, deregulation and devaluation. A familiar package in the global South, the central goal of neoliberal reforms in South Asia is a shift in both growth and development to the market, unseating the state from its coveted position.

The first wave of liberalization in Sri Lanka (1977–88), for instance, centred around the promotion of private enterprise and foreign direct investment. Ownership patterns were targeted, giving foreign investors as much as 100 per cent foreign ownership in investment projects. The tax structure was simplified in favour of foreign investors, permitting tax exemptions on investments and imports. Similarly, the import regime was relaxed, as were exchange rates and exchange payments. Tariffs were drastically slashed and licensing was curtailed to a handful of items. State monopolies over imports, except for food grains and oil, were also removed. Protectionism gave way to open competition. Interest rates were also raised to promote savings, and ceilings were placed on the growth of the public sector. New institutional arrangements, notably the establishment of the Export Development Board and the Greater Colombo Economic Commission, were designed to create and run investment processing zones.[19] Although the major aim of liberalization was to institute a market logic in areas previously secured by the state, the actual process of implementing neoliberal reforms entailed concessions to established structures of patronage, including a vibrant welfare tradition.[20] This facet produced the expected consequence of buttressing an already politicized administrative process. On the other hand, violent ethnic conflict interrupted the liberalization drive. Ethnicity would exercise a durable impact on Sri Lanka's political economy[21] throughout the tenure of the liberalization drive.

The structure of patronage in India was the product of a complex array of collusions between state actors and dominant propertied interests.[22] More recently, the presence of a 'farmer lobby' in the state structure has also been linked to the politicization of 'bullock capitalists'.[23] But it is the so-called license-*raj* that was the most recognizable feature of the Indian economy.[24] A 'regime of licenses and quotas',[25] the license-*raj* spawned a labyrinthine set of bureaucratic entanglements, generally stifling private initiative while rewarding specific industrialists.

The impetus for altering the overall structure of patronage came with the slowdown of the economy, the rise of new social classes, and international pressures including stiff foreign competition, but mainly from the emergence of a technocracy under new political tutelage. Resistant to change, however, the bureaucracy and large oligopolist segments of the established Indian bourgeoisie, were less than eager to welcome reforms. Hence, the first phase of liberalization in India (1980–91) was on a modest scale, focusing on partial deregulation of industry and trade in order to boost export-oriented growth. Attempts were made to diversify the financial sector and to promote the stock market.[26] Despite the centre's decision to rescind the existing deep-sea fishing policy in reaction to fishermen's protests, it continued to allow foreign vessels to operate in Indian waters, and in fact permitted Indian industrialists to import fishing vessels and cooperate with foreign companies.[27] In essence, this phase was conspicuous by the recognition of the existence of a bureaucratic maze ready to subvert liberalization efforts. State managers were not willing to part with economic carrots to maintain their grip over the character of the industrialization process.

In Pakistan's case, the first phase of liberalization (1980–88) also consisted of unsuccessful measures to release the bureaucracy's hold over the economy. These measures consisted of devaluation of the currency, marginal relaxation in the import regime, institution of export promotion measures, growth in private investment, and a reduction in the role of public enterprises.[28] These reforms were designed to reverse a decade-long slump in private industrial development in the 1970s.

To situate liberalization, Pakistan's 'robber barons' were largely a creation of the state. Receiving unprecedented favour and perks throughout the 1960s under President Ayub, 22 families came to enjoy a virtual grip over industry, banking and insurance.[29] In 1969, a wave of protest, in no small measure linked to growing inequality, toppled Ayub's government, bringing a military government into power in the country's already uncertain political history. Insurgency and brutal civil war in the eastern half of the country followed, resulting in the dismemberment of Pakistan, and the establishment of the state of Bangladesh in December 1971. Under Zulfikar Ali Bhutto, private capital received a major setback as populism undermined a business climate conducive to investment.[30] Bhutto's state socialism envisioned capital accumulation without capitalists. Nationalization of key industrial and banking units brought industrial growth to a near standstill, as did Bhutto's often personalized vendetta against individual industrialists.

The economy survived, owing in large measure to foreign remittances from migrant Pakistani workers in the Gulf, a trend underscoring the fragility of domestic economic growth.[31] Actual liberalization had to wait for Bhutto's removal from power in 1977, following an urban-led mass protest movement. But the first wave of liberalization failed to dislodge bureaucrats and the landed interests, only widened the circle of patronage to include serving and retired military elites and political classes drawn specifically from rural localities and provinces. The economic reforms benefitted only those who stood in close proximity to political power under the watchful eyes of the military establishment. Although Pakistan's structural adjustment programme has been succeeded by multiple reform packages under ten different governments, the essential character of patronage has remained intact, adding extra layers to absorb new political constituencies.

The second major phase of liberalization in Sri Lanka followed an army insurgency and civil war. Under the aegis of the International Monetary Fund (IMF) a new package was put in place in 1988, but again insurgency prevented its implementation. Under new political leadership the militant insurgency was crushed with brutal force. In mid-1989 another stabilization package was introduced, stressing tighter controls on money supply, balance of payments and budget deficits. Reductions in tariffs, corporate and income taxes, currency devaluation, and opening up of financial and commodity markets followed. Agricultural prices of important items were adjusted to the global market, imports were relaxed, and in March 1994 currency convertibility in the current account was achieved.[32]

Nothing illustrates the dramatic change in Indian political economy better than the second wave (1991–95) of liberalization. Building upon the technocratic 'vision' undergirding Rajiv Gandhi's government, a series of proposals sought to create an entirely new climate of operation for the national economy, as well as dealing with global economic forces, especially attitudes towards export promotion and foreign direct investment (FDI). Confronting the spectre of rising inflation and a balance-of-payments crisis in mid-1991, India's new government introduced a reform package allowing fiscal, trade and tax measures aimed at making the state more efficient in gaining revenues.[33] Moreover, privatization of some public services such as the telecommunications sector became a precursor to redefining the ethos of India's cultural contact with the West. A globalizing 'leisure class' would soon become the conduit of MTVized modalities of aesthetic and dietary expression.

With the abolition of the license-*raj*, domestic capital was now freed from licensing restrictions. In addition, import tariffs were reduced, the currency devalued, and the ceiling on FDI was raised to 51 per cent of the total equity in several sectors, especially tourism. Allowing private capital in infrastructural development – including power generation – broke the monopoly of the state sector. The public sector also came under heavy assault, required to trim its size in employment and expenditures. The idea of a relaxed exchange rate regime to attract private and foreign investment, handling fiscal deficits via tariff cuts and reductions in excise duties, further underlined a different temper of economic management.[34] Notably, the stock market was opened to permit Indian firms to borrow from international capital markets, and non-resident Indians (NRIs) were given access to the domestic economy via investment.[35] These reforms also envisaged the privatization of the insurance industry and early retirement packages in the public sector.[36] The World Bank's prescription to raise the prices of food, transportation and energy was also adopted.[37]

Since 1995, neoliberal reforms have become more extensive in scope. In India, for instance, the state must aggressively provision a physical and social infrastructure to facilitate private capital accumulation. A common refrain is the inadequacy of these necessary prerequisites for industrial upgrading relative to East and Southeast Asia.[38] Agriculture, once protected from excessive intrusions from the outside, is now open to receive private investment from giant agro-businesses, and food processing industries are also being set up.[39] Moreover, giant pharmaceutical multinationals have been targeted, sparking controversies over drug testing on indigenous peoples, and charges of multinational corporations' practice of stealing local medical herbs.[40]

Despite temporary setbacks, the process of implementing neoliberal reforms remains unabated in all the South Asian countries. In fact, wrangling over the pace, direction and character of specific reform proposals has become an integral part of the political process itself, reflected in electoral campaigns, parliamentary deliberations and public debates in the media.

CONFLICT, COMPROMISE AND CONVERGENCE

Residues of populism, bureaucratic opposition and grassroots challenges from social movements offer the major challenges to liberalization in South Asia, but the picture is not self-evident. In nearly all the South Asian countries, prior populist commitments to specific constituencies have interceded to dilute the neoliberal medicine. The importance of state workers in urban areas can hardly be exaggerated. Hence, retrenchment of public enterprises has not been too drastic. In both Sri Lanka and Pakistan, for instance, state employees have not been made completely expendable. The Indian government, too, has been reluctant to magnify its unemployment situation by eliminating public enterprises. With the state reducing its payrolls in public offices and enterprises due to shrinking budgets, many educated youth already find themselves without hope.[41]

Opposition to reforms has also been sector-specific. India's efforts to privatize the insurance sector, for example, has been bitterly opposed by progressive forces.[42] Until recently, farmers and industrial workers have also opposed neoliberal reforms, as have public workers with the passing of the Industrial Relations Act, which would eliminate ailing public-sector enterprises. Trenchant opposition has come from local industrialists who fear becoming an appendage of global capital.[43] Similarly, privatization of the power sector, under pressure from the World Bank, has been opposed by several farmer groups.[44]

Within the state bureaucracies, support for neoliberal reforms has generally been lukewarm and, in some cases, quite hostile. In Pakistan, for instance, attempts by the prime minister to deregulate airlines, rail, water and power were actively challenged by federal and state bureaucrats under a pro-public-sector president on numerous occasions. Non-cooperation in implementation has been another strategy to subvert the pace of reforms. Finally, court challenges to the 'legality' of denationalization have been a favourite weapon in the hands of pro-bureaucratic forces.

The most sustained and vocal opposition to neoliberal reforms, however, has come from grassroots action groups, especially new social movements of ecologists. In India, the National Alliance for People's Movement (NAPM) has spearheaded the campaign against the New Economic Policy (NEP) under the leadership of Medha Patkar, an outspoken critic of multilateral social engineering in India. Rallying depressed social groups in the country's hinterland, NAPM has sought to prevent what it terms the 'marginalization' of the majority of the population, degradation of labour and the destruction of the environment. Using both traditional and unorthodox political methods to pressurize state governments and MNCs, NAPM has been quite successful in blocking neoliberal efforts, including several 'mega-projects'.[45] Activists have also linked the growing incidence of violence against women from the lower castes to neoliberal globalization. The latter is blamed for injecting a culture of consumerism and greed among the *nouveau riche*.[46] *Dalit* (so-called 'untouchable') groups, too, have rejected neoliberal reforms, especially in the public sector. It is mainly in this sector that *dalits* saw the prospect of overcoming age-old discrimination in education and employment, via state policies of preferential treatment. Left to the mischievous whims of the market, they now anticipate a reversal of fortune and marginalization in society.[47] In India, the so-called 'Backward Classes' and *dalits* have not welcomed the reforms, since the latter have tended to empower upper castes, reversing the state's efforts to create a level playing field in the area of education and employment.

Recognizing opposition to neoliberal reforms, the globalizing elites and their junior partners have used liberalization as an ideological weapon. Promises of rapid economic growth have been blended with calls for efficient management and 'good governance'. A coalition of technocrats, middle-class professionals and globalizing industrialists has publicized 'structural adjustment' programmes under IMF/World Bank sponsorship as the *only* available course of action. What has been dubbed as the TINA (There Is No Alternative) principle in South Asia, is largely a brain-child of neoliberal conceit.

Memories of dirigists' perdition have effectively subverted creative possibilities for devising socially responsible and culturally sensitive policies for the vast majority of South Asians. On this view, critiques of neoliberalism have appeared illogical, irrational and politically retarded. Often, though, expediency has been a reliable substitute for ideological purity; acceptance of neoliberal reforms has been quite forthcoming even from groups previously opposed to liberalization, as in the case of rural farmers in Maharashtra, led by Sharad Joshi. On the other hand, industrial workers under 'reformist' leadership have shown a willingness to negotiate with (both domestic and foreign) companies to become more 'productive'.[48] Hence, initial protests against NEP are giving way to a new social compact between workers and industrialists.

In short, a remarkable convergence now characterizes the economic 'vision' of the leading political players in South Asia. Political platforms and electoral rhetoric reflect a new attitude toward globalization.[49] Clearly, a 'pragmatic consensus' on economic reforms marks the current political horizon. To the more cynical, the domestic convergence on neoliberal reforms may reflect opportunities. In essence, however, disparate social forces in virtually all the South Asian capitals acknowledge the difficulties of avoiding globalization. There can be little dispute that populist politics of the 1970s, and to some extent the 1980s, led to considerable structural weaknesses in the economy. In the 1990s, these weaknesses paved the way for pressures from the IMF and the World Bank.[50] Now, the state in South Asia is under titanic pressure to trim its own capacity. Paradoxically, the same state must also ease the burdens of social dislocation wrought by greater integration into the global political economy.[51]

THE NEW CULTURAL DIVIDE

Globalization necessitates a revision of the social compact between social groups under new regimes of liberalization and privatization, with detrimental effects to sectors least capable of competing in a marketplace. Belief in state-led development, once enshrined in the South Asian political unconscious, appears shaken. Exacerbating existing structures of inequality, neoliberal globalization can also be linked to new forms of marginalization and social division.[52] There is substantial evidence that the major losers of economic reforms have tended to be the industrial workers, small-scale producers and state workers. Potentially, enterprises enjoying state protection and bureaucrats, especially white-collar workers,[53] are also the casualties of neoliberal excess. Living standards of the urban classes have already shown signs of deterioration. Although highly-skilled labourers have gained, especially in telecommunications and other capital-intensive industries, the rest of the working poor have become quite vulnerable. There are fears that temporary workers in public enterprises will suffer the most, given further retrenchment.[54] The most obvious effect of reforms, however, has been the phenomenal increase in the size of the unorganized sector,[55] a trend multilateral agencies ingeniously script as the voluntary initiative of groups in a rising 'civil society'.

At the macroeconomic level, South Asian economies confront the most likely prospect of a debt trap.[56] Rising debt service, combined with a diminution in the state's capacity to regulate domestic finance, is likely to undermine long-range development planning. Increasingly, provincial (state) governments are seeing new international avenues for funds, giving them considerable autonomy.[57] This trend suggests loss in the capacity of the 'national' state to fulfill its developmental role, a crucial aspect in a southern context. Once *the* chief architect of economic planning, development and welfare, the state must now accommodate the market in allocating resources. Once aspiring to be the gatekeeper of the 'national' interest and the principal player in political economy, the state is now the great facilitator of international capital movements, technology and investment, to help the national economy adapt to the rhythms of globalization.[58]

The new mood attending questions of inequality and redistribution reveals a deeper shift in the role of the state. A central target of planning in the pre-liberalization phase, economically-generated inequality is now regarded as a necessary evil of growth. The inclusion of 'security nets' in liberalization packages registers this basic change. Across the board, there is now greater reliance on the private institutions of civil society (market, voluntary groups and NGOs) in place of the state. Ironically, the new inequality lends quiet legitimacy to non-state actors in the economy.

In short, with the growing power of global capital and multilateral agencies – particularly the IMF and the World Bank – the arteries of autonomous economic decision-making in the South are becoming narrower. In vital areas of economic control, the state's role is being reduced, despite its seeming omnipresence.[59] Received social compacts, protective of large sections of the poor, are now under fire.[60] While the sanctity of the global marketplace is being welcomed, welfare-planning receives an unceremonious farewell. As champions of the new era, aggressive entrepreneurs of a different generation and temperament impose their instrumental rationality on society.[61]

As the undermining of the state in South Asia continues to produce contradictory effects, it is mainly in the *cultural* arena that neoliberal globalization presents its most effective challenge to the region. Specifically, transnational cultural penetration, expressed via the medium of homogenized lifestyles, consumerism and westernization, is articulating new forms of social inequity. With durable structures of inequality already in place, these new forms are tied primarily to the rise of a globalizing elite and a growing marginalization of large segments of the underclass. A culture of contentment, linked to the global cultural economy, is emerging in South Asia. A materialist orientation is fast replacing embedded social relationships. With this orientation comes an ethos of indifference towards the poor, the infirm, the elderly and social actors who cannot successfully battle against market rationality. The new globalizing elite is also redefining aesthetic expression, as demonstrated in film, television and fashion. Invariably, local cultural expression is being subordinated to an imperious regime of homogenized global culture.

CONCLUSION

In its innocence, neoliberal globalization offers efficient alternatives to dirigiste planning and economic organization. It also disrupts the lethargy of South Asia's political economy by injecting technology, capital and ideas into previously unchartered economic zones. To the extent that neoliberal reforms weaken the 'administrative' state in favour of initiative in civil society, it is likely to produce positive results. Exposure to the global political economy provides opportunities to rethink economic management in basic ways. In the context of durable structures of inequality in South Asia, though, a viable alternative to the state remains in doubt. Despite major deficiencies, the state has been the primary agent of reducing social divisions based on caste, class, gender, religion, ethnicity and region.

Furthermore, civil society in South Asia is the site of not only democratic projects, but also fairly illiberal social agendas and programmes. Under the stress of globalization, a spate of exclusivist social groupings have made their appearance on the political and cultural scene. Religious nationalism in nearly all the South Asian countries may be a more visible expression of the tenor of the new political ethos. Offering solace to some, redemption to others, sectarian politics presents the most ominous threat to the construction of democratic polities. In this vein, the role of the state cannot be understated. Social divisions in civil society require intervention; without a redistributive programme of action under the aegis of a democratized state, economic inequities will only spread.

As noted, the capacity of the state is under severe strain under the regime of neoliberal globalization. Unless this trend is reversed, opposition to liberalization may not be very effective. It is within this framework that the call to strengthen civil society *against* the state among NGOs seems misplaced;[62] ironically, the attack on the state in South Asia from various quarters only tends to fortify the neoliberal project. Rethinking this strategy may be the most urgent task to be groppled with in respect to neoliberal globalization. Abstract typologies of resisting globalization, therefore, only obfuscate reflexive engagement with the strategic problems of our times.

Notes and References

1. Given neoliberalism's project of constraining worker freedoms and its inegalitarian bias, it is quite ironic that its adherents show an affinity with liberalism. The latter is clearly premised on the idea of extending social freedoms (including worker rights) and promoting egalitarian social arrangements, not stifling them.
2. Stephen Gill, 'Globalization, Market Civilization, and Disciplinary Neoliberalism', *Millennium: Journal of International Studies*, vol. 24 (1995) pp. 399–423.
3. Arjun Appadurai, *Modernity at Large: Cultural Dimensions of Globalization* (Minneapolis: University of Minnesota Press, 1996).
4. John G. Ikenberry, 'The International Spread of Privatization Policies: Inducements, Learning, and Policy Bandwagoning', in E. N. Suleiman and J. Waterbury (eds), *The Political Economy of Public Reform and Privatization* (Boulder: Westview, 1990).
5. Deepak Lal, 'The Political Economy of Liberalization', *World Bank Economic Review*, vol. 1 (1987) pp. 273–99.
6. Mustapha Kamal Pasha, 'Security as Hegemony', *Alternatives*, vol. 24 (July – September 1996) pp. 283–302.
7. Gunnar Myrdal, *Asian Drama: An Inquiry into the Poverty of Nations* (New York: Twentieth-Century Fund, 1968).
8. Ronald J. Herring, 'Economic Liberalization Policies in Sri Lanka: International Pressures, Constraints, and Supports', in W. P. Glade (ed.), *State Shrinking: A Comparative Inquiry into Privatization* (Austin: University of Texas, Institute of Latin American Studies, 1986).

9. International Monetary Fund (IMF), 'Nepal Reform Strategy Emphasizes Investment', *IMF Survey*, 21 February 1994.
10. David Dunham and Saman Kelegama, 'Does Leadership Matter in the Economic Reform Process? Liberalization and Governance in Sri Lanka, 1989–93', *World Development*, vol. 25 (1997) pp. 179–90.
11. Hamza Alavi, 'The State in Post-Colonial Societies: Pakistan and Bangladesh', *New Left Review*, vol. 74 (July–August 1972) pp. 59–81.
12. Mohammad Waseem, *Politics and the State in Pakistan* (Islamabad: National Institute of Historical and Cultural Research, 1994).
13. It is important to note here that the state in South Asia was never a 'developmental state' *a la* East Asia, neither strong enough to resist pressures from civil society nor taking capitalist development as its *raison d'etre*.
14. S. Akbar Zaidi, 'This IMF Business: Who is Really Responsible?', *Economic and Political Weekly*, vol. 31 (1996) pp. 2728–29.
15. Clearly, such an investigation is beyond the scope of this chapter. Here we concentrate on broad trends. For background, see Ranajit Guha (ed.), *A Subaltern Studies Reader, 1986–95* (Minneapolis: University of Minnesota Press, 1997); Francine R. Frankel, *India's Political Economy, 1947– 77: The Gradual Revolution* (Princeton, NJ: Princeton University Press, 1978); Hassan Gardezi and Jamil Rashid (eds), *Pakistan: The Roots of Dictatorship. The Political Economy of a Praetorian State* (London: Zed Books, 1981); Ayesha Jalal, *The State of Martial Rule: The Origins of Pakistan's Political Economy of Defence* (Cambridge: Cambridge University Press, 1990); M.G. Quibria (ed.), *The Bangladesh Economy in Transition* (Delhi: Oxford University Press, 1997); and Ole Borre, Sushil R. Panday and Chitra K. Tiwari, *Nepalese Political Behavior* (Aarhus, Denmark: Aarhus University Press, 1994).
16. Akmal Hussain, 'The Dynamics of Power: Military, Bureaucracy, and the People', in K. Rupesinghe and K. Mumtaz (eds), *Internal Conflicts in South Asia* (London: Sage, 1996).
17. Subhendu Dasgupta, 'A Class in Pursuit of Power: Industrial Bourgeoisie of Bangladesh', in Ramakant and B.C. Upreti (eds), *National Building in South Asia*, vol. 2 (New Delhi: South Asian Publishers, 1991), p. 289.
18. The above general features of South Asian political economy must also be perceived in the context of a preponderant security complex, in nearly all the South Asian states. In the case of India and Pakistan, security has been the key negative feature of political economy, conditioning the social process in basic ways. Mustapha Kamal Pasha, 'Globalization and Poverty in South Asia', *Millennium: Journal of International Studies*, vol. 25 (1996); pp. 635–56. The effect of persistent ethnic unrest, insurgency and violence in Sri Lanka on its economy can hardly be exaggerated. Stanley J. Tambiah, *Leveling Crowds: Ethnonationalist Conflicts and Collective Violence in South Asia* (Berkeley: University of California Press, 1996). Bangladesh had its own share of political turmoil, originating from the days of its very inception. Lawrence Ziring, *Bangladesh from Mujib to Ershad: An Interpretive Study* (Dhaka: University Press, 1992).

19. Sriyani Dias, 'Economic Liberalization and the Development of Manufacturing in Sri Lanka', *Asian Survey*, vol. 31 (1991), pp. 611–29.
20. D. Dunham and S. Kelegama, 'Does Leadership Matter in the Economic Reform Process?', *op.cit.*
21. S. J. Tambiah, *Leveling Crowds*, *op.cit.*
22. Pranab Bardhan, *The Political Economy of Development in India* (New York: Blackwell, 1984).
23. Lyold Rudolph and Suzanne R. Rudolph, *In Pursuit of Lakshmi: The Political Economy of the Indian State* (Chicago: University of Chicago Press, 1987).
24. Stephen D. McDowell, 'The Decline of the License Raj: Indian Software Export Policies', *Journal of Communication*, vol. 45 (1995), pp. 25–50.
25. M.N. Panini, 'The Social Logic of Liberalization', *Sociological Bulletin*, vol. 44 (1995), p. 38.
26. R. Nagaraj, 'What Has Happened Since 1991? Assessment of India's Economic Reforms', *Economic and Political Weekly*, vol. 32 (1997), pp. 2869–79.
27. Sarthi Acharya and Niru Acharya, 'Structural Adjustment and Small Producers: Reflection from Case Studies', *Economic and Political Weekly*, vol. 44 (1995), pp. 45–52.
28. S. Akbar Zaidi, 'The Structural Adjustment Programme and Pakistan: External Influence or Internal Acquiescence?', *Pakistan Journal of Applied Economics*, vol. 10 (1995), pp. 21–46.
29. Rashid Amjad, *Industrial Concentration and Economic Power* (Lahore: South Asian Institute, 1974).
30. Shahid Javed Burki, *Pakistan Under Bhutto, 1971–77* (New York: St Martin's Press, 1980).
31. Jonathan S. Addleton, *Undermining the Centre: The Gulf Migration and Pakistan* (Karachi: Oxford University Press, 1992).
32. D. Dunham and S. Kelegama, 'Does Leadership Matter in the Economic Reform Process?', *op.cit*, pp. 180–81.
33. R. Nagaraj, 'What Has Happened Since 1991?', *op.cit.*
34. Jaganath Pathy, 'The Consequences of the New Economic Policies on the Peoples of India: A Sociological Appraisal', *Sociological Bulletin*, vol. 44 (1995), pp. 11–31.
35. R. Nagaraj, 'What Has Happened Since 1991?', *op.cit.*
36. M. N. Panini 'The Social Logic of Liberalization', *op.cit.*
37. J. Pathy, 'The Consequences of the New Economic Policies', *op.cit.*
38. Jayati Ghosh, 'India's Structural Adjustment: An Assessment in Comparative Asian Context', *Economic and Political Weekly*, vol. 32 (1997), pp. 113–20.
39. S. Acharya and N. Acharya, 'Structural Adjustment and Small Producers', *op.cit.*
40. A.V. Varghese, 'U.S. Health Institutes Find No Toehold', *The Hindu*, 8 December 1997.
41. 'Dwindling Jobs, Receding Hopes', *The Hindu*, 15 September 1997, p. 25.
42. 'Left Protests Opening Up of Insurance Sector', *The Hindu*, 2 March 1997, p. 7.

43. J. Pathy, 'The Consequences of the New Economic Policies', *op.cit.*
44. *The Hindu*, 25 February 1997, p. 9.
45. 'Indians Must Boycott MNC Goods: Patkar', *The Hindu*, 8 February 1997, p. 5.
46. Sarabjit Pandher, 'Nasty Ways of the Neo-Rich', *The Hindu*, 1 September 1997.
47. M. N. Panini, 'The Social Logic of Liberalization', *op.cit.*
48. *Ibid.*
49. Hasan Suroor, 'Left Set to Abandon Old Ideologies?', *The Hindu*, 30 October 1997, p. 15.
50. M. N. Panini, 'The Social Logic of Liberalization', *op.cit.*
51. *Ibid.*
52. S. Acharya and N. Acharya, 'Structural Adjustment and Small Producers', *op.cit.*, J. Pathy, 'The Consequences of the New Economic Policies', *op.cit.*
53. D. Lal, 'The Political Economy of Liberalization', *op.cit.*
54. Ajit Kumar Singh, 'Social Consequences of New Economic Policies: With Particular Reference to Levels of Living of Working Class Population', *Economic and Political Weekly*, vol. 28 (13 February 1993).
55. G. Parthasarthy, 'Unorganized Sector and Structural Adjustment', *Economic and Political Weekly*, vol. 31 (1996), pp. 1859–69.
56. Ashwini Deshpande and Prabirjit Sarkar, 'Structural Adjustment in India: A Critical Assessment', *Economic and Political Weekly*, vol. 30 (1995), pp. 3151–55.
57. M. N. Panini, 'The Social Logic of Liberalization', *op.cit.*
58. On this point, see Robert W. Cox, *Production, Power, and World Order: Social Forces in the Making of History* (New York: Columbia University Press, 1987), for the general theoretical argument.
59. Rajni Kothari, 'Under Globalization: Will Nation State Hold?', *Economic and Political Weekly*, vol. 30 (1995), pp. 1593–1603.
60. Nona Grandea, *Adjustment and Poverty in South Asia* (Ottawa: North–South Institute, 1993).
61. Hanumantha C.H. Rao and Hams Linnemann (eds), *Economic Reforms and Poverty Alleviation in India* (New Delhi: Sage, 1996).
62. J. Pasha, 'Security as Hegemony', *op.cit.*

14 State–Socialist Transition and Labour Relations in China

Xiaobo Lu

One of the most important historical events in the last decade of the twentieth century has been the collapse of communist regimes throughout the world and the subsequent transitions from politically authoritarian and economic state socialist systems. Nobody expected this transition to be smooth, and the transition raises more questions than answers. Among the most critical questions is that of what to do with the previously interventionist (indeed, in some cases, totalitarian) state. From Moscow to Beijing, from Hanoi to Budapest, post-communist leaders are asking the same question – what is the proper role of the state in their emerging capitalist economies? Given its interventionist past, the state in socialist systems tends to be regarded as a multi-armed monster which not only suppresses people's creative energies, but also stifles the market and competition. Its reduction and retreat seems to be a necessary condition for the transition to succeed. The experience of the past decade suggests, however, that such may not be a cure-all formula to remedy the inherited ills left by years of stagnant central planning. Far from a foregone conclusion, the state's role in a transitional economy and society is still being shaped and defined.

The post-communist transitions are taking place in a world that is becoming more interconnected than ever. More significantly, they are occurring while other states are undergoing their own reforms. For developing countries, to which some of the former state socialist countries belong, the daunting task is to build a state with a commitment to economic development and a strong transformative capacity in the face of an increasingly competitive international environment. For the industrialized countries, the state has undergone changes in the mode of governance as a consequence of transition from the 'positive' to the 'regulatory' state.[1] For the post-communist countries, the challenge is even more formidable: they must not only drastically reduce their overstaffed bureaucratic machine, retreating from state over-intervention, but also protect property rights, macro-manage the economy, and regulate the emerging marketplace, all of which require an effective role of the state. This poses a central dilemma for the former socialist states now under transition.

This chapter will address this central dilemma through an analysis of the case of labour relations in China. The analysis in this chapter is based on the premise that political choice as well as institutional legacies in state socialist countries including China affect the sequence and methods of transformation of industrial relations. I will first highlight some basic features of industrial relations under state socialist regimes and in transitional economies, with a focus on China. I will then discuss how the reforms launched in 1978 have changed pre-existing industrial relations. I argue that neither the changing international political economy nor the transition from state socialism has diminished the role of the state. Moreover, the state will continue to play a significant role in redefining and managing industrial relations. The pace, scope and sequence of changes in industrial relations are determined not only by leadership choice, but also by structural constraints derived mainly from the pre-reform past as reflected in the entrenched *danwei* (work unit) system in China.

THE STATE, WORKERS AND THE ENTERPRISE UNDER STATE SOCIALISM

In contrast to capitalism, the state in state socialist systems did not act in concert with labour and management to determine the rules of industrial relations. The state instead was the dominant actor in a three-way relationship. Both trade unions and enterprise management played an auxiliary role in the state-sponsored production process. Under state socialism, the labour process is combined with a specific type of political economy in which the party/state apparatus appropriates and distributes resources through centralized planning and command. It produced a distinct labour process characterized as the dual control system of managers and party mobilized to meet production targets through a variety of mechanisms.[2] The state controlled employment and work compensation. Enterprises had limited autonomy to hire and fire, while workers had little freedom in choosing their jobs.

Second, profitability generally appeared not to have been the only, nor even the most important, goal for firms in state socialist systems.

Rather, they sought full employment and job security. Most workers had lifetime employment. Enterprise paternalism – firms providing social services and welfare including housing, vacation facilities and food subsidies – can be found in many transition economies, ranging from the well-developed Russian industrial system to less-industrialized economies such as Vietnam.[3]

Third, industrial relations were defined by the absence of a labour market. Labour was not regarded as a commodity whose value could be dictated by supply and demand. Relationships between workers and their employers were often purported to be those between individuals and organizations or citizens and the state, not employee and employer or labour and management. More emphasis was given to employee participation in industrial affairs than to confrontation between labour and management. Given the existence of a bargaining relationship between enterprises and the state, the incentive was strong for a 'triple alliance between managers, unions, and party within the enterprise' to promote the interests of the enterprise to the central planners.[4] As a result, the direct producers – the purported 'masters of the nation' and 'masters of the enterprise' – were deprived of any institutionalized way of defending their interests against managerial despotism.[5] If and when labour disputes did occur, they were presented and handled as any other disputes in an administrative organization-namely, individual petitions to higher levels of organizational leadership.

Trade unions served a political role, functioning as a 'transmission belt' between the state and workers.[6] Unions were nonetheless reduced to a minimal welfare organization with limited roles in industrial relations. Occasionally, trade unions would become more participatory at the enterprise level and adversarial at the national level. However, the many 'trade union reforms' in most of these socialist countries never went beyond the model of 'dualistic functions'– namely, a 'transmission belt' of the state which advocated workers' interests.[7] Only near the end of communist rule in many former socialist states did the official unions begin to shed their 'transmission belt' function and become genuinely adversarial.

The nature of the relationship between the state and trade unions in particular, and communist politics in general, has been analysed in the light of 'state corporatism'.[8] It was posited that communist states adopt corporatist rule by creating vertical functional institutions and placing them under central control, with the express purpose of preempting the horizontal coalescing of class interests. This argument overlooks, at least in the Chinese case, the fact that the *cellular* structure of work units (mostly in China but also found in other former state socialist systems) have exerted a more defining impact on state–union–worker relations. Workers' interests were more fragmented between or within different enterprises[9] rather than 'organized into a limited number of singular, compulsory, noncompetitive, hierarchically ordered categories'.[10] The communist state relied on neither corporatism nor pluralism. Instead, it relied heavily on the *danwei* system which generated cellular social and political dynamics. When they did occur, labour protests as well as protests by other social groups often took place with workers from one enterprise during the Maoist period.[11] Rarely were they organized by unions or joined by workers from other enterprises.

CHINESE INDUSTRIAL RELATIONS BEFORE THE REFORMS

For nearly three decades, industrial relations in the People's Republic of China (PRC) were characterized by what was common in state socialist systems – an economy dominated by state-owned enterprises (SOEs), employee dependence on the enterprise, state- controlled union organizations, and relative labour peace. Despite sporadic working-class protests in PRC history since 1949, there were no organized labour movements.

While China shared many features of labour relations in a typical state socialist system, it also had unique characteristics. Perhaps the most significant is the *danwei* system, which made both entrance and exit extremely difficult for urban employees. It has had a number of consequences: the combination of *both* political and social dependence created by the *danwei* system posed barriers to collective action, in contrast to the former Soviet Union where enterprise paternalism was largely attributed to labour shortages; and disincentives for participating in collective action were mainly economic in nature.[12] It also helped to create divisions within the working class – between newer and older workers, between locals and outsiders, and between permanent and temporary and contract labourers. Chinese enterprises maintained a system of enclosed welfare communities which prohibited the free entrance of non-members.

During the Maoist period, Chinese workers were more tied to the enterprise than their counterparts in other state socialist countries. The dynamics of power relations within enterprises were also different in China and the Soviet Union. While Chinese workers were very much at the mercy of managers, Soviet workers had more control of the labour process. Herein lies one of the key differences between industrial relations in China and other state socialist countries – labour supply. Due to labour shortages, Soviet enterprise managers competed constantly with incentives of welfare provisions to attract employees, especially skilled ones.[13] Persistent labour shortages, not legal guarantees, made it very difficult to dismiss a worker.

China had more controlled workers' councils during the Maoist period. Even though workers' councils – which were supposedly a 'basic form of democratic management and an authoritative body for workers to participate in decision making and to monitor managers' were revived after the reforms began in the late 1970s, and had been established in almost all SOEs by 1986, they met primarily for the sake of formality and are basically used as rubber stamps. More recently, a survey found that with the SOE reforms many newly – transformed 'modern corporations' (65 per cent of those surveyed) have reduced the authority of workers' councils.[14] In many instances, they just deal with social and welfare issues such as employee housing allocation. They are rarely taken seriously by either workers or managers as having any major influence. At best, they were (and still are) 'consultative forums that impose limited obligations on top management'.[15] If the experience of other transition economies can offer any perspective for Chinese enterprises after privatization, *de facto* or *de jure*, it is the diminishing role of the workers' councils.[16]

The stature of trade unions in China was even more precarious throughout PRC history than their counterparts in other former state socialist countries. Though there were times when the leadership of the All China Federation of Trade Unions (ACFTU) leaned towards being more of a 'workers' interest representative and protector', trade unions were often subject to political wrangling, with their orientation being dictated by the political needs of the day. From time to time, unions were accused of being 'economistic'–putting the short-term interests of workers before the long-term interests of the nation. They never exerted their 'representative functions' after the radicalization of the Chinese political leadership in 1958. A typical statement of the function of labour unions would read:

> The most fundamental and important mission of trade unions is to organize and educate workers in order to improve productivity and guarantee fulfillment of the state production plan. On the basis of

> improving production, unions shall pay attention to the mundane interests of workers and serve the their needs. Unions shall lead workers to fight for the future of socialism.[17]

In a 1958 speech to purge former leaders of the ACFTU, the new chairman stated:

> Labour unions must summit themselves *unconditionally* to the party leadership. Union work is part of the party's mass work. Unions at all levels (from the ACFTU on down) should be *in essence the union affairs department of the party committee*. All must work under the unified leadership of the party, serving the needs of the core tasks and political mission of the party.[18]

The desired relationship between the Communist party, management, trade unions and ordinary workers was made clear in another speech by an official in 1957: 'The director makes the report, the party committee gives instructions, the trade union issues the call, the masses give the pledge'.[19] Indeed, trade unions became instrumental in Maoist attempts to radically transform Chinese urban society. In one of the most telling instances, unions played a significant role in carrying out a massive downsizing of the urban workforce in 1959 without instigating social unrest. In what communist leaders themselves later marveled at as an 'incredible achievement', the government was able to remove nearly ten million workers, many of whom had to relocate back to the countryside, with the help of the unions in arranging layoffs.[20]

Trade unions' political role of serving the needs of the regime was often overshadowed by its welfare caretaker role at the enterprise level. Working closely with management they were an important part of 'enterprise paternalism', for which the *danwei* system was known. Some summarized this role figuratively as 'issuing film tickets, managing meal coupons, and collecting bathing tickets'.[21] But again, even in this capacity, the unions' role was mainly redistributive rather than representative.

EMERGING INDUSTRIAL RELATIONS IN A TRANSITION ECONOMY

The reforms have drastically changed China's industrial relations. Today, after nearly two decades, there is a relatively open labour market in which employers can hire freely without being dictated to by the state. Even though the Chinese state still plays a significant role in managing labour relations as do its counterparts in large industrializing countries – a recent national survey of business managers found that over half of them regard government labour agencies as 'intervening too much'–its concerns and priorities have changed. With a gradualist approach and a 'growing out of the central planning' strategy, the Chinese government has been pushing a comprehensive reform of the state sector since 1992. No longer are full-employment and job – security policies endorsed. At the firm level, Tayloristic management practices are adopted. Unlike other industrializing countries such as Thailand and Malaysia,[22] however, its concerns have been less about cost containment than trying to attract more foreign investment. The most challenging task for the Chinese state has been redefining industrial relations within an emerging market economy. The basic thrust of government efforts has been constructing a legal framework aimed at effectively regulating increasingly divergent interests among the state, corporations and workers.

A series of new labour laws, including the Labour Law (which, after 15 years, 30 drafts and a few political near- deaths later, took effect on 1 January 1995), began to lay a basic framework of regulating emerging labour relations in a market economy. It is no coincidence that only after the adoption of the objective of a 'socialist market economy' at the 14th party congress of the Communist party of China in 1992, did the Labour Law receive a final push in the National People's Congress – the official legislature. In the next few years, the government plans to set up a comprehensive structure of labour regulations that will suit the needs of a market economy.

A major change from the pre-transition period is the 'contractualization' of labour. Beginning in 1983, new employees were required to be hired on a contract basis while employees hired previously remain permanent, in effect creating a dual-track system of 'tenured employees' (*guding zhigong*) and 'contracted employees' (*hetong zhigong*). Instead of state guarantee and assignment of employment, now all industrial workers are to be hired on a contract basis. For the first time in PRC history, employers can legally discharge someone for economic reasons, while employees have the right to resign. Neither was this legitimate nor practical under the old labour regime, for employers could exact a heavy cost on individuals who wanted to transfer out of the enterprise with such tactics as holding on to employees' personnel records or taking back housing. Gradually, tenured workers are also being transformed into contract workers. By June 1997, 96.8 per cent of all industrial workers (*qiye zhigong* or employees in enterprise units[23]) have become contractual employees, while nearly half of the entire workforce is now contract-based[24] (see Table 14.1).

The enactment of the new Labour Law created a whole array of institutions, including minimum-wage regulations, social security funds, labour mediation and arbitration bodies ('enterprise labour mediation committees', and 'labour arbitration commissions', both re-established in 1987 after a 32-year absence), and a labour law enforcement monitoring system ('labour supervision agency'). There are now 270 000 labour mediation committees and 3159 labour arbitration commissions nationwide.[25] The most significant change, though, is the introduction and gradual phasing-in of collective bargaining and contracts (see Table 14.2).

With these institutions functioning, cases of labour disputes and violations of labour law have risen dramatically in the last few years. Between 1987 and 1993, there were over one million labour dispute cases.[26] According to the latest official statistics, the first half of 1997

Table 14.1 Employees on labour contracts (per cent of total employees)

Year	*All Sectors*	*SEUs**	*CEUs*	*Other*
1983	0.6	0.6	0.3	n/a
1984	1.8	2.0	1.0	8.4
1985	3.3	3.7	2.2	11.4
1986	4.9	5.6	2.7	14.5
1987	6.6	7.6	3.6	18.1
1988	9.1	10.1	5.8	20.7
1989	10.7	11.8	7.0	25.1
1990	12.1	13.3	8.1	26.3
1991	13.6	14.9	8.9	28.0
1992	17.2	18.9	11.0	29.8
1993	21.0	21.9	15.5	37.4
1994	25.9	26.2	20.1	45.6
1995	40.9	40.1	37.4	62.8

Note: SEU = state economic units. This category includes both enterprises (*qiye*) and non-production (*shiye*) units. CEU = collective economic units.

Source: *Zhongguo tongjin nianjian* (*Statistical Yearbook of China*) (Beijing: Zhongguo tongji chubanshe, 1996); *Zhongguo laodong tongji nianjian* (*Labour Statistic Yearbook of China*) (1995–96) (Beijing: Zhongguo laodong chubanshe, 1996); *Zhongguo gonghui tongji nianjian* (*Trade Union Statistical Yearbook of China*) (Beijing: Zhongguo tongji chubanshe, 1994).

Table 14.2 Labour dispute cases brought to labour arbitration commissions (1992–97)

Year	*Number of cases*	*Collective disputes*
1992	8 150	548 (6.7%)
1993	12 358	684 (5.5%)
1994	19 096	1 482 (7.7%)
1995	33 033	2 588 (7.8%)
1996	n/a	n/a
1997 (January – July)	26 600	1 821 (6.8%)

Source: *Zhongguo laodong tongji nianjian* (*Labour Statistical Yearbook of China*) (1992–94) and (1995–96) (Beijing: Zhongguo laodong chubanshe, 1994 and 1996, respectively); *RMRB*, 25 July 1997.

saw a 59 per cent increase from the same period last year in labour disputes, involving 26 600 cases and 97 000 employees.[27] Labour supervision agencies handled 196 700 cases of labour law violation which were brought in 1996 – a 264 per cent increase from 1995. Among these cases, 117 800 received administrative penalties including 83 000 fines and 1729 units closed for rehabilitation, while 412 units had their licenses revoked.[28] In addition to those investigated by labour supervisory agencies, labour-related litigation also increased. Before the labour law went into effect in 1995, approximately 10 000 labour litigation cases were brought to court annually. Since 1995, the courts have handled three times that many labour-related litigations each year.[29]

In reality, implementation of labour laws has faced resistance and distortion. One of the major targets is irregularities in the non-state sector including foreign-invested enterprises (FIEs) and domestic private firms, the sources from which the new industrial relations themselves were perceived to have originated. Unions, though numerous, still have limited functions in representing workers' interests *vis-à-vis* those of the state and management. Trade unions, especially those in the state sector, are not armed with their most powerful weapon: collective bargaining. Most labour protests and strikes, increasing rapidly in recent years, are spontaneous and not organized by unions.

Many state-owned firms have been slow to implement contracts because large numbers of workers are reluctant to give up their lifetime guaranteed employment. The long-standing reliance on the enterprise has put workers, especially those who are non-skilled, in a weak bargaining position. On the other hand, the power of managers has been greatly enhanced. In many firms, the 'social and political dependence on the enterprise'[30] which characterized pre-reform industrial relations has actually intensified.[31] Driven by the abundant supply of labour, some employers (mostly non-state-sector firms) require workers to pay a 'job security deposit' (*fengxian diyajin*) as part of their job commitment to the firm. According to an official report, the government discovered 230 million yuan worth of such funds nationwide and ordered employers who collected job security deposits to return the monies to employees.[32] Cases of 'internal takeovers' by factory managers – de facto privatization and its labour relations consequences–have been reported.[33] After 1996, when labour contracts expired in some SOEs, many managers tried to avoid renewing contracts and to lay off older employees by replacing them with cheaper temporary workers from the countryside.[34]

Ideological constraints still exert influence on the future direction of the current transition, especially the nature of 'market socialism', a frequently-used yet contentious concept. Some leaders insist that the bottom line is to maintain the '*socialist* nature' of the Chinese economy ('market socialism'), and that public ownership must be the main form of property rights.[35] Privatization is seen only as a secondary means. Most SOEs, large or small, are not to be *privatized*. Despite the continuing growth of the private sector in China's economy, the public sector, especially SOEs, remains dominant. Not only does it employ 90 per cent of the urban working population among which 67 per cent are employed by SOEs, but the public sector remains the single largest contributor to the national economy. SOEs still contribute 60 per cent of annual national revenue.[36] For many urban workers, the lack of guaranteed jobs still violates the social contract of the People's Republic.[37] Not very long ago, guaranteed employment was the main indicator of workers' 'masters of the nation' status and a cornerstone of state socialism.

Structural constraints also hamper the remoulding of industrial relations in an emerging market economy. China faces immense employment problems because of continuous and severe labour-market supply pressures, large-scale rural development, rising urban unemployment and labour redundancy as well as growing income and social inequalities between different segments of the population. Surplus labour from both the countryside and the industrial sector will generate tremendous pressure on the government which intends to keep the targeted unemployment rate under 5 per cent during the next four years. It is estimated that in order to revitalize the inefficient state sector, 20 to 25 per cent of the urban state-sector labour force – some 15 to 30 million employees–must be laid off.[38] In the first nine months of 1997, more than eight million state–sector workers were either unemployed or semi-unemployed.[39] China must also find ways to accommodate millions of mobile workers from rural areas who are outside the *danwei* social benefits system. In 1995, there was already an excess labour force of 175 million people – almost half of the agricultural labour force–in the rural areas. The real unemployment rate in the agricultural sector is about 34.8 per cent.[40] Hundreds of millions of farmers will have to leave agriculture by the year 2000, for better or worse.

Although the state sector as a whole is still able to maintain labour peace, it is no longer immune to worker protests and strikes. Labour unrest has thus become a serious potential threat to the regime. A deputy minister of labour admitted that, in recent years, labour collective actions including strikes, protests and collective petitions have been on the rise. Mostly caused by unsolved labour disputes, these actions 'bear not only economic but also political implications', according to this official.[41] Most labour collective actions were in the form of petitions and sit-ins at government offices, and street protests. In 1996 there were 3000 street demonstrations by workers, among which some 300 were large-scale ones involving more than a thousand people. Some of these labour protests involved workers from several factories, an unprecedented occurrence in the PRC where most labour collective actions (with the exception of the Cultural Revolution) were enterprise-based 'cellular protests'.

Chinese industrial relations are as much political as economic. After the collapse of the former communist regimes in Eastern Europe and the 1989 mass demonstrations in China, the Chinese communist leadership greatly increased its vigilance against possible social unrest. Putting laid-off workers 'on the street' would present a serious risk to the stability of the communist regime itself. In this regard, enterprise-reform advocates face opposition from both conservatives and SOE workers who, being used to guaranteed employment and social welfare, are making every effort to hold on to such benefits. Indeed, much of the resistance to SOE reforms comes from the workers in these enterprises whose lives are dependent on their units. Leaving the factory would mean, in many cases, losing health care, housing and other benefits. Women workers are particularly hard hit when it comes to downsizing or closure. According to official surveys, the proportion of women among laid-off workers is now higher than that among active employees.[42] Family income, which is mostly composed of two salaries, would seriously decline if wives lost their jobs.

So far, most of the collective actions by workers have been spontaneous and not organized by unions. The state, however, remains highly suspicious of any attempt to organize labour groups without official sanction. The feared scenario is one of independent labour unions challenging the legitimacy of official unions and the authority of the regime as in the case of the Solidarity movement in Poland. In this sense, the role of the unions has changed the least. Trade unions remain mainly welfare caretakers and political 'transmission belts' of the state. In non-state sectors, unions are fewer in number (see Table 14.3). In 1992 a new trade union law was promulgated replacing the previous law of 1950. The new law ostensibly stipulated some roles that are comparable to any free union movement.[43] Yet few resources are guaranteed with which such active roles can be made effective.[44] The fact that recent years have seen a dramatic increase both in labour disputes brought to labour arbitration bodies and labour law violations handled by courts, as well as in collective actions, indicates that the internal problem-solving mechanism between management and employees remains ineffective with a weak union role representing the interests of workers. Even though collective bargaining is to be established in the state sector within the next five years, without it labour disputes will continue to be individually-based and unions' roles will be limited. As Table 14.2 shows, while the number of labour dispute cases involving collective disputes have been on the rise, they remain constant in proportion to individual disputes.

By the end of 1995, only 350 firms had experimented with collective bargaining and contracts, most of them in the non-state sector,[45]

Table 14.3 Unions at the firm level (1993)

Total	*SOE*	*COE*	*TVE*	*SHF*	*POE*	*FIE*
626 666	478 753	116 591	19 566	3 272	224	8 260
(% of all unions)	(76%)	(18%)	(3%)	(0.5%)	—	(1%)

Note: SOE = state-owned enterprises, COE = collective-owned enterprises, TVE = township and village enterprises; SHF = share-holding firms; POE = - privately-owned enterprises, FIE = foreign-invested enterprises.

Source: *Zhongguo gonghui tongji nianjian* (*Trade Union Statistical Yearbook of China*) (Beijing: Zhongguo tongji chubanshe, 1994).

though collective bargaining and contracts are not entirely novel to state socialist countries including China. Comprehensive implementation of these instruments still remains a politically delicate matter. At a labour bureau chiefs' meeting in 1994, the Minister of Labour revealed that whether and how to implement collective bargaining was highly controversial during the drafting of the Labour Law. Opponents of the rapid implementation of collective bargaining argue that many SOEs have very murky property rights which could lead to positioning the government, rather than management, at the opposite end of the bargaining table.[46] The government, it is argued, may risk being made a political adversary of the workers. The government eventually decided not to push too hard in the first few years after the Labour Law took effect while allowing a few experiments.[47]

GLOBALIZATION AND CHINESE LABOUR RELATIONS

Internationalization of national economies has affected industrial relations in many countries. The reasons why the consequences of such an impact differs lie in, among other things, how the state in each country has responded to both internal and external pressures. Since the early 1980s, there has been a steady inflow of foreign direct investment (FDI) into China (see Tables 14.4 and 14.5). By the end of June 1997, foreign-invested enterprises, which include equity and contractual joint ventures, and wholly foreign-owned firms, amounted to 293

Table 14.4 Sources of foreign investment in China (1995)

Country of origin	*Amount (billion $)*	*Per cent*
Hong Kong	20.18	53.4
Japan	3.21	8.5
Taiwan	3.16	8.4
United States	3.08	8.2
Singapore	1.86	4.9
Korea	1.04	2.8
United Kingdom	0.91	2.4
Germany	0.39	1.0
France	0.28	0.8
Australia	0.23	0.7

Source: *Zhongguo tongji nianjian* (*Statistical Yearbook of China*) (Beijing: Zhongguo tongji chubanshe, 1996).

Table 14.5 Structure of foreign investment in China (1995)

Sector	*Number**	*Per cent of total investment*
All sectors	233 564	100.0
Manufacturing	166 786	71.4
Services	16 802	19.3
retail and restaurants	13 280	5.6
real estate	15 131	6.4
social service	14 769	6.3
health and welfare	509	—
education and entertainment	1 524	—
finance	85	—
Agriculture and fishing	5 661	2.4

Note *This category indicates officially approved FIEs including both those in operation and those in the process of becoming operational.

Source: *Zhongguo jingji nianjian* (*Economic Statistical Yearbook of China*) (Beijing: Znohgguo tongji chubanshe, 1996).

556. Half of them are already in operation, with the utilized foreign investment totalling $197.9 billion. Today, foreign-owned assets account for 13 per cent of total social assets in China, and FIEs account for as much as 47 per cent of China's total imports and exports.[48] A further dimension of China's economic internationalization is the growth of export-oriented manufacturing. Today, five major manufacturing sectors in China – garments, office equipment, leather products, electronics and textiles – export over 30 per cent of their products overseas.[49]

Compared to state-owned enterprises, FIEs enjoy considerable autonomy in the management of their labour forces.[50] While most domestic companies were still under strict state plans in the late 1970s, foreign companies were the first–according to the 1979 Joint Venture Law – to have the power to 'fire and hire' and to determine wages and bonuses as the market dictated. The impact of FIEs on Chinese industrial relations was particularly salient in the early years of the reforms when industrial relations in the state sector remained virtually unchanged. Despite the absence of a labour market, FIEs were permitted to freely hire people and set higher wages. As many workers hired by FIEs had come from the state sector, FIEs, with certain limits, began chipping away at the enclosing walls of the *danwei*. They contributed to increasing labour mobility, a precursor to a more fully-fledged labour market a decade later.

The presence of foreign companies also created new industrial relations distinct from those in the SOEs. The clashes between the two kinds of management highlighted the early reform period. Since most of the early FIEs were in the form of joint ventures,[51] both Chinese managers and workers in these companies often found that the new practices in labour management by their foreign partners 'ignored human feelings' and were at odds with what they had been used to. It was within the early joint ventures where conflicts between the new practices based on emerging labour relations and the old institutions of state socialism first unfolded. Many of these joint ventures were formed in existing state-owned enterprises. As often was the case, one shop or division would be converted into a joint venture, with the rest of the larger enterprise remaining state- owned. This in effect created a coexistence of two kinds of labour relations in what previously had been one company, causing tension between workers of two different types of enterprises over different remuneration and management techniques.

The situation began to change with more wholly-foreign- owned firms in operation as a result of the government's determination to bring in more foreign investment. One of the direct factors involved was the decentralization of the foreign investment approval process and the opening up of more sectors to overseas investors. Competition to attract foreign investment among local governments led to more accommodating and less-restrictive policies towards foreign investors. In the early 1990s, some large joint ventures sent managers to the United States, Singapore, Thailand and the Philippines to learn about labour-relations management in multinational corporations (MNCs).

Today, among the estimated 100 million employed labourers who work for private companies, 5.6 million are in FIEs.[52] The novel concept of differentiation and conflict of interests between capital and labour, derived from privately-owned domestic or foreign companies which prompted the government to re-evaluate existing industrial-relations regulations. Since the early 1980s, FIEs have provided a testing ground for many new labour regulations. From their very beginning, the Chinese government has attempted to regulate labour relations in FIEs as a part of its efforts to direct and regulate foreign investment. It adopted a dual-track policy – in that the sequence and process of implementing labour regulations is different when applied to the state and non-state sector, especially FIEs. In addition to the labour regulations that are applied to all types of companies, there are special regulations on FIE labour relations which are primarily concentrated around occupational safety,[53] remuneration,[54] and the enforcement of written contracts.

In fact, the rules for collective bargaining and contracts and the decision to begin pilot projects for establishing collective bargaining mechanisms were both aimed at foreign-owned companies. In 1994, collective bargaining first began to be implemented on a limited scale in FIEs. Thus far, the state sector still has not started such a process.

Despite the fact that in some provinces as many as 96 per cent of foreign-invested companies have organized unions,[55] most FIEs still have a low rate of unionized labour. As Table 14.3 indicates, only 1 per cent of existing unions in China in 1993 were in FIEs. Of the 170 000 FIEs employing over ten million workers, labour unions barely accounted for 12 per cent.[56] Among cases of violations of the labour laws, 52 per cent were by non-state companies.[57]

THE DILEMMAS OF THE STATE

What will be the role of the state in future labour relations? Can it balance the need to reform, the propensity to develop rapidly, the avoidance of social unrest, the attraction of foreign investment and the protection of workers rights? In recent years, mainstream scholarship on industrial relations has been increasingly sanguine about the growth of globalization. The message is clear: the nation state as a regulator of production relations is fast becoming ineffective and obsolete as information, capital, raw materials, semi-finished goods and skilled workers become increasingly globally mobile.

The case of changing Chinese industrial relations indicates that there is no reason to believe that globalization will soon make the state irrelevant or obsolete. Similarly, the belief that the changing role of the state from a 'positive' to a 'regulatory' one in industrialized countries should be a model for the rest of the world, and that the remedy for the former state socialist systems is to wither the once interventionist state to a minimal role must be viewed with great caution. As a large industrializing country, China's labour process and industrial relations are defined by the *transition* of both political and economic regimes. This makes China, along with some other former state socialist countries, distinct from both industrialized capitalist societies and newly-industrializing countries. Industrialized countries have experienced a relatively *reactive* state during early industrialization when pre-industrial employment relationships based on personal status were replaced by contractual arrangements. Reacting to the relegation of labour to its treatment as a commodity, the state first acted to countermand the harshness of certain of these contractual arrangements – mostly what it deemed 'abuses' of the market system – including restrictions on child and female labour, working-hour limits and occupational safety.[58] In the late stages of industrialization, however, the state became more active. It expanded the scope of its intervention to take on issues such as unemployment compensation, job-training, and workplace discrimination. This process, which some scholars call the 'juridification of labour relations',[59] took more than a century to evolve.

Such sequencing does not always apply to newly- industrializing countries. Patterns of late industrialization in developing countries have generally resulted in labour repression by the state; and external competition and cost – cutting measures affected labour relations in these countries.[60] In China, the 'juridification of the labour relations' process has been more intense – the state has taken on virtually simultaneously all of the formidable tasks which its western counterparts did incrementally and sequentially.

The Chinese state thus encounters several dilemmas: external competition and cost-cutting were not the determinant factors for the state's role in labour relations in China unlike in many industrializing countries. Instead, the active role of the state in a transition economy is dictated by the needs of both dismantling the old labour regime dominated by the state itself, and reconstructing a new one that still requires some government intervention. As Peter Evans succinctly puts it, while neoliberal economists are not wrong in pointing out the existence of state predation, they are wrong in their diagnosis of its roots.[61] A state in transition needs not, and should not, be a minimal one. The logic of emerging market orders dictate that an active and effective role for the state in regulating and maintaining order in the marketplace must be present during the transition.

Another paradox the Chinese state faces is that to transform socialist enterprises (SOEs) into 'modern corporations' capable of competing in an increasingly tough international economic environment, it must accelerate the pace of enterprise reform which has been piecemeal and sluggish until recently. It must also, as the government decided recently, take more drastic measures such as privatization and forced closure of many loss- making SOEs. Yet at the same time, such a rapid transition may also cause dislocations for millions of workers who are used to lifetime employment and welfare benefits provided by their enterprises. In the near future, deterioration of conditions for the working class may continue, given the much needed structural reforms and China's ample labour supplies.

The gradualist transition strategy that China has adopted offers both opportunities and dilemmas. That the Chinese state has been able to maintain relative labour peace during the reforms is due in part to its refusal to push for wholesale privatization of the state sector, and to its insistence on playing an active role in building up a social safety net. Deliberate avoidance of potential labour unrest has also meant the delay or slowdown of state-sector reforms in the past decade, thereby further worsening the entrenched problems of the SOEs. The number of loss-making industrial enterprises has risen steadily since the early 1990s. According to official statistics, 43.7 per cent of the 104 700 currently operating SOEs sustained losses in 1996.[62] At a recent high-level meeting of officials, a vice-premier revealed that the first quarter of 1996 saw, for the first time in history, a net loss of 3 billion yuan by the state sector.[63] On the other hand, with the intensified SOE reform efforts of the last two years, and despite the efforts by the state to control the pace and scope of these reforms, what used to be relatively peaceful labour relations appear to have become increasingly confrontational. It is workers in the state sector, not conservative leaders, who are now the most vocal opponents of a rapid transformation of SOEs. Recent reports indicate that because of strong resistance from workers, state authorities in some areas could not move forward with privatization plans as endorsed by the 15th party congress in September 1997.[64]

Under state socialism, workers' interests were purported to be indistinguishable and inseparable from those of the state. Even though unions and worker's councils nominally existed, they rarely engaged in real negotiations or dispute-mediation with management. Such a lack of experience and procedures in internal negotiations and mediation has shown its effect in the increasing amount of external arbitration and court cases as well as so called 'petitions to higher authorities' (*shangfang*, a common mode of expressing grievances since pre-revolutionary times) and other forms of street demonstrations. This has two consequences: the state has to be more active than it intends, and labour peace becomes more difficult to maintain without an effective internal mediation mechanism.

The efforts of the Chinese state to manage emerging industrial relations will also be affected by China's huge labour supply. The main concerns of the government in regulating emerging labour relations have less to do with pressures to suppress labour costs in order to attract more investment than in many other newly-industrializing countries. The vast labour pool China possesses simply makes such concerns irrelevant. On the contrary, the Chinese state has been playing, and will continue to play, an active role precisely because the working class is in a perennial disadvantageous position *vis-à-vis* management.

The goal of the state in managing industrial relations appears to be an active but indirect one – that is, actively legislating and enforcing labour laws while leaving actual negotiations and mediation to employers and employees. As its efforts in the past few years indicate, the Chinese state is trying to set up a tripartite framework of labour-relations maintenance. This raises the question of the future role of organized labour in transition economies such as China's. Undoubtedly, the government is granting, albeit ever so cautiously, some new powers to officially sanctioned labour unions. It will allow a more active role for trade unions in representing and protecting workers' interests with regard to capital and management. The key, however, is the autonomy of trade unions which traditionally were ineffective and at the mercy of the government. The 'depoliticization' of trade unions is underway. It is unlikely, however, that unions will gain full autonomy from the state any time soon. They will not be allowed to organize collective actions such as large-scale strikes.

The lesson here is clear. During economic and political transitions, the contraction or dismantling of certain types of state controls are necessarily associated with the expansion or development of state capabilities in other areas. The transformation of the state should be analysed in a disaggregate manner: it involves downsizing and the abolition of old institutions, but on the other hand it may also require the creation of some entirely new (market-promoting and maintaining) agencies; furthermore, other cases call for reorganization.[65] This is quite different from the simplistic understanding of the transformation process that advocates a minimal role of the state, a view generally shared by neoliberal economists.

Notes and References

1. G. Majone, 'From the Positive to the Regulatory State: Causes and Consequences of Changes in the Mode of Governance', *Journal of Public Policy*, vol. 17 (1997), pp. 139–67.
2. C. Smith and P. Thompson (eds), *Labour in Transition: The Labour Process in Eastern Europe and China* (London: Routledge, 1992).
3. Xiaobo Lu, 'Enterprise Paternalism and Transition to Market Socialism: The Political Economy of State Sector Reform in State Socialist Systems', *Mondes en Developpement*, vol. 99 (Winter 1997), pp. 41–56.
4. M. Burawoy, 'View from Production', in *Labour in Transition*, *op. cit.*
5. *Ibid.*
6. M. Warner, *The Management of Human Resources in Chinese Industry* (New York: St Martin's Press, 1995); A. Verma, T. Kochan and R. Lansbury, *Employment Relations in the Growing Asian Economies* (New York: Routledge, 1995); and A.A. Blum (ed.), *International Handbook of Industrial Relations: Contemporary Developments and Research* (Westport, Conn.: Greenwood, 1981).
7. A. Chan, 'Revolution or Corporatism? Workers and Trade Unions in Post-Mao China', *Australian Journal of Chinese Affairs*, vol. 29 (1993), pp. 31–61.
8. D. Chirot, 'The Corporatist Model and Socialism', *Theory and Society*, 9 (1980). pp. 363-81; V. Bunce and J. Echols, 'Soviet Politics in the Brezhnev Era: "Pluralism" or "Corporatism"', in D. Kelly (ed.), *Soviet Politics in the Brezhnev Era* (New York: Praeger, 1980); A. Pravda and B. Ruble, *Trade Unions in Communist States* (Boston: Allen & Unwin, 1986); and Chan, 'Revolution or Corporatism?', *op.cit.*
9. See, for example, Perry's finding that during two of the four major labour unrest periods (that is, 1956–57, 1966–69), a main cause of grievances was differential treatment of temporary, contracted workers and permanent workers in the same enterprises. E. Perry, 'Labour's Battle for Political Space: The Role of Worker Associations in Contemporary China', in D. Davis, R. Kraus, B. Naughton and E. Perry (eds), *Urban Spaces in Contemporary China* (Washington, DC: Woodrow Wilson Centre Press, 1995).
10. Philippe Schmitter, cited in Chan, 'Revolution or Corporatism?', *op.cit.*, p. 35.
11. Lu, 'Enterprise Paternalism', *op. cit.*
12. X. Lu and E. Perry (eds), *Danwei: The Changing Chinese Workplace in Comparative and Historical Perspective* (Armonk, NY: M.E. Sharpe, 1997).
13. D. Flitzer, 'Economic Reform and Production Relations in Soviet Industry, 1986–90', in *Labour in Transition*, *op. cit.*
14. L. Jiang, Xueyi Lu and T. Shan (eds), *1996–97 Zhongguo shehui xingshi fenxi yu yuce* (*Analysis and predictions of China's social situation in 1996–97*) (Beijing: Zhongguo shehui kexue chubanshe, 1997).
15. C. Smith and P. Thompson (eds), *Labour in Transition*, *op. cit.*, p. 237.
16. L. Florek, 'Problems and Dilemmas of Labour Relations in Poland', *Comparative Labour Law*, vol. 13 (Winter 1992), pp. 111–28.

17. Zhonghua Quanguo Zonggonghui (All China Federation of Trade Unions), *tianguo yilai zhonggong zhongyang guanyu gongren yundong wenjian xuanbian* (Selected CCP central committee documents on workers movements) (Beijing: Gongren chubanshe, 1989) p. 662.
18. *Ibid.*, p. 669, emphasis added.
19. Li Xue-feng, as quoted in Smith and Thompson (eds), *Labour in Transition*, *op.cit.*, p. 235.
20. Zhonghua, *Jianguo yilai zhonggong zhongyang guanyu gongren yundong wenjian xuanbian*, *op.cit.*, p. 718.
21. M. Warner, *The Management of Human Resources*, *op.cit.*, p. 36.
22. S. Frenkel and J. Harrod, *Industrialization and Labour Relations: Contemporary Research in Seven Countries* (Ithaca: ILR Press, 1995).
23. In China, all for-profit economic entities – industrial and commercial – are referred to as '*qiye danwei*' or 'enterprise units'.
24. *Renmin Ribao* (*People's Daily*), (RMRB) (Beijing), 7 July 1997.
25. *RMRB*, 25 July 1997.
26. Jiaxin Wang (ed.), *Zhongguo laodong nianjian 1992–94* (*Chinese labour yearbook* (Beijing: Zhongguo laodong chubanshe, 1996).
27. *RMRB,* 25 July 1997.
28. *RMRB,* 9 July 1997.
29. *RMRB,* August 1996.
30. A Walder, *Communist Neotraditionalism*: *work and authority in Chinese industry* (Berkeley: University of California Press, 1986).
31. Bojun Wang, 'Shichangua dachao zhongde zhigong quanyi baozhang' (Worker rights protection in the market reform), *Taosuo yu Zhengming* (*Inquiries and Debates*), vol. 4 (1995), pp. 23–7.
32. *RMRB,* 8 April 1997.
33. L. Jiang, X. Lu and T. Shan, *1996–97 Zhongguo shehui xingshi fenxi yu yuce*, *op.cit.*
34. *Ibid.*
35. In China, the 'public sector' or 'public ownership' refers to both state-owned and collective enterprises. The latter is a somewhat ambiguous category.
36. *RMRB*, May 1996 and 3 July 1996.
37. Douglas Guthrie also found that at the firm level, such a sense of social contract remains strong among both managers and workers. See D. Guthrie 'Organized Uncertainty and Labour Contracts in China's Economic Transition', *Sociological Review* (forthcoming).
38. *Qiaobao* (*Overseas Chinese Daily*) (New York), 4 November 1997; *Liaowang* (*Outlook New Weekly*) (Beijing), vol. 25 (1996); and Fang, W. ed. *Guanyu gaohao guoyou qiye de diaocha* (Investigations on how to improve SOEs) (Beijing: Zhongguo wenshi chubanshe, 1995).
39. *Ming Pao*, 4 November 1997.
40. *Qiaobao*, 4 November 1997.
41. J. Wang, *Zhongguo laodong nianjian 1992–94*, *op.cit.*
42. *RMRB*, 9 November 1995.
43. *RMRB*, 9 April 1997.
44. E. Perry, 'Labour's Battle for Political Space', *op.cit.*

45. *Zhongguo laodong tongjin nianjian* (*Labour statistic yearbook of China*) (Beijing; Zhongguo laodong chubanshe, 1996).
46. *Ibid*
47. J. Wang, *Zhongguo laodong nianjian 1992–94*, *op.cit.*, One incident illustrates the wariness of the state about unsanctioned calls for collective bargaining. In March 1994, a 39–year-old street vendor was detained for interrogation because he printed T-shirts with the slogan 'collective bargaining is a workers' right' (see WWW web site: http://www.cleanclothes.org/1/s-asia).
48. *RMRB*, 31 July 1997.
49. *RMRB*, 28 July 1997.
50. J. Howell, 'The Myth of Autonomy: The Foreign Enterprise in China', in *Labour in Transition*, *op.cit.*
51. In China, there are three types of foreign investment companies: *equity joint ventures*, where the Chinese and foreign partners jointly invest in and operate the corporation sharing profits, losses and risks; *contractual joint ventures*, where Chinese and foreign partners cooperate in joint projects, sharing output, earnings or profits according to contracts; and *wholly-owned foreign enterprises*.
52. L. Jiang, X. Lu and T. Shan, *1996–97 Zhongguo shehui xingshi fenxi yu yuce*, *op.cit.*
53. With the inflow of foreign capital into China and increasing numbers of FIEs, there were increasing cases of physical abuse, longer working hours, delayed payment or impoundment of workers' salaries, and poor working conditions before 1994. The Ministry of Labour issued a 'Regulation on Labour Management in FIEs' in 1994 to address this and other related issues.
54. In 1991, the Ministry of Labour issued a ruling putting a salary ceiling on workers in FIEs in order to avoid too big a gap between employees in the SOEs and FIEs. A year later, a vice-premier revised it by saying that the salary ceiling is only applicable to the FIEs not operating efficiently. For profitable FIEs, such a salary cap 'can be broken' (J. Wang, *Zhongguo laodong nianjian 1992–94*, *op.cit.*, p. 205). This indicates that the government has been struggling to come to terms with the socio-economic effects of the new market economy.
55. *RMRB*, 9 June 1997.
56. *Beijing Review* (Beijing), 11 July 1997.
57. *RMRB*, 8 April 1997.
58. J. Niland, R. Lansbury and C. Verevis (eds), *The Future of Industrial Relations* (Thousand Oaks: Sage Publications, 1994).
59. S. Simits, 'The Juridification of Labour Relations', *Comparative Labour Journal*, vol. 7 (1986), pp. 93–142.
60. F. Deyo, *Beneath the Miracle: Labour Subordination in the New Asian Industrialism* (Berkeley: University of California Press, 1989); S. Frenkel and J. Harrod, *Industrialization and Labour Relations*, *op.cit.*, and J. Schor and J. You (eds), *Capital, the State, and Labour: A Global Perspective* (Brookfield: Edward Elgar, 1995).
61. P. Evans, *Embedded Autonomy: State and Industrial Transformation* (Princeton: Princeton University Press, 1995), pp. 247–9.

62. *RMRB*, 23 January 1997.
63. *RMRB*, 13 September 1996.
64. *SJRB*, 24 October 1997.
65. L. Whitehead, 'Political Democratization and Economic Liberalization: Prospects for their Entrenchment in Eastern Europe and Latin America', unpublished manuscript, 1995.

Select Bibliography

Agbese, P.O. and J.O. Ihonvbere (1988) *The State and Structural Adjustment in Nigeria* (Washington, DC: Howard University Press).

Appadurai, A. (1996) *Modernity at Large: Cultural Dimensions of Globalization* (Minneapolis: University of Minnesota Press).

Bardhan, P. (1984) *The Political Economy of Development in India* (New York: Blackwell).

Boyer, R. and D. Drache (1996) *States Against Markets: The Limits of Globalization* (London: Routledge).

Bryan, D. (1995) *The Chase Around the Globe: International Accumulation and the Contradictions for Nation States* (Boulder: Westview Press).

Brynen, R., Korany, B. and Noble, P. (eds) (1995) *Political Liberalization and Democratization in the Arab World*, vol. 1 (Boulder: Lynne Rienner).

Bulmer-Thomas, V. (ed.) (1996) *The New Economic Model in Latin America and its Impact on Income Distribution and Poverty* (New York: St Martin's Press).

Burghat, F. and W. Dowell (eds) (1997) *The Islamic Movement in North Africa* (Austin: University of Texas Press).

Campbell, B.K. and J. Loxley (eds) (1989) *Structural Adjustment in Africa* (London: Macmillan).

Centeno, M.A. (1994) *Democracy Within Reason: Technocratic Revolution in Mexico* (University Park: Pennsylvania State University Press).

Connor, W. (1994) *Ethnonationalism: The Quest for Understanding* (Princeton: Princeton University Press).

Cornelius, W., Craig, A. and J. Fox (eds) (1994) *Transforming State–Society Relations in Mexico: The National Solidarity Strategy* (La Jolla: Center for US–Mexican Studies, University of California at San Diego).

Cothran, D. (1994) *Political Stability and Democracy in Mexico: The 'Perfect Dictatorship'?* (Westport, Conn.: Praeger).

Cox, R.W. (1987) *Production, Power, and World Order: Social Forces in the Making of History* (New York: Columbia University Press).

Davis, E. and N. Gavrielides (eds) (1991) *Statecraft in the Middle East: Oil, Historical Memory, and Popular Culture* (Miami: Florida International University Press).

Deyo, F. (1989) *Beneath the Miracle: Labour Subordination in the New Asian Industrialism* (Berkeley: University of California Press).

Diamond, L., Lipset, M. and J. Linz (1988) *Democracy in Developing Countries* (Boulder: Lynne Rienner).

Dicken, P. (1992) *Global Shift: The Internationalization of Economic Activity* (New York: Guilford Press).

Dorraj, M. (ed.) (1995) *The Changing Political Economy of the Third World* (Boulder: Lynne Rienner).

Dorraj, M. (1994) 'Privatization, Democratization and Development in the Third World: Lessons of a Turbulent Decade', *Journal of Developing Societies*, vol. 10, no. 2 (Spring), pp. 173–82.

Eckstein, S. (1994) *Back from the Future: Cuba under Castro* (Princeton, NJ: Princeton University Press).

Evans, P. (1995) *Embedded Autonomy: State and Industrial Transformation* (Princeton, NJ: Princeton University Press).

Falola, T. and J.O. Ihonvbere (1985) *The Rise and Fall of Nigeria's Second Republic, 1979–84* (London: Zed Books).

Fine, B. (1980) *Economic Theory and Ideology* (London: Edward Arnold).

Gill, S. (1995) 'Globalization, Market Civilization, and Disciplinary Neoliberalism', *Millennium: Journal of International Studies*, vol. 24, pp. 399–423.

Glade, W.P. (ed.) (1986) *State Shrinking: A Comparative Inquiry into Privatization* (Austin: University of Texas, Institute of Latin American Studies).

Grandea, N. (1993) *Adjustment and Poverty in South Asia* (Ottawa: North–South Institute).

Grayson, G. (1998) *Mexico: From Corporatism to Pluralism* (Fort Worth: Harcourt Brace).

Green, D. (1995) *Silent Revolution: The Rise of Market Economics in Latin America* (London: Cassell).

Halebsky, S. and R.L. Harris (eds) (1995) *Capital, Power, and Inequality in Latin America* (Boulder: Westview).

Handelman, H. (1997) *Mexican Politics: The Dynamics of Change* (New York: St Martin's Press).

Harvey, N. (ed.) (1993) *Mexico: Dilemmas of Transition* (London: University of London, Institute of Latin American Studies).

Herbst, J. (1993) *The Politics of Reform in Ghana, 1982–91* (Berkeley: University of California Press).

Heredia, C. and M. Purcell, *Structural Adjustment in Mexico: The Roots of the Crisis* (Washington, DC: The Development Gap).

Hirst, P. and G. Thompson (1995) 'Globalization and the Future of the Nation State', *Economy and Society*, vol. 24, no. 3 (August).

Hirst, P.Q. and G. Thompson (1996) *Globalization in Question: The International Economy and the Possibilities of Governance* (Cambridge, Mass.: Basil Blackwell).

Horowitz, D.L. (1991) *A Democratic South Africa? Constitutional Engineering in a Divided Society* (Berkeley: University of California Press).

Hunter, S.T. (ed.) (1988) *The Politics of Islamic Revivalism: Diversity and Unity* (Bloomington: Indiana University Press).

Huntington, S. (1991) *The Third Wave: Democratization in the Late Twentieth-Century* (Norman: University of Oklahoma Press).

Ihonvbere, J.O. (1984) *Nigeria: The Politics of Adjustment and Democracy* (New Brunswick, NJ: Transaction Publishers).

Ihonvbere, J.O. and T.M. Shaw (1998) *The Illusions of Power: Nigeria in Transition* (Lawrenceville, NJ: Africa World Press).

LaBotz, D. (1995) *Democracy in Mexico: Peasant Rebellion and Political Reform* (Boston: South End).

Lijphart, A. (1985) *Power Sharing in South Africa* (Berkeley: University of California Press).

Lu, X. and E. Perry (eds) (1997) *Danwei: The Changing Chinese Workplace in Comparative and Historical Perspective* (Armonk, NY: M.E. Sharpe).

Lustig, N. (1992) *Mexico: The Remaking of an Economy* (Washington, DC: The Brookings Institution).

Middlebrook, K. (1995) *The Paradox of Revolution: Labor, the State, and Authoritarianism in Mexico* (Baltimore: Johns Hopkins).

Mittelman, J.H. (1994) 'Global Restructuring of Production and Migration', in Y. Sakamoto (ed.), *Global Transformation: Challenges to the State System* (New York: United Nations University Press), pp. 276–98.

Mittelman, J.H. (ed.) (1996) *Globalization: Critical Reflections* (Boulder, Col.: Lynne Rienner).

Mittelman, J.H. (1995) 'Rethinking the International Division of Labour in the Context of Globalization', *Third World Quarterly*, vol. 16, pp. 273–94.

Mohanty, C., Russo, A. and L. Torres (eds) (1991) *Third World Women and the Politics of Feminism* (Bloomington: Indiana University Press).

Moonshipouri, M. and M. Dorraj (1997) 'Democracy and Human Rights in the Third World: A Comparative Assessment', *Journal of the Third World Spectrum*, vol. 4, no. 1 (Spring), pp. 85–111.

Mosley, P., Subasat, T. and J. Weeks (1995) 'Assessing Adjustment in Africa', *World Development*, vol. 23, no. 9.

Nelson, J.M. (ed.) (1990) *Economic Crisis and Policy Choice: The Politics of Adjustment in the Third World* (Princeton, NJ: Princeton University Press).

Ohmae, K. (1990) *The Borderless World: Power and Strategy in the Interlinked Economy* (New York: HarperCollins).

Olukoshi, A. and L. Laakso (eds) (1996) *Challenges to the Nation-State in Africa* (Uppsala: Nordiska Afrikainstitutet).

Onimode, B. (ed.) (1989) *The IMF, the World Bank, and the African Debt* (London: Institute for African Alternatives).

Otero, G. (ed.) (1996) *Neoliberalism Revisited: Economic Restructuring and Mexico's Political Future* (Boulder: Westview).

Ould-Mey, M. (1994) 'Global Adjustment: Implications for Peripheral States', *Third World Quarterly*, vol. 15, no. 2.

Pasha, M.K. (1996) 'Globalization and Poverty in South Asia', *Millennium: Journal of International Studies*, vol. 25, pp. 635–56.

Rao, H.C.H. and H. Linnemann (eds) (1996) *Economic Reforms and Poverty Alleviation in India* (New Delhi: Sage).

Ravenhill, J. (ed.) (1986) *Africa in Economic Crisis* (New York: Columbia University Press).

Ray, D. (1986) *Ghana: Politics, Economics, and Society* (Boulder: Lynne Rienner).

Reding, A. (1991) 'Mexico: The Crumbling of the Perfect Democracy', *World Policy Journal*, vol. 8 (Spring), pp. 255–84.

Roett, R. (1995) *The Challenge of Institutional Reform in Mexico* (Boulder: Lynne Rienner).

Roett, R. (1993) *Political and Economic Liberalization in Mexico: At a Critical Juncture?* (Boulder: Lynne Rienner).

Rosen, F. and D. McFadyen (eds) (1995) *Free Trade and Economic Restructuring in Latin America* (New York: Monthly Review).

Rothchild, D. (ed.) (1991) *Ghana: The Political Economy of Recovery* (Boulder: Lynne Rienner).

Ruigrok, W. and B. van Tulder (1995) *The Logic of International Restructuring* (London and New York: Routledge).
Salame, G. (ed.) (1994) *Democracy Without Democrats? The Renewal of Politics in the Muslim World* (London: I.B. Tauris).
Schor, J. and J. You (eds) (1995) *Capital, the State, and Labour: A Global Perspective* (Brookfield: Edward Elgar).
Scott, J.C. (1990) *Domination and the Arts of Resistance: Hidden Transcripts* (New Haven: Yale University Press).
Scott, J.C. (1976) *The Moray Economy of the Peasant: Rebellion and Subsistence in Southeast Asia* (New Haven: Yale University Press).
Scott, J.C. (1985) *Weapons of the Weak: Everyday Forms of Peasant Resistance* (New Haven: Yale University Press).
Sheahan, J. (1991) *Conflict and Change in Mexican Economic Strategy* (La Jolla: Centre for US–Mexican Studies, University of California at San Diego).
Skidelsky, R. (ed.) (1977) *The End of the Keynesian Era: Essays on the Disintegration of the Keynesian Political Economy* (New York: Holmes & Meier).
Smith, C. and P. Thompson (eds) (1992) *Labour in Transition: The Labour Process in Eastern Europe and China* (London: Routledge).
Stahl, K. (1996) 'Anti-poverty Programmes: Making Structural Adjustment More Palatable', *NACLA Report on the Americas*, vol. 29, no. 6 (May/June).
Stallings, B. and R. Kaufman (eds) (1989) *Debt and Democracy in Latin America* (Boulder: Westview).
Standing, G., Sender, J. and J. Weeks (1996) *Restructuring the Labour Market: The South African Challenge* (Geneva: International Labour Office).
Suleiman, E.N. and J. Waterbury (eds) (1990) *The Political Economy of Public Reform and Privatization* (Boulder: Westview).
Swatuk, L.A. and D.R. Black (eds) (1997) *Bridging the Rift: The New South Africa in Africa* (Boulder: Westview).
Tambiah, S.J. (1996) *Leveling Crowds: Ethnonationalist Conflicts and Collective Violence in South Asia* (Berkeley: University of California Press).
Teichman, J. (1995) *Privatization and Political Change in Mexico* (Pittsburgh: University of Pittsburgh Press).
Thomas, C. (1989) *Restructuring the World Economy and its Political Implications in the Caribbean* (London: Mancel).
Veltmeyer, H., Petras, J. and S. Vieux (1997) *Neoliberalism and Class Conflict in Latin America* (New York: St Martin's Press).
Vilas, C. (1996) 'Neoliberal Social Policy: Managing Poverty (Somehow)', *NACLA Report on the Americas*, vol. 29, no. 6 (May/June).
Weeks, J. (ed.) (1989) *Banks, Governments, and Multilaterals Confront the Crisis* (New York: New York University Press).
Weeks, J. (1981) *Capital and Exploitation* (Princeton, NJ: Princeton University Press).
Weeks, J. (1998) *Economic Integration in Latin America: Impact on Labour* (London: SOAS).
World Bank (1994) *Adjustment in Africa: Reforms, Results, and the Road Ahead* (Oxford: Oxford University Press).
World Bank (1995) 'Workers in a Changing World', *World Development Report 1995* (Oxford: Oxford University Press).

World Bank (1995) *World Development Report 1995: Workers in an Integrating World* (Washington, DC: World Bank).

World Bank (1996) *World Development Report 1996* (Oxford and New York: Oxford University Press).

Yeebo, Z. (1991) *Ghana: The Struggle for Popular Power* (London: New Beacon Books).

Index